ARE TWO LEGAL PROFESSIONS NECE

Peter Reeves is a practising Solicitor and has had a long association with Ruskin College, Oxford, where he is a visiting lecturer in law.

Martin Smith, M. A. (Oxon.), is Deputy Law Librarian of Bodleian Law Library, Oxford.

Also published by Waterlows

Legal and Social Policy Library
Pornography and Politics *by A. W. B. Simpson*
Fair Charges? *by M. R. Ludlow*
Unlawful Sex, *the Report of a Howard League Working Party*
Marketing Legal Services *edited by S. C. Silkin*

For further information write to Waterlow Publishers Limited,
27 Crimscott Street, London SE1 5TS
Tel. 01-232 1000

Are Two Legal Professions Necessary?

PETER REEVES, *Solicitor*

WATERLOW PUBLISHERS LIMITED

First Edition 1986
© Peter Reeves 1986
Bibliography © Martin R. Smith 1986

Waterlow Publishers Limited
PO Box 55,
27 Crimscott Street,
London SE1 5TS
A member of the British Printing & Communication Corporation PLC

ISBN 0 08 039218 0

British Library Cataloguing in Publication Data

Reeves, Peter
    Are two legal professions necessary?—(Legal and social policy library)
    1. Lawyers—England
    I. Title   II. Series
    340′.023′42   KD460

Printed in Great Britain by A. Wheaton & Co. Ltd, Exeter.

Foreword

BY SIR DAVID NAPLEY

This book presents in a well researched, balanced, interesting and persuasive form, an argument in favour of the fusion of the two branches of the legal profession. My own view on this subject has been somewhat ambivalent. I suspect that in the long term, fusion is inevitable since public opinion favours it, believing that the present system is too expensive and in many respects unjust.

Whatever doubts one may have on the question of fusion there can be no doubt that the present system requires radical overhaul. I have been advocating for the best part of 30 years that both branches should have a common education, and be free to practise as they wish as lawyers. If they could then demonstrate, by examination or otherwise, special aptitudes and skills in particular specialisations, including advocacy, they should be free to go to the Bar which would, as a consequence, be reduced in numbers, as it should be. The Bar has over a long period sought to present itself as a band of specialists comparable to specialists in the medical profession as compared with general practitioners. It is a wholly false analogy. Doctors have common training, and consultancy or specialist status is acquired only by further examination and individual selection upon the basis that special skills, ability and experience are established to the satisfaction of their peers. The decision to become a barrister, on the other hand, is made, in almost all cases, at the undergraduate stage when the person concerned has neither knowledge nor experience of the practice of law and no basis for judging where his or her aptitudes really lie. Less than 1,000 of the 5,000 lawyers called to the Bar over a period of years become true specialists. To suggest that the remaining number either immediately upon qualification, and in some cases even later, fall into that category is insupportable.

At page 50 the author reminds us that Justice has put forward the suggestion that an Advisory Appointments Committee or a Judicial Commission should be constituted to advise and recommend upon all judicial appointments. I believe, beyond that, if meaningful reform in the public interest is to be achieved someone must take a long hard look at the Lord Chancellor's Department itself in the hope that a body might be brought into existence with a view to redressing the overwhelming influence which the Bar brings to bear for the preservation of its entrenched position.

This book is published at a time when more meaningful public discussion of the inadequacies of the present system is being pursued than ever before in my lifetime. In crystallising the issues, marshalling the arguments from both sides, it performs a valuable service, and all those who have the interests of justice and the public weal at heart would be well advised to read it and consider with care the message which it contains.

SIR DAVID NAPLEY   London
                                                                   November 1985

Preface

Proposals for the reform of the structure of the legal profession have, for decades, been met with hostility within the profession and with indifference from without. The mistaken idea of the roles of the solicitor as general practitioner and the barrister as specialist, so indelibly imprinted on the mind of the public, is accepted without question.

When the extensive overlapping of the work of solicitors and barristers is considered it seems remarkable that they have remained apart for so long. For this reason detail has been included of the nature of the separate systems of training and working arrangements. Latent feelings of dissatisfaction and antagonism have also been described. I do not endorse them and admittedly, taken alone, these are not reasons for altering the organisation of the profession. They do, however, serve to indicate a misdirection of effort engendered by the system.

Paradoxically, a profession concerned with the exercise of judgement rarely approaches its own problems with impartiality. This strange intransigence, I must confess, has provided the motive for writing this book. Although by no means the first attempt to examine the many aspects of the divided profession, it comes at a time when the call for reform is more persistent and reaching a wider audience.

The bibliography is extensive and has been included for the benefit of students of the subject. The notes of each reference also serve to record the debate upon fusion over the past thirty-five years. I freely acknowledge the use made of many ideas and conclusions contained in the sources mentioned.

To those who have given help and advice in the formation of this book I express my gratitude. In particular the comments, suggestions and information given by friends belonging to both branches of the profession and officers of the professional bodies have helped immensely. To Martin Smith for preparing the bibliography and unearthing long-forgotten works I take this opportunity of recording my appreciation and thanks.

Yarnton, Oxford
November 1985

Table of Contents

Index of Abbreviations

Code of Conduct: Code of Conduct for the Bar of England and Wales 1981 3rd Edition incorporating amendments to 31st Dec. 1984

Consolidated Regulations: Consolidated Regulations of the Honourable Societies of Lincoln's Inn, Inner Temple, Middle Temple and Gray's Inn.

Evidence to the Benson Commission (e.g. "Legal Action Group, Evidence to the Benson Commission") Evidence to the Royal Commission on Legal Services

Gazette: The Law Society's Gazette

Benson Commission: The Royal Commission on Legal Services

Benson Commission Report: The Royal Commission on Legal Services, Final Report Oct. 1979 (Cmnd. 7648)

Senate Evidence: Senate of the Inns of Court and the Bar, Evidence to the Royal Commission on Legal Services

Index of periodicals cited in the bibliography (with abbreviations)

American Bar Association Journal (*A.B.A.J.*).
American Bar Foundation Research Journal (*A.B.F. Research J.*).
Australian Law Journal (*Austral. L.J.*)
Current Legal Problems
The Economist
Fordham Law Review
The International Lawyer (*Internat. Lawyer*)
Journal of Contemporary Law (*J. Contemp. L.*)
Law Society's Gazette (*Law Society's Gaz.*)
Law Journal (*L.J.*)
Law Quarterly Review (*L.Q.R.*)
Law Times (*L.T.*)
Modern Law Review (*M.L.R.*)
New Law Journal (*N.L.J.*)
New York State Bar Journal (*N.Y. State B.J.*)
New Zealand Law Journal
Osgoode Hall Law Journal (*Osgoode Hall L.J.*)
Solicitors' Journal (*Sol. Jo.*)
The Times
University of Tasmania Law Review (*Univ. of Tasmania L.R.*)

CHAPTER 1

Historical

1. Early Times

The legal profession in England and Wales has a long and curious history. Slowly and without sudden upheavals, it evolved over a period of six centuries. The various tasks involved in the administration of justice and the general work of a lawyer were first performed by distinctive groups of practitioners. Gradually they merged, both in name and function until only the barrister[1] and solicitor remained.[2] This division reflects a basic pattern in the structure of the profession which has been discernible from early times. The barrister has an exclusive right of audience before the superior courts and is alone eligible to serve as a member of the higher judiciary and as a law officer in Parliament.[3] A solicitor, although entitled to practise as an advocate, has a restricted right of audience limited to the inferior courts and, to a lesser degree, the Crown Court. Eminent legal historians have traced the influences which led to this separation and the establishment of what Lord Gardiner has described as "the two legal professions . . ."[4] It is not the intention of these observations to give a detailed account of the manner in which the structure of the profession developed. Reference, however, is made to the period before the professional associations which exist today were founded. This is necessary to show that the separation is the result of a combination of competing sectional interests and historical accident and not by design.

Professor Sir W. S. Holdsworth, in *A History of English Law,* indicates that the development of a divided profession stems from the difficulty, in primitive systems of law, of recognising the idea that one

---

1. Barristers are first referred to in Black Books of Lincoln's Inn in Trinity Term 1455 'duo de optimis barrei'; in 1 *Lincoln's Inn Black Book* (1465) 26, 41 'utter barresters' and in Statute of Sewers 1531–23 Hen. 8 c. 5 which stipulates that a commissioner of sewers shall be 'admitted in one of the four Inns of Court for an utter barrister.' *Halsbury's Laws of England* 4th ed. Vol. 3 (1973) p. 588.
2. Solicitors who first appeared in the fifteenth century in the courts of equity are thought to have been business agents rather than lawyers. *Ibid,* vol. 44 (1983) p. 6.
3. The offices of Lord Chancellor, Attorney General and Solicitor General have by custom and for a long period been occupied by persons who are or have been barristers.
4. The Rt. Hon. Lord Gardiner, 'Two Lawyers or One', 1970 *Current Legal Problems* Vol. 23 p. 1.

man can stand in place of another. He explains that:[5]

> "It was only gradually that an attorney was allowed to take the place of his client for all purposes (he could not in early days even disclaim or admit on behalf of his client). On the other hand the idea that one man can assist another in legal proceedings is in harmony with many old ideas concerning law and law suits . . ."

The first statutory reference to a relaxation of the principle which insisted upon the personal attendance of the parties to proceedings before a court is to be found in the Statute of Merton 1235 which states:[6]

> "It is provided and granted that every Freeman which oweth suit to the County, Trything, Hundred and Wapentake, or to the Court of his Lord, may freely make his Attorney to do those suits for him . . ."

These were the inferior courts. The right to engage an attorney was progressively extended by statute to the higher courts. In 1285 the first general power of appointment of an attorney was enacted in the following terms:[7]

> "Such as have lands in divers shires . . . may make a general Attorney to sue for them in all Pleas in the Circuit of Justices moved or to be moved for them or against them during the Circuit: which Attorney or Attorneys shall have full power in all Pleas moved during the Circuit, until the Pleas be determined or that his master remove him . . ."

It has been suggested that at this stage the attorney acted as advocate. Generally this was not the case but there does not appear to be any clear rule forbidding the practice. It seems that arguments were usually conducted by countors or sergeants. There is, however, evidence in the court rolls of the period which shows that the functions of the various types of practitioner were not always distinct and separate. Professor Holdsworth comments upon this question:[8]

> "A study of the rolls makes it plain that it was not normal for those men who had become Serjeants to act as Attornies though here and there in a particular action an exception may perhaps be noticed."

This is consistent with the belief that it was not abnormal for barristers, other than sergeants, to act as attorneys. For a period, divisions within the profession might have disappeared altogether. This did not happen and during the latter part of the sixteenth century and throughout the seventeenth century the structure began to assume and resemble that of today.

---

5. Professor Sir W. S. Holdsworth, *A History of English Law*, 3rd. ed. 1923 Vol. II, p. 312.
6. 20 Hen. III c.10 1235.
7. 13 Edw. I St.1, c.10 1285.
8. Prof. Holdsworth, *op. cit.* Vol. II, p. 312.

Professor Holdsworth describes the development in this way:[9]

"At the lower end we see a growing distinctness in the profession of the attorney, a growing separation between the attorneys and the barristers and the rise of three new classes in the legal profession—pleaders, conveyancers and solicitors—the first two of which approximate to the profession of barrister and the third to that of the attorney. At the upper end, the commanding position of the sergeants was modified by the growth of the pre-eminence of the law officers of the Crown and the rise of the new class of King's counsel. As the result of these changes the grouping of the legal profession begins to assume almost its modern form."

2. Emergence of Modern Structure

The close connection of attorneys with the courts and their staff became more evident at this time. A statute of 1605 imposed restrictions upon their activities and prescribed penalties for their fraudulent or negligent conduct. The widening division is evidenced by the preamble to that statute which stated that the regulation of attorneys was needed because:[10]

"... the subjects grow to be overmuch burthened and the practice of the just and honest councillor at law greatly slandered."

The control of attorneys and solicitors by the courts was then well established. It has remained so and is enshrined in the modern description of "*A Solicitor of the Supreme Court of Judicature.*"

The barrister was in a different position. Never regarded as an officer of the court, he (they were all male) was not concerned with the administrative work involved in an action and had no contact with court officials. His concern was with the understanding and application of the law and the pleading of cases in the courts. Barristers were drawn from the privileged strata of society. In the main they were the sons of men who enjoyed the benefits of inherited wealth or who were successful and prosperous in trade or commerce.[11]

Throughout the seventeenth century these differences were accentuated. They affected relationships within the profession and those with the lay client. Barristers could not sue for their fees[12] although solicitors were entitled to do so.[13] In 1614 the Benchers of the four Inns of Court stated without equivocation that:[14]

"there ought always to be preserved a difference between a counsellor at law, which is the principal person next unto sergeants and judges in

9. *Ibid.* Vol. VI, 432.
10. 3 Jas. I, c.7 An Act to Reform the Multitudes and Misdemeanours of Attornies.
11. Prof. Holdsworth, *op. cit.,* 1924 Vol. VI, p. 436.
12. *Moor v Row* (1629–1630) I Ch. Rep. 38.
13. *Bradford v Woodhouse* (1619) Cr. Jac. 520.
14. E. B. V. Christian, *A Short History of Solicitors,* 1896 (Reeves & Turner, London), p. 89.

administration of justice and attorneys and solicitors which are but ministerial persons of an inferior nature, therefore it is ordered that henceforth no common attorney or solicitor shall be admitted of any of the four Houses of Court."

By the eighteenth century the demarcation line between attorneys and solicitors on the one hand and barristers on the other was clear and definite. Attorneys and solicitors were finally excluded from membership of the four Inns of Court in 1793.[15] They were relegated to the subordinate Chancery Inns which provided the earliest system of education and acted as their professional organisation. By this time these Inns had declined in status and eventually became mere dining clubs. The last to disappear was Clifford's Inn, which was sold. The proceeds were invested and the annual income divided between the Law Society and The Council of Legal Education to be used for educational purposes.[16]

In 1739, solicitors and attorneys combined to form the Society of Gentlemen Practisers in the Courts of Law and Equity. The earliest records of the Society's proceedings stated its aims in the following minute:[17]

> "The meeting unanimously declared its utmost abhorrence of all male (fide) and unfair practice, and that it would do its utmost to detect and discountenance the same."

The need for self-discipline is shown in the protest by the Society's committee against those members of the profession who had stood in the pillory or had been convicted of highway robbery and yet continued to practise. A significant development affecting the working relationship between the two branches of the profession was the insistence by the Gentlemen Practisers Society that a brief should not be accepted by a barrister from a lay client direct. This rule, introduced to protect the professional interests of attorneys was, much later, justified by the Bar in more profound terms. Sir Richard Webster, Attorney General, maintained that it existed because a barrister:[18]

> "cannot himself make proper enquiry as to the actual facts; it is essential that he should be able to rely on the responsibility of a solicitor as to the statement of facts put before him."

This illustrates the way in which rules of professional etiquette have arisen for the purpose of protecting sectarian interests and have later been justified on the ground that they are fundamental to the public interest.

15. Halsbury, *op. cit.*, Vol. 44 (1983) p. 5, para. 1.
16. *Ibid.* p. 7 note 1.
17. E. B. V. Christian, *op. cit.*, p. 121.
18. Sir Richard Webster A. G., *Law Times*, 7 July 1888. p. 176.

3. Establishment of the Professional Associations

At this stage, it is appropriate to leave the earlier period of genesis of the profession and enter its modern phase of development. The Gentlemen Practisers Society, which was dissolved in about 1817, is recognised as the germ of The Law Society.[19] A group of attorneys and solicitors led by Bryan Holmes, who was previously a member of the Honourable Society of New Inn and the Gentlemen Practisers Society, founded The Law Institution in 1825. From this beginning, The Law Society, as it is known today, arose. A Royal Charter of 1845 gives its title as:

> "The Society of Attorneys, Solicitors, Proctors and others not being Barristers practising in the Courts of Law and Equity of the United Kingdom."

The separation was complete. At this time practitioners were almost always both attorney at law and solicitor in equity—to give them their full description. The older designation of attorney had, for some, acquired unpleasant associations and this resulted in most attorneys "taking refuge in the gentler name of solicitor."[20] By the Judicature Act 1873 the title of attorney was interred and all practitioners in this branch of the profession became solicitors. As they began to close their ranks and achieve recognition as a profession, the Bar, for the first time, became organised collectively. There had been no body representing barristers until the Bar Committee was formed in 1883. The General Council of the Bar replaced this committee in 1895 and was constituted as an elected body, deriving its authority from general meetings and empowered:[21]

> "to deal with all matters affecting the profession and to take such action as may be deemed expedient."

The four Inns of Court remained and continued to be responsible for the education and admission of students and their call to the Bar. The Bar Council, as it came to be known, ruled upon questions of professional etiquette which affected the relations of its members with solicitors. The resulting decisions were published for the guidance of barristers in an official Annual Statement. In this way, uniformity of professional conduct and etiquette was maintained.

With the existence of separate professional associations, the division between barristers and solicitors became definite and fixed. Rules and conventions were established governing the working arrangements between what had come to be known as the two branches of the profession. Strictly enforced, the pattern was set and has changed little.

---

19. E. B. V. Christian, *op. cit.*, p. 120.
20. *Ibid.*, p. 224–5.
21. Twelfth Annual Statement of the Bar Committee and First of the General Council of the Bar 1895, p. 3.

The structure as it now exists has evolved from the confused and unregulated activities of lawyers and their sub-professional associates over the centuries. At no time was a plan for the structure of the profession and provision of legal services conceived and based upon the public interest. Instead, conflicts which arose from the clash of social and economic interests were resolved by partitioning the profession. The concern of the protagonists was only incidentally directed towards the establishment of an efficient and effective legal system. Their main interest was to preserve the identity of each group and protect what were seen to be their respective interests.

The separateness of the Bar has been emphasised by the concept of solicitors as officers of the court—a fact which they are never allowed to forget. This long established position arose from the need to control the activities of unorganised and sometimes errant individuals. It now serves to discipline solicitors and, to a great extent, duplicates the strict supervision and disciplinary powers of The Law Society. This again illustrates how customs and practices can persist when the reasons for their introduction no longer exist.

At the time The Law Society was founded, the apparent satisfaction of attorneys and solicitors with their improved status was not universal. The right of audience issue was seen by an influential minority as fundamental to the improvement of their professional opportunities. Edwin Wilkins Field, a well known and active reformer:[22]

> "inveighed against the exclusion of attorneys from the Bar and argued that here, as in the United States and Colonies, every lawyer should have the right to plead in court and address the jury. He soon found support; the sense of injustice to the profession in its exclusion from all judicial appointments had long been felt by solicitors; they were a proscribed class."

Other eminent lawyers and commentators, including Walter Bagehot, spoke in similar terms. The language used was robust and the proposals for reform radical. Walter Bagehot wrote of the divisions in the profession as "artificial hedges which cramped and hurt clients".[23] Lord Selbourne went as far as to suggest that the Inns of Court should become corporations and their funds used for the improvement of legal education by the creation of a new university of law where solicitors and barristers could be educated together.[24]

A concession to the aspirations of solicitors was made in granting them parity with barristers as advocates in the County Courts, established in 1846. Fusion, at this juncture, was a realistic objective.[25]

---

22.   E. B. V. Christian, *op. cit.*, p. 210.
23.   W. Bagehot, 'Bad Lawyers or Good', *Literary Studies* (1898 ed.) Vol. III, p. 278.
24.   *Supra* p. 14.
25.   J. R. Forbes, 'The Divided Legal Profession in Australia', *The Queensland Lawyer* Vol. 4. Book supplement (Law Book Company, Brisbane) 1977, p. 12.

This probably explains why opposition from the Bar and judiciary was strenuous and bordered on hostility. The division between the two branches of the profession had never been based solely upon function. It was also of a social nature with the Bar believing that its ancient rights and privileges were under threat.[26] In retrospect the establishment of solicitor advocates in the County Courts was a significant landmark. Overnight, the myth that as a group solicitors were unsuited and ill-equipped to perform this type of work was dispelled.

Despite strenuous efforts on the part of those who sought the creation of a unified profession, the established order prevailed. A dispirited Edmund Christian, at the end of this turbulent period, wrote:[27]

> "It seems certain that the twentieth century will begin and it may end, with barristers in sole possession of the right of audience in the superior courts and solicitors still sitting (as Dickens said) silent, like Truth, at the bottom of the well."

Fusion is a reform which has always attracted support. At times the debate subsided but it has never ceased. With an improvement in the status and prosperity of solicitors during the 1890s little was heard of the subject. J. R. Forbes points out that economic factors were a major influence in subduing the call for fusion during this period. He describes how:[28]

> ". . . a great increase in the quantity and (financial) quality of conveyancing in the closing years of the century removed the temptation for fusionists to test the still-fresh cement of judgements and practices constituting division."

4.   A Period of Consolidation

This began a period of consolidation. In the provinces solicitors served the interests of prosperous tradesmen and farmers. In the Metropolis the landed classes and wealthy were among their clients. Relations with the Bar improved and a deferential acceptance of the divided profession stilled critical voices of earlier years. Rulings of the Bar Council upon basic questions of etiquette strengthened the independence of its members. Fusion as an issue was raised less frequently and without rancour. This tranquil scene did not last—it was disturbed and then lost forever in the tumult of World War I.

After the Armistice fusionists again became active. At a meeting of The Law Society in 1919, a motion proposing fusion was passed by a large majority. A postal ballot followed which overturned the decision with

---

26.   *Ibid.* p. 19.
27.   E. V. B. Christian, *op. cit.* pp. 215–6.
28.   J. R. Forbes, *op. cit.* p. 18.

about two thirds voting against the proposal. Clearly the controversy was set to continue as it still had the support of a sizeable minority. In 1922, a Bill to unify the legal profession was introduced in Parliament.[29] At the time Lloyd George, a solicitor, was Prime Minister. On the occasion of the first reading a speaker referred to him as a man of brilliance who could not attain an appropriate level in the law because he was a solicitor. Nothing more was heard of the Bill after its first reading.

During the inter-war period, attempts were made to extend the rights of audience of solicitors. They were not successful. It was in the 1930's that the mass conveyancing market expanded rapidly. Practices became dependent upon this work as a major source of income, so diverting attention from fusion.

5. World War II and After

On the outbreak of World War II and for its duration, lawyers concentrated upon the war effort. Plans for post war reforms were under constant discussion but the legal system did not figure among them. With the end of the war and the return of those who had served in the armed forces normality was soon restored. After a period of austerity in the economic life of the country, attention was once more directed to the structure of the legal profession and the service it provided. Correspondence and articles in legal journals reflected a growing interest in fusion. Few expressed views which allowed for compromise between total separation and outright amalgamation. It was in 1949 that the next positive sign of a slow move towards fusion was seen. The office of stipendiary magistrate had, until then, been reserved for barristers. In that year, solicitors of seven years' standing also became eligible to serve.[30] Although only a minor reform in extent, it heralded an important principle. For the first time it was acknowledged that solicitors were suitable by virtue of their training and experience to hold judicial office.

The professional bodies continued to maintain a united front in their opposition to fusion. A revived interest in the topic was, however, evident. The correspondence columns of *The Times,* for instance, published about thirty-six letters from November 1959 until January 1960 about the functioning of the divided profession. Writers included representatives of the four Inns of Court, the Chairman of the Bar Council, the President of The Law Society and many practitioners. In the second half of 1968 two works were published[31] which attracted the

---

29. The Legal Practitioners Bill 1922.
30. Justice of the Peace Act 1949 s 29.
31. B. Abel Smith and R. Stevens, *In Search of Justice* (Allen Lane, The Penguin Press, London) 1968. Prof. M. Zander, *Lawyers and the Public Interest* (Weidenfeld & Nicholson, London) 1968.

attention of those who believed that the legal profession should be re-structured. The respective authors were highly critical of the legal system and stressed the advantages which would flow from fusion. Lord Gardiner, then Lord Chancellor, responded to their views in a Presidential address to the Bentham Club.[32] He summarised advantages of the divided professions as:

"(1) The services of the whole of a specialist Bar are open to the smallest firm of solicitors as they are to the largest.
(2) The Bar has always been a highly competitive profession where influence is useless and only skill can ensure success.
(3) The barrister's opinion is more independent than that of the solicitor whose most important client may be this client: the barrister is in any case unlikely to see the same client again.
(4) The barrister's easy access to law libraries is greater and he can work without the distraction of telephone calls from clients or their correspondence to answer.
(5) A divided profession makes specialisation easier."

The exclusive advocacy rights possessed by the Bar remained intact. They were regarded as an indispensable feature of the divided profession. At this time a possible way of securing an extension of solicitors' rights of audience without the intervention of Parliament was rediscovered. Some of the Courts of Quarter Sessions which then existed were open to solicitor advocates. It had long been held that these courts were self-regulating and had power to allow solicitors to appear before them. This was confirmed when in 1945 Lincoln (Parts of Kesteven) Sessions withdrew the rights of audience solicitors enjoyed there. The Bar endeavoured to have solicitors excluded from Lincoln (Parts of Holland) Sessions in 1962 and again in 1964, but without success. This hidden conflict was not new. As far back as 1889 a Mr. Bott sought to regain his right as a solicitor to appear at Oswestry Quarter Sessions but failed.[33]

The British Legal Association, following Mr. Bott's example, organised a national campaign in 1969 to secure the right of audience for solicitors at selected Quarter Sessions throughout the country.[34] Individual applications were made by members of the Association in places as far apart as Teesside and Portsmouth, Bristol and Bedfordshire but they all met the same fate as that of Mr. Bott and were rejected. This unusual display of militancy coincided with a relaxation of the rules governing the transfer of solicitors to the Bar.[35]

---

32. Lord Gardiner, *op. cit.*, p. 21–2.
33. *Re. Botts Case* (1889) 24 Law Journal 28.
34. *BLA Solicitor*, January 1969, p. 8, March 1969, p. 8. *Evening Standard*, 2 April 1969, p. 10. *Daily Mail*, 7 May 1969. P. H. Reeves, 'The Right of Audience at Quarter Sessions' 1968 *New Law Journal* 819.
35. *Infra* p. 38.

6.   The Royal Commissions

The higher criminal courts of Assizes and Quarter Sessions came under
scrutiny in the 1960s. They were not meeting the demands of a rising
crime rate combined with the existing concentrations of population and
twentieth century communications. The Circuit system, from which
Assizes had arisen, can be traced back to the thirteenth century.[36]
The Royal Commission on Assizes and Quarter Sessions was appointed
in 1966 under the chairmanship of Lord Beeching to enquire into and
report upon the reforms needed to dispose of the business of the courts
more efficiently. The terms of reference were wide enough to include a
review of the rights of solicitors and barristers to practise as advocates in
the courts concerned. In its submission to the Commission, The Law
Society put forward a case "for some extension of solicitors' right of
audience" and stressed the advantages which this would bring to the
public. The Commission's report recommended that solicitors should
have limited rights to appear before the proposed Crown Court,
comparable with those already existing, and also be eligible to serve as
Recorders and Circuit judges.[37] The report was acted upon and the
Courts Bill introduced in Parliament. Initially there was no provision for
solicitors to act as advocates in the new Crown Court which was to
replace Assizes and Quarter Sessions. It soon became apparent that this
was not acceptable to The Law Society and eventually an enabling clause
was included giving the Lord Chancellor power to issue directions
permitting solicitors to appear before sessions of the Crown Court either
generally or in a particular place.[38] Two practice directions have been
made. They restored to solicitors rights of audience comparable with
those they had enjoyed in the old courts of Quarter Sessions. In addition,
new but very limited rights were granted to conduct appeals from
Magistrates' Courts to the Crown Court.[39] In contrast to this minor
improvement in a solicitor's opportunity to practise advocacy a major
advance was made in the area of judicial appointments. The recommendation that solicitors should be eligible to serve as Recorders and as
Circuit judges was accepted and enacted.[40]

The new Crown Court system removed some of the causes of
discontent. The media, though, continued to criticise legal services
generally. Complaints of delay, high cost and inefficiency constantly
appeared in the press. Conveyancing procedures and in particular alleged
excessive charges were condemned.

---

36.   Magna Carta Chap. XVIII.
37.   Royal Commission on Assizes and Quarter Sessions, Report, 1969, Cmnd. 4153 p.
          127–8, para. 401 and p. 84, para. 248.
38.   Courts Act 1971 s. 12.
39.   *Infra* p. 29–30.
40.   Courts Act 1971 s.16 and s.21.

The Government reacted to this mood by appointing the Royal Commission on Legal Services under the chairmanship of Sir Henry Benson (now Lord Benson) in 1977. The response to requests for evidence was widespread and large. Nearly 3,500 persons and organisations made submissions, of which over 2,000 came from private individuals. The latter were not published, having been regarded as confidential. With few exceptions, the remaining evidence and records of the Commission were deposited with the Public Record Office. Sets of the published evidence have also been supplied to other bodies, including the Bodleian Library, Oxford and the library of the Middle Temple.[41] In its Final Report the Benson Commission rejected both fusion and a general extension of solicitors' right of audience as a way of improving legal services.[42] On the rights of audience issue opinion was divided. Seven of fifteen members concluded that a solicitor should have the right to appear in the Crown Court on behalf of a defendant pleading guilty.[43] Three members went further and thought that this right should apply to all but the more serious and complex defended cases.[44]

The Benson Commission, after a long and wide ranging enquiry, did not recommend any radical changes in the structure or practices of the divided profession. In one area this satisfaction with the status quo was met with some scepticism. Critics of the conveyancing system were not convinced by the Commission's reasoning. A majority had concluded that the monopoly should be maintained.[45] This did not prove to be acceptable to public or political opinion. To the surprise of the legal establishment, Austin Mitchell's Bill for the introduction of licensed conveyancers passed a first reading in Parliament. The Government's promise to implement the proposals in the Bill in return for its withdrawal was a shock to solicitors. Reacting quickly, The Law Society pointed out that this would mean a fundamental change in the allocation of work to the legal profession. At the time the Benson Commission was deliberating, the Society's submission upon the rights of audience issue was made upon the assumption that the conveyancing monopoly would not be disturbed. The drastic change contemplated justified a change of attitude towards this question. For this reason, the campaign to secure parity on advocacy rights with the Bar in all courts was begun.

There is little doubt that the universal right of audience for solicitors will bring fusion closer. Lord Gardiner put forward this view when he wrote:[46]

41. Benson Commission Report, p. 7, para. 1.23.
42. *Ibid.*, pp. 201–2, paras. 17.45–6 and p. 219, para. 18.60.
43. *Ibid.*, p. 807 ND 2.14–6.
44. *Ibid.*, p. 818 ND 5.22.
45. *Ibid.*, p. 266, para. 21.61.
46. Lord Gardiner, *op. cit.* p. 3–4.

"It would mean that solicitors could do everything a barrister can do while a barrister would remain unable to do most of the things solicitors do. On these terms what possible object would anyone have in being a barrister?"

The Law Society reached the same conclusion and added that fusion, if it came, would not be against the public interest.

7. Legal Education

The divided profession and independence of the Inns of Court have contributed to the ascendancy of the Common Law system over Roman Law in England and Wales and also to the form and nature of legal and professional education. Weber explains the influence in this way:[47]

"The reason for the failure of all attempts to codify English law in a rational way as well as the rejection of Roman law lay in the successful resistance of the great centrally organised Lawyers' guilds, a monopolistic stratum of honoratiores, who have produced from their ranks the judges of the great courts. They kept the legal education as a highly developed empirical technique in their own hands and combatted the menace of their social and material position which threatened to arise from the ecclesiastical courts and for a time also from the universities in their attempt to rationalise the legal system."

There is a connection between the legal educational activities of the Inns of Court in early times[48] and the separate law schools provided by the governing bodies of the divided profession today. In the Middle Ages, the universities of Oxford and Cambridge had law faculties. Their association with continental scholars and universities fostered the teaching of Roman Law in England to the exclusion of local law. As a consequence, it was the Inns of Court which provided the organised teaching of the Common Law to their student members. In 1598 there were six Inns of Court and eight Inns of Chancery. Gradually the educational work which they undertook declined because of the difficulty in providing able instructors. Suitable practitioners were reluctant to neglect their professional work to supervise moots and exercises. Eventually, the Civil War, with the disruption it caused, ended the educational activities of the Inns. Apprenticeship replaced tuition of a formal kind in both branches of the profession. For solicitors and attorneys this type of training in the form of articles of clerkship became compulsory by statute in 1729.[49] Having been finally excluded from

---

47. V. Aubert ed. *Sociology of Law* (Penguin Books, 1969) p. 157. Excerpt from Max Rheinstein (ed), Max Weber, *Law in Economy and Society* (Harvard University Press 1954) pp. 349-56.
48. Report of the Committee on Legal Education, Mar. 1971, Cmnd. 4549, p. 4, para. 10 *et seq.*
49. 2 Geo II c. 23 An Act for the Better Regulation of Attornies and Solicitors.

membership of the four Inns of Court in about 1801 they joined the Chancery Inns. By this time these Inns had declined as teaching institutions. During the following period, The Law Society was founded and eventually became responsible for the professional education of solicitors.[50]

In the mid eighteenth century, Blackstone and Viner attempted to introduce Common Law studies at Oxford University. On Viner's death, a chair in Common Law was endowed and Blackstone became the first Vinerian professor, a post which, in recent years, was occupied by Sir Rupert Cross, a solicitor. Blackstone's Commentaries were the lectures which he gave from 1758 to 1765. It was not until 1826 that the first modern university school in England was established at University College, London. In 1833, a chair of Law was created at King's College, London.

Concern over the state of legal education resulted in the appointment of a Select Committee on Legal Education in 1846.[51] Its report revealed an almost total lack of institutional law teaching. At the Inns of Court there was no formal instruction or examination of any kind for students before they were called to the Bar. The keeping of terms by eating a certain number of dinners in Hall had, however, become a requirement before call. With solicitors, the position was also considered to be unsatisfactory. Such examinations as articled clerks were bound to take served, in the Committee's words:[52]

". . . merely as a guarantee against absolute incompetency."

Articles of clerkship were regarded as inadequate because of lack of supervision and direction by the principal.

The Committee decided as a general policy that "special institutions" should be entrusted with the provision of professional training and the control of qualifying examinations. In this context the role of universities was considered and the view taken that academic study had as its end:[53]

". . . not so much the acquirement of knowledge as the creating and maintaining the habit of acquiring it; nor is it less true that a few subjects well mastered, outweigh in real utility many indifferently or partially attended to . . . It would indeed be a total misapprehension of the purposes and character of this University Legal Education to consider it a substitute for, or even appropriate to, the peculiar purposes of the professional student. In this, as in other departments, the special institution is absolutely necessary."

Over the past 130 years, this policy of confining academic legal education

---

50. *Handbook of the Law Society*, 1938 (Council of the Law Society), p. 21.
51. Report from the Select Committee on Legal Education 25 Aug. 1846 H. of C. p. 686.
52. *Ibid.*, p. 686.
53. *Ibid.*, p. xlv and p. xlvii.

to the universities and institutions of higher education and of providing special institutions for professional education and training in law has been followed. The universities responded by creating law faculties and instituting law degrees which included Common Law studies. The Inns of Court began to re-introduce formal teaching for student barristers and in 1852 The Council of Legal Education was formed. The Law Society, at this stage, because of internal differences, did not found a teaching institution.

In 1870, a proposal was put forward by The Legal Education Association to establish a "General School of Law" based upon the Inns of Court to provide joint education for Bar students and articled clerks. The Middle Temple and Gray's Inn supported the scheme. The Council of the Law Society opposed it but, at a general meeting, they were outvoted by younger members.[54] A motion to establish the suggested school then came before the House of Commons supported by Sir Roundell Palmer (later Lord Selbourne L.C.). Mr. G. B. Gregory, a solicitor, said in opposition to the proposal:[55]

> "The scheme . . . was supported by young and ambitious spirits, who desired an absolute fusion of the two branches of the profession."

The motion was defeated. Several later attempts to revive the idea failed, the last one being in 1875. Renewed efforts were made to create an institution to provide joint legal education by amalgamating the teaching responsibilities of the Council of Legal Education and The Law Society as part of a separate university in London to be called "Gresham University". The Law Society supported the plan but as the Inns of Court would not co-operate the move was abandoned.

When the buildings of Clifford's Inn and New Inn, both Chancery Inns, were sold, a large sum of money became available for the purposes of legal education. A joint committee of the Law Society and the four Inns of Court was appointed to draw up a scheme to use this money for the creation of a school of law. A draft charter was prepared but the proposal was defeated by the opposition of the Inner Temple. Attempts to unify legal professional education during this period came to an end when the Haldane Commission on University Education in London observed:[56]

> "The proposal to found a great school of law in London has been made more than once and has come to nothing. In our view the real seat of learning, and the source of scientific instruction, is a university and we think it is as a faculty of the university in its proper relation to all

54. Report, *op. cit.* (note 51 *supra*), p. 10. para. 23.
55. Hansard Parl. Deb. (1871) ccviii, col. 250.
56. Royal Commission on University Education in London, Final Report 1913, Cmnd. 671, para. 338.

other departments of learning, that a great school of law can be developed, and the scientific study of law pursued in a spirit of freedom and independence."

Following these unsuccessful attempts to institute joint education and training, the Inns of Court and The Law Society continued upon their separate ways. They each retained the responsibility for the provision of teaching establishments and the conduct of qualifying examinations. The Council of Legal Education founded the Inns of Court School of Law for barristers, and The Law Society's School of Law was established for solicitors.

In 1967, a Committee on Legal Education was appointed under the chairmanship of Mr. Justice Ormerod, to consider the legal education of the two branches of the profession generally and in particular:[57]

"The contribution which can be made by the Universities and Colleges of Further Education; and the provision of training by The Law Society and the Council of Legal Education, the co-ordination of such training, and of qualifying examinations relating thereto . . ."

A majority of the Committee favoured the proposal that the vocational stage of legal education should be provided within the university and college of further education structure. Arguments advanced in support were directed mainly to the superior resources and facilities of these institutions and the belief that this was the only practical way of achieving a common educational scheme for the two branches of the profession. It was felt that an independent law school suffered "the disadvantage of being mono-technic with limited facilities." Accordingly the following recommendation was made:[58]

". . . inquiry and negotiation should begin at once with a view to establishing by 1977 vocational courses in not less than four university centres into which the Inns of Court School of Law and College of Law would merge; these centres would conduct the vocational courses and award certificates or diplomas which, with a law degree or its equivalent, would qualify for practice."

This proposal was not adopted and the two independent professional training institutions remain.

The opposition to joint professional education can be viewed as a by-product of the divided profession. Those who do not support fusion will have perceived that the characteristics of the two distinct branches would become blurred and eventually disappear if all lawyers received the same vocational education and training. In order to maintain the social customs and working methods of the Bar it is essential to separate entrants to the profession at the beginning of their training.

57. Report, *op. cit.*, (note 48 *supra*) p. 1, para. 1.
58. *Ibid.*, p. 96, para. 24.

CHAPTER 2

The Profession Overseas

1. The English Connection

Casual references are made to other jurisdictions with comparable legal systems when fusion is discussed. Lord Gardiner mentions the position in the United States, Australia and New Zealand, but only briefly.[1] The Benson Commission contains a few comments upon the position in New Zealand and the United States.[2] A systematic review of legal education with reference to fusion is to be found in the Ormerod Report on Legal Education.[3] Direct comparisons of the structure of legal professions are not otherwise easy to find. Those who oppose fusion, however, usually refer only to the disadvantages which they believe exist in countries with a unified profession. These are often vague and so cannot be regarded as convincing evidence to support the dual system as it operates in England and Wales.

There is, however, a common factor among the countries which have only one legal profession. None of them show any sign whatsoever of restructuring upon the lines of the English system. It is only in Australia that practitioners are compulsorily divided and then only in three states. The historical reasons for separation are remarkably similar to those of England and Wales. A study by John Forbes of the Australian situation[4] begins with a comprehensive and absorbing account of the development of the profession in England. In relating this to the position in Australia state by state, the two branches, where they exist, are shown to have arisen from a determination to defend and preserve class rights.

2. Australia

Australia does not have a national legal profession. There are six federal states each with its own profession.[5] Of a total of about 16,000 practising lawyers, about 1800 practise as barristers. In the states of South Australia (population 1.2 m), Tasmania (population 0.4 m) and Western Australia

---

1. Lord Gardiner, *op. cit.*, p. 5, 9.
2. Benson Commission Report, p. 200–1, paras. 17.43–4.
3. Report on Legal Education, *op. cit.* (note 48 p. 12), p. 155–77 Appendix D.
4. J. R. Forbes, *The Divided Legal Profession in Australia* (Law Book Co., 1979), p. 1–27.
5. J. R. Forbes, *op. cit.*, p. 29.

(population 1.1 m), there is fusion. In Western Australia, some practitioners by choice restrict their activities to those usually undertaken by the Bar in England and Wales. This arrangement is the result of an innovation of a Mr. Francis Burt in about 1958. It has resulted in the provision of an advocacy service for other firms of solicitors. Some put this development forward as a reason why fusion is not appropriate in England. It is difficult to understand the logic in this argument. Western Australia is sparsely populated and not comparable with the highly industrialised and densely populated United Kingdom. This group of advocates still remains part of a unified profession. There is no question of its members being forced to decide upon advocacy as a career before admission.

In New South Wales (population 4.75 m) and Queensland (population 2 m) there are compulsorily divided professions. Practitioners are admitted as solicitors or barristers. Solicitors are entitled to appear in all courts of their respective states and in the High Court of Australia. Generally speaking, they do so mainly for the purpose of conducting procedural and formal matters.

The state of Victoria (population 3.6 m) has, since 1891, admitted practitioners as solicitors and barristers. It has, since then, been customary for those who wish to become advocates to sign a Roll of Counsel. It will be noted that this takes place after admission. The choice is that of the individual and not dictated by the system.

The topic of fusion is frequently discussed in Australia and its introduction supported by many practitioners. John Forbes puts forward forceful arguments in favour of rationalising the profession in this way where it still remains divided. The defects which he outlines in the system are the ones to be found in this country. The division, he suggests, may continue to be supported by the profession unless there is a radical change in the extent or nature of the work of solicitors. His observation was prophetic. The possibility of fusion has never been so actively discussed in England as it is now. The re-allocation of conveyancing work taking place is the cause of this renewed interest. In Australia, the position is not static and proposals have been put forward in New South Wales for a common admission scheme, which is a step towards unification in that state.

3. New Zealand

New Zealand (population 3.1 m) has a unified legal profession which was first introduced in 1841 by a Supreme Court Ordinance. The qualifying examination entitles those who pass to be admitted as solicitors and barristers. The distinction has no practical effect. A few practise as barristers but this is a voluntary option and the number who do so is not significant. There is no indication that the profession will, on this account, ever become separated upon English lines. A practitioner who becomes Queen's Counsel may only practise as a barrister. However to be eligible for this distinction it is not necessary to have practised exclusively as a barrister previously. The judiciary is selected from the legal profession as a whole.

4.   Canada

Canada (population 23 m) also has a unified legal profession. The rank of Queen's Counsel is retained and all practitioners are solicitors and barristers. The judiciary is appointed from the whole profession and no moves towards separation are contemplated.

CHAPTER 3

The Profession

PART 1—SOLICITORS

1. Organisation

The Law Society has a dual role. It is the governing body of the solicitors' profession and also its professional association. A register, or Roll as it is called, of admitted solicitors is kept by the Society. A name cannot be removed from the Roll except by order of the Society or on death.[1] A person entered on the Roll is not entitled to practise without first obtaining a practising certificate. This is issued by the Society annually upon an applicant satisfying certain conditions. These include the production of an accountant's certificate stating that the applicant's accounts, so far as money belonging to clients is concerned, are in order and comply with prescribed rules. Newly qualified solicitors must have undergone mandatory post qualification training within three years of admission before a third practising certificate will be issued.[2]

A solicitor, though not obliged to be a member of The Law Society, is subject to its disciplinary powers. The Society is governed by a council of 70 members, 56 being elected by members representing 31 constituencies in England and Wales. Each member serves for four years. The Council itself has power to elect the remaining 14 members from those with specialist knowledge of legal practice or areas of the law. Its responsibilities include the education and training of entrants, post qualification training, professional discipline, the administration of a compensation fund and a professional indemnity scheme. Apart from statutory obligations, the Society services a Law Reform Committee and is frequently consulted by the Government on questions of policy. For its members, representations are made to the Government when necessary upon matters affecting their interests. A journal, *The Law Society's Gazette,* is published weekly and each month an issue is combined with the Law Guardian and entitled *Guardian Gazette.* This is supplied to members of the Bar and the judiciary, and contains information and notices relating to Bar matters. The Law Society's Hall in Chancery Lane

---

1. Solicitors Act 1974, s. 2 and 80.
2. P. 25 *infra.*

is maintained with social and library facilities and the Society is generally concerned with its members' interests.

The work of the Society is carried out by special and standing committees comprised of Council members and co-opted members drawn from the general membership. A number of committees are also in existence which are concerned with topics upon which the profession has an interest or collective view. The subjects they cover include criminal law, company law and other specific areas of the law and practice. Disciplinary matters are within the province of the Professional Purposes Committee.

Solicitors are regarded as officers of the Supreme Court.[3] The High Court and Court of Appeal have jurisdiction to hear applications relating to their conduct and exercise disciplinary powers. They are also bound to observe practice rules made by the Law Society under statutory authority[4] which include detailed provisions relating to money held on behalf of clients. For the protection of clients, a compensation fund, administered by the Society, compensates those who have lost money through a solicitor's dishonesty. The responsibility for enforcing practice rules is that of the Society, which has the power to impose penalties.

2.   Finances

The finances of the Law Society are less complex than those of the Bar. Income is derived mainly from the practising certificate fee of £125, a contribution of £30 to the compensation fund and a membership subscription of £18 for town members and £12 for country members. Membership of the Society is not compulsory and currently stands at 39,406. The Society's annual accounts for the year ending 31st December 1984 contain the following analysis of income and expenditure by activity:[5]

	£	£
Income		
Statutory fees	3,222,382	
Subscriptions	421,175	
Gazette—income from advertisements, subscriptions, etc.	2,508,500	
Income from insurance advisory service	938,627	
Investment income	459,603	
Miscellaneous income	270,762	
National information campaign	29,556	
		7,850,605

3. Halsbury *op. cit.* 4th Edition Vol. 44 (1983) p. 191–3, paras. 252–4.
4. Solicitors Act 1974, s. 53.
5. The Law Society, Annual Report of the Council and Accounts for 1984–5, (The Law Society, London) p. 63.

Grant from The Law Society Charity
for educational purposes   794,900

                                                                              8,645,505
Expenditure
Administration expenses   7,018,630
Establishment expenses   1,009,034
National information campaign   213,714

                                                                 8,241,378
Covenanted donations to The Law
Society Charity   889,536

                                                                              9,130,914

Deficit   (485,409)

Taxation Credit   1,694

Deficit   (483,715)

The assets of the Society are shown in the consolidated balance sheet
reproduced below:[6]

	£	£
Fixed Assets		
Freehold land and buildings		241,631
Leasehold property		1
Equipment and furniture		433,810
Library		12,000
		687,442
Current Assets		
Investments	435,726	
Stocks	149,815	
Debtors	2,274,746	
Joint deposit account	289,459	
Short-term deposits	4,271,068	
Bank balances and cash	65,636	
	7,486,450	

Freehold buildings are included at the net book value on 31st
December 1938 plus subsequent additions at cost. Leasehold properties
are shown at cost. Investments are listed at cost, the actual market value
being £1,127,831. The properties are used for the general purposes of the
Society with part devoted to the provision of a library, common room
and catering facilities for members.

6. *Ibid.*, p. 65.

3.   Education and Training

The legal education and training requirements to qualify as a solicitor are prescribed by The Law Society under statutory authority.[7] The present scheme was introduced in 1979 and is governed by regulations and later amendments made by the Society.[8] An entrant to the profession must first enrol as a student and then pass academic and vocational stages of training to qualify for admission. To enrol, a candidate must be eighteen years old, have a good knowledge of English and be a suitable person to become a solicitor. The Society may require an applicant to attend an interview before a committee or panel to consider his or her suitability before issuing a certificate of enrolment.

Once accepted as a student, the possession of a degree in law constitutes the academic stage. About ninety-eight per cent of all students enrolling are graduates and of these about seventy-five per cent have law degrees. Graduates in subjects other than law must pass the Common Professional Examination, usually in six subjects and normally after a full-time course of study for one year. A school leaver without a degree is required to take the full Common Professional Examination after two years' full-time study at a Polytechnic. This examination was originally intended to enable non-law graduates to become either a solicitor or barrister. It is, however, rarely used now as a means of becoming a student barrister.

Another source of entrants is from the ranks of legal executives and assistant justices' clerks who have attained the age of twenty-five years. Fellows of the Institute of Legal Executives or holders of the Diploma of Justices' Clerks Assistants are, for the academic stage, required to pass the Common Professional Examination. A mature student of twenty-five or over may be permitted to take the Common Professional Examination and may be allowed exemption from any subject in which the applicant has already passed an examination of equivalent standard. In addition, he or she must have attained a good standard of education and have "had considerable experience or shown exceptional ability in an academic, professional, business or administrative field." An interview may be required before a panel or committee appointed by the Society to consider whether such an applicant is suitable for admission as a mature student.

The second stage of training, which is vocational, consists of a period of articles of clerkship, a compulsory full-time course in legal subjects and the Final Examination. Approved courses are provided by the College of Law and at designated Polytechnics. Examination scripts are marked

---

7.   Solicitors Act 1974, s. 2 and 80.
8.   Qualifying Regulations 1979 as amended 1982 and 1984.

centrally, regardless of the venue of the course. This ensures a uniformity of standards of marking. Courses are planned to give teaching in areas of the law which are of importance in practice combined with practical instruction. Papers in the Final Examination are based upon the courses as taught and are set by examiners appointed by The Law Society under the following headings:[9]

After 31st August 1985 the Examination shall consist of the following seven papers under the following Heads and the length of time to be allowed for the answering of each paper shall be as shown:

Head A: The Solicitor's Practice	
Accounts	2 hours
Head B: The Solicitor and the Business Client	
1. Business Organisations and Insolvency	3 hours
2. Consumer Protection and Employment Law	2 hours
Head C: The Solicitor and the Private Client	
1. Conveyancing (divided into two parts of 2 hours each, the marks of which shall be aggregated)	4 hours
2. Wills, Probate and Administration	3 hours
3. Family Law	2 hours
Head D: Litigation	
Litigation (divided into two parts of 2 hours each, covering respectively Civil Procedure and Criminal Procedure, the marks of which shall be aggregated)	4 hours

To succeed in the examination all papers must be passed at one session which is held annually in July. A maximum of two subjects, in which a candidate fails, may be referred and taken in the following February if a specified minimum standard has been reached. This process can be repeated three times. In the event of failure, the whole Final Examination must be taken again without any concession for earlier passes, unless the Society waives or varies this rule "in exceptional circumstances."

Articles of clerkship have always been an important feature of a solicitor's training. It was as long ago as 1729 that they became compulsory.[10] Service as a clerk bound by contract to a practitioner for a term of five years was then stipulated as a qualification for admission as a solicitor or attorney. The term 'articles', which is still used to describe what is in modern terms in-service training, has not altered over the centuries. The effectiveness and control during the period served has improved beyond measure. Until recent times, it was only necessary to

9. The Law Society Final Examination Rules 1984, Rule 3 (2).
10. 2 Geo. II c. 23, An Act for the Better Regulation of Attornies and Solicitors.

produce evidence that the required term had been served. A premium was often demanded by the principal, which could be as much as five thousand pounds according to present day values, and no salary was paid.

Today, an articled clerk receives a modest salary which must be at a level acceptable to The Law Society. Each year, minimum figures are published for central London, outer London and the provinces. They lie between a grossed up maintenance grant paid to an under-graduate living in lodgings and the salary of a newly qualified solicitor. The Law Society will not register a deed of articles if less than the recommended figure is to be paid, including the amount of an annual review. This is an effective control for if articles are not registered they are invalid for qualification purposes.

Service under articles is governed by the terms and conditions set out in a formal document being an agreement entered into between a trainee solicitor and a qualified practising solicitor.[11] A model form, reproduced in Appendix A, is published by The Law Society and some of the conditions it contains are mandatory. An agreement must, inter alia, stipulate the salary to be paid, give details of the basic legal topics available for instruction, provide for the maintenance of training records and include a conciliation clause setting out a procedure to be followed if any difficulty or dispute should arise between the parties. The normal term of articles is two years. A law graduate entrant must serve at least eighteen months of this period immediately after taking the final examination. If the academic stage has been completed by passing the Common Professional Examination the whole term of articles may be served before taking the Final Examination. Usually, however, most entrants follow the scheme laid down for law graduates. All articles must be registered with The Law Society within one month after signing. The principal solicitor must have held a practising certificate for five years immediately before the beginning of the term and is normally restricted to having two clerks at any one time.

Apart from the specific legal topics and basic skills which are specified in a deed of articles it is expected that training will be given in office routines and procedures. A principal is under a duty to supervise work undertaken and to ensure that the practical training is properly organised. Training records must be kept by the articled clerk and The Law Society provides a model diary and check lists for guidance and specimens are reproduced in Appendices B and C. When the term under articles has ended, a certificate of training, signed by the principal, is required by the Society. Should it be considered that inadequate

11.   *Guide for Principals Taking Articled Clerks*, The Law Society.

instruction has been given in the topics mentioned in the deed of articles the Society can ask for the training records to be produced. These are then taken into account in deciding whether further training is needed.

An established conciliation procedure exists to deal with problems which may arise between a principal and articled clerk. Local Law Societies co-operate by appointing solicitors to act as conciliation officers to whom disputes may be referred. Should it not be possible to resolve a difference at this stage, The Law Society has power to order the discharge of articles but this is rarely used.

A solicitor's legal education does not end upon being qualified. On 1st August 1985 a system of mandatory continuing education was introduced.[12] Courses must be attended during the three years following admission. These consist of two compulsory subjects—professional conduct and office management and efficiency—and a wide range of optional ones. The latter include advocacy, child care procedure, Legal Aid, ancilliary applications in matrimonial cases, Industrial Tribunal procedure, Common Market Law and many other areas of legal practice. A points system operates, a prescribed number being awarded for each course. A minimum total is set for each year. This must be achieved within three years of admission. The attendance requirements are modest and it is expected that practitioners will continue to attend courses voluntarily after the three year period.

A barrister of the English Bar who wishes to become a solicitor must first be disbarred. If the applicant practised at the Bar in England and Wales (other than as a pupil) for at least three years during the previous five years, concessions may be granted. Upon satisfying the Society that he or she is a suitable person to become a solicitor, then only such examinations as the Society considers necessary need to be taken to qualify for admission. A barrister whose "experience in the practice of English law is such that it is unnecessary for him to serve under articles of clerkship" may be required to complete satisfactorily courses prescribed by the Society and be employed by a practising solicitor for up to two years before being admitted. Other barristers who are not within these categories are not allowed any concession and they must qualify in the normal way. This is only a résumé of the regulations which are set out in full in Appendix D.[13]

Students encounter problems in finding articles with suitable firms. A survey conducted in 1978 by the Trainee Solicitors' Group revealed that about one third of articled clerks secured their articles through personal contact. About ninety per cent of all articles are taken in private

---

12. R. N. Page, 'Compulsory Continuing Education' 82 *Gazette* 2141–44 (1985). The Law Society Post-Admission Training Regulations 1985.
13. Qualification Regulations 1974 R. 56 as amended in 1982.

practices.[14] A register is kept by The Law Society listing solicitors who employ trainees and entitled Register of Solicitors Employing Trainees (ROSET). It is up-dated each year and lists over 3,000 firms, giving information of their size, recruitment policies and the kind of work undertaken. Other sources of articles are local government departments, Magistrates' Courts and, to a lesser degree, industry, commerce and law centres.

The present entry scheme, as outlined and introduced in 1978/79, is, it is considered, now fully reflected in the number of solicitors admitted in 1984 i.e. 2,728. There had been a steady increase over the years since 1974 when there were 1,848 admissions apart from exceptionally high numbers of over 3,000 in 1980 and 1981. Admissions in the future will be directly related to the places at approved teaching institutions for the compulsory one year law course required before taking the Final Examination. At present these number 3,352. It has been estimated that annual admissions will eventually rise to about 3,000, but this estimate is not based upon ascertainable data.

The number of women entrants shows a significant increase. During 1983, approximately 44 % of the 3,472 prospective students who applied for enrolment were women. Of the 194 Oxford University graduates who embarked upon the Law Society course in 1984, 50 % were women.[15] In the same year 2,623 deeds of articles were registered and of these 49.6 % were those of women. Of the 47,600 solicitors on the Roll in 1983 a sample analysis of those aged under 65 showed that about 17% were women concentrated in the lower age groups. In 1984, of the 2,728 admissions, 39.3% were women. The records examined suggest that a relatively high proportion of women take employment in local government, nationalised industries and commerce.[16]

4. Discipline

An established procedure exists to handle complaints against solicitors. The Professional Purposes Department first decides whether professional mis-conduct is involved. If so, an attempt is made to settle the matter by correspondence with the solicitor concerned. If the client does not accept the solicitor's explanation, the facts are referred to the Professional Purposes Committee. If the committee does not uphold the complaint, the client is informed of his or her right to ask the Lay Observer to examine the case.

14. *Trainee Solicitors Handbook*, The Law Society Trainee Solicitors Group, 1984.
15. University of Oxford Appointments Committee Report 1983–84 p. 7.
16. P. G. Marks, 'A Statistical Summary of the Solicitors' Profession' 81 *Gazette* 2607–8 (1984) and 82 *Gazette* 2903–14 (1985).

If the Professional Purposes Committee decides that a complaint is justified, it has power to reprimand the solicitor and to impose restrictions upon a practising certificate, governing the manner in which the solicitor may practise e.g. not to practise without a partner or, alternatively, to bring the complaint before the Solicitors' Disciplinary Tribunal.[17] This tribunal is an independent body established by statute whose members are appointed by the Master of The Rolls. They must be solicitors of ten years standing or lay persons or barristers who are not solicitors. An officiating tribunal must have at least three members, one being a lay member. The procedure followed is similar to that of a trial in court, the parties being present and represented if they wish. A hearing is held in private but findings are made public and published in the *Law Society's Gazette*.

A complaint may also be referred to the Lay Observer, an independent official appointed by the Lord Chancellor:[18]

> ". . . to examine any written allegations by or on behalf of a member of the public concerning the Society's treatment of a complaint about a solicitor or an employee of a solicitor made to the Society by that member of the public or on his behalf."

This office is funded by the Government and operates from the Royal Courts of Justice in London. A Lay Observer has power to examine and report upon complaints received within three months of the date on which the Society has notified the complainant of its decision. Consideration of a case is based upon the Society's entire file of papers and any other information supplied on request. A written report is then made and sent to the complainant and the Society. The Observer does not have the power to take any other action. An annual report is submitted by the Observer and laid before each House of Parliament, but this must not identify any individual or firm.

5. Practising Arrangements

Unlike barristers, solicitors have an unfettered right of establishment and are allowed to practise together in partnership. It is an offence if an unqualified person wilfully:[19]

> ". . . pretends to be, or takes or uses any name title, addition or description implying that he is qualified or recognised by law as qualified to act as a solicitor. . ."

17. Solicitors Act 1974, s. 3.
18. *Ibid*. s. 45.
19. *Ibid*. s. 21.

A total of 44,837 practising certificates was issued in the year ending 31st October 1984.[20] Of these 25,656 held professional indemnity insurance certificates. Insurance is compulsory for principal solicitors in private practice and covers the solicitors they employ.

Partnerships vary in size and the present distribution is set out below.[21]

	No. of Firms	*No. of Principals*
Sole Practitioner	4,146	4,146
2 Partners	1,834	3,668
3 Partners	1,087	3,261
4 Partners	652	2,608
5 Partners	415	2,075
6 Partners	241	1,446
7 Partners	193	1,351
8 Partners	110	880
9 Partners	78	702
10 Partners	84	840
11–15 Partners	159	1,979
16–19 Partners	52	891
20 and Over	57	1,809

The figure of 4146 shown to be sole practitioners includes a significant number who work part-time or only occasionally do legal work. It has not been possible to ascertain the numbers and distribution of qualified and unqualified staff employed by partnerships.

The profession undertakes a wide range of work of immense variety. Some of this is reserved exclusively to solicitors, and legal protection is given to prevent unqualified persons competing with them. It is a statutory offence for a person who is not qualified to:[22]

> "(a) act as a solicitor, or as such issue any writ or process, or commence, prosecute or defend any action, suit or other proceeding, in his own name or in the name of any other person, in any court of civil or criminal jurisdiction; or
>
> (b) act as a solicitor in any cause or matter, civil or criminal, to be heard or determined before any justice or justices or any commissioners of Her Majesty's revenue."

and also "for reward" to "draw or prepare any . . . instrument relating to . . . any legal proceedings."[23] These statutory provisions effectively prevent anyone who is not a solicitor conducting proceedings in the courts on behalf of a litigant.

20. The Law Society Annual Report of the Council and Accounts for 1984–5, p. 42.
21. Source, The Law Society, Dec 1984.
22. Solicitors Act 1974, s. 20.
23. *Ibid.* s. 22(1)(b).

Restrictions also affect the legal procedure for obtaining a grant of probate of a will or, where there is no will, letters of administration. Should the issue of a grant be disputed and differences fall to the court to be decided, the matter becomes contentious. A non-qualified person cannot then act in relation to any proceedings which ensue. Where an application is not contentious, it is an offence if an unqualified person, for or in expectation of reward:[24]

"(a) takes instructions for a grant of probate or of letters of administration: or
(b) draws or prepares any papers on which to found or replace such a grant"

None of these restrictions prevent an individual acting in a personal capacity as a litigant or administrator or executor of a deceased person's estate.

In the courts, the respective rights of audience enjoyed by solicitors and barristers act to prevent unqualified persons, with some exceptions in the Magistrates' Courts and County Courts, acting as advocates. Litigants can appear in person before any court or tribunal. They are also allowed to have the assistance of a lay friend or relative who may:[25]

"take notes, quietly make suggestions and give advice . . ."

but this does not extend to addressing the court.[26] Summarised, the courts in which a solicitor may appear and represent a party to proceedings are:—

(a) the House of Lords, but only to apply for leave to appeal;
(b) the Court of Appeal, but only to make applications to a single judge in chambers in the Criminal Division;
(c) the High Court in open court for specified bankruptcy applications and in chambers before a judge, official referee, master or registrar;
(d) the Crown Court, but limited to specified sessions and cases, as detailed below;
(e) the County Courts, Magistrates' Courts, Employment Appeals Tribunal (a division of the High Court) and nearly all statutory tribunals.

The right of solicitors to conduct cases in the Crown Court is governed by practice directions set out in Appendix E, made by the Lord Chancellor under the provisions of the Courts Act 1971, s. 12.[27] Since 1st January 1972, they are permitted to appear before sessions of the Court held at Caernarvon, Barnstaple, Bodmin or Doncaster. Summarised, the right is restricted to:

24. *Ibid.* s. 23.
25. *McKenzie v McKenzie* [1970] 3 WLR 472.
26. *Meray v Persons Unknown* [1974] C.L.Y. 3003.
27. Practice Directions 7 December 1971 [1972] 1 All ER 144 and 9 February 1972 [1972] 1 All ER 608.

(a) appeals from magistrates' courts;
(b) proceedings on committal by a magistrates' court of a person to be
     sentenced or "to be dealt with";
(c) offences stipulated in the class 4 category as designated by the
     Lord Chief Justice with the concurrence of the Lord Chancellor.
     Generally speaking these exclude offences of a grave nature;
(c) civil cases in which the Crown Court has original or appeal
     jurisdiction.

At Lincoln, the right is extended to the cases mentioned above only
where they originate from magistrates' courts situated in the County of
the Parts of Holland and, in civil cases, where before the Courts Act 1971
they were within the province of the court of quarter sessions for the area.

In addition to the rights outlined, which are restricted to particular
sessions of the Court, there is a limited general right of audience. This
permits solicitors to "conduct, defend and address the court" in civil and
criminal appeals, committals for sentence and cases to be dealt with
which, in each instance, originate in a magistrates' court. This right can
only be exercised by the solicitor, his or her partner or an employee who
conducted the original proceedings in the magistrates' court. According
to the honorary secretary of the Criminal Courts Solicitors' Association,
this general right is used extensively in London.[28]

Conveyancing, until recently, was almost the exclusive province of
solicitors. This near monopoly was maintained by making it an offence
for an unqualified person to prepare or draw a document relating to land
for or in expectation of the payment of a fee.[29] It was of great importance
to solicitors as a considerable proportion of fees earned were derived
from conveyancing. This was changed by legislation enacted pursuant to
the undertaking given by the Government when Austin Mitchell's House
Buyers' Bill[30] was withdrawn. The Benson Commission's firm recommendation that conveyancing should remain with solicitors was ignored.
Accepting the principle that their near monopoly should be broken the
Conveyancing Committee, under the chairmanship of Professor Julian
Farrand, was appointed to consider the necessary legislation. The main
proposals of the Committee form the basis of part II of the
Administration of Justice Act 1985.

This Act established the Council for Licensed Conveyancers to
régulate the provision of conveyancing services by licensed conveyancers.
The Council has a maximum of twenty one members of whom no more
than eleven can be licensed conveyancers. It has a statutory duty to
regulate the standard of competence and professional conduct of persons

---

28. A. Edwards, 'Rights of Audience' (Letter) 82 *Gazette* 1528 (1985).
29. Solicitors Act 1974, s. 22.
30. *Infra* p. 91.

who are licensed to provide conveyancing services as defined in the Act namely:[31]

> "(3) References in this Part to conveyancing services are references to the preparation of transfers, conveyances, contracts and other documents in connection with, and other services ancillary to, the disposition or acquisition of estates or interests in land; and for the purposes of this subsection—
>
> > (a) "disposition"—
> > > (i) does not include a testamentary disposition or any disposition in the case of such a lease as is referred to in section 54(2) of the Law of Property Act 1925 (short leases); but
> > > (ii) subject to that, includes in the case of leases both their grant and their assignment; and
> > (b) "acquisition" has a corresponding meaning."

The Council's obligations extend to the formulation of rules governing the education and training of those seeking to practise as licensed conveyancers including examinations to be passed and practical training and experience. The establishment of separate accounts for clients' money and the circumstances under which interest arising therefrom must be paid to a client are specified. The Council must also make rules for professional indemnity in respect of claims against licensed conveyancers and for the compensation of clients for loss in consequence of negligence or fraud.

A controversial section allows the Council to permit the provision of conveyancing services by 'recognised bodies' managed and controlled by licensed conveyancers either alone or with persons who are not licensed. It has, however, been stated that this will not permit lending institutions to act for their own borrowers. Further legislation is contemplated to deal with this situation.

The restraints imposed for the protection of the client are equal to those of The Law Society. In one respect licensed conveyancers are quasi lawyers for they are entitled to legal professional privilege in the following terms:[32]

> "**33.**—Any communication made—
> > (a) to or by a licensed conveyancer in the course of his acting as such for a client; or
> > (b) to or by a recognised body in the course of its acting as such for a client,"

shall in any legal proceedings be privileged from disclosure in like manner as if the licensed conveyancer or body had at all material times been acting as the client's solicitor.

---

31. Administration of Justice Act 1985. s. 11(3).
32. *Ibid.* s. 33.

An Investigating Committee is responsible for the preliminary investigation of alleged failure to comply with the Council's rules or conditions. A Disciplinary and Appeals Committee hears and determines cases referred to it by the Investigating Committee. The Committee has the power to disqualify and there is a right of appeal to the High Court. There are no other restrictions which prevent competition arising from sources outside the profession. The administration of estates provides an example of an area in which there is open competition. Banks and trust corporations, who meet certain statutory financial requirements, are entitled to act as professional executors and administrators. Although not permitted to obtain a grant of probate or letters of administration, they may perform and charge for other work involved in administering an estate. Such competition does not appear to diminish the demand for the services of solicitors. The profession, in fact, continues to expand.

The average firm provides at local level the type of legal services which over decades have been needed in most rural and urban areas. Barristers are used frequently in litigious matters and for the representation of clients in court. Specialist opinions are sought upon legal problems and documents settled. Solicitors have contact with sets of chambers and may know the barristers they consult personally. In unusual or special matters, the opinion of a chambers clerk is often relied upon to select a suitable barrister. Should a brief be returned, a degree of latitude will be given to the clerk in selecting a substitute. It is this relationship between the clerk and solicitor which contributes greatly to the prosperity of a set of chambers. As one writer has observed, "As long as the Bar forbids advertising, the clerk will be required to publicise the Barrister"[33]

The freedom which solicitors enjoy to provide services where they are needed no doubt contributes to their success in combatting competition, as the continuing growth of the profession testifies. Many firms have been established for long periods and their permanence is a characteristic of the profession. This has been achieved without the need to foster ancient customs and rituals. There are few concessions to traditionalism. In recent years, for instance, the title Commissioner for Oaths was abolished and all solicitors were permitted to exercise the functions once associated with this appointment. Elaborate dress is not worn in court or on ceremonial occasions, there is no hierarchical structure and outdated terminology has been discarded. The profession is able to present a contemporary image to the public, uncomplicated by associations with the past.

---

33. J. A. Flood *Barristers' Clerks—The Law's middlemen* 1983 Manchester University Press p. 133.

PART 2—BARRISTERS

1. Organisation of the Bar

The organisation of the Bar is complex. Seven separate bodies are involved in training and regulating the profession. The method of election to the groups which control each of these entities varies from one to the other. Their functions are not, in all instances, clearly defined and some have powers which are exercised independently. They have distinguished titles, being known respectively as the four Inns of Court, the Senate of the Inns of Court and the Bar, the Bar Council and the Council for Legal Education. There are also six Circuits which are autonomous groups of practising barristers.

The Inns of Court are voluntary unincorporated societies of equal status. They are known as The Honourable Societies of Lincoln's Inn, The Inner Temple, The Middle Temple and Gray's Inn. Each society owns and occupies a group of buildings known by the name of the Inn and, in the case of Inner Temple and Middle Temple, they are held under a Royal Charter granted by James I. The Inns are said to provide a collegiate environment for students and young barristers with a limited degree of training in the form of moots, lectures and practical exercises. They do, however, have other functions of a social nature which benefit all of their members. Each Inn is responsible for the management of the extensive holding of property under its control and ownership. This involves the administration and letting of office and residential accommodation and maintenance of common rooms for the use of members. Chambers are provided for practising members, and the acquisition of property for this purpose is funded and library facilities are maintained. Accommodation and catering facilities to enable members to associate regularly for educational and social purposes are provided. Scholarships and bursaries are awarded to students and young barristers.

As now constituted, the Inns have three classes of membership; student, barrister (or hall member) and bencher (or master of the bench). Each Inn is governed by its benchers, who are elected for life by existing benchers. 300–400 benchers are actively involved in running their Inns and of these about one third are practising barristers and the rest judges or retired members. Common regulations[1] adopted by the Inns govern the admission of students and their call to the Bar. The senior officer of an Inn is the Treasurer who is appointed by the benchers annually. An under-treasurer (in Lincoln's Inn, the sub-treasurer) is the head permanent official. The property of each Inn is vested in its benchers.

---

1. Consolidated Regulations.

Although the Inns are independent bodies, they are represented upon the Senate of the Inns of Court and the Bar, which is the central governing body of the profession. The Senate's membership includes six representatives appointed by the Inns of Court, three 'hall representatives' of each Inn who are not benchers, the representatives of the Bar who are elected by members of the Bar and three Circuit judges. The Senate is financed by subscriptions £344,475, contributions from the Inns, £160,000, and other income, £82,847. These figures are for the year ending 5th April 1985.[2] The Senate is responsible for the direction of the legal education of students of the Inns, and keeps under review and, if thought fit, amends the Consolidated Regulations of the Inns of Court. It lays down general policy in all matters affecting the profession (other than in matters over which Bar Council or Inns have exclusive jurisdiction) and the conduct of disciplinary procedures. The Senate also stipulates qualifications for admission to the profession, the location, provision and use of chambers. It is through the Senate that official contact with the Law Society is maintained. The Inns have undertaken to accept and adhere to the policy determined by the Senate upon these matters. Each Inn, however, retains the power to manage its own property, bursaries, scholarships and domestic affairs. Decisions of the Senate which involve expenditure above a sum already agreed with an Inn cannot be enforced.

The Council of Legal Education, acting as a committee of the Senate, conducts the education, training and examination of student members of the Inns. The Council is bound to follow directives upon policy made by the Senate and is constituted as an educational charity. The Inns of Court School of Law is under its management. All aspects of the legal education of the profession including pupillage, the provision of facilities for continuing education and refresher courses and the limited educational activities of the Inns are under the Council's review. Twelve of its members (eight being nominated by the Inns) and the chairman are elected by the Senate, the Dean is an ex officio member and a minimum of twelve but not more than sixteen members are co-opted. The Senate and the Inns are responsible for the Council's finances and its income is derived from invested capital, tuition fees and examination fees charged to students.

The Bar Council is concerned with the affairs of the Bar and specifically:[3]

> "to maintain the standards, honour and independence of the Bar, to promote, preserve and improve the services and functions of the Bar, and to represent and act for the Bar generally as well as in its relations with others and also, in all matters affecting the administration of justice."

2. Senate of the Inns of Court and the Bar, Annual Statement 1984–5, p. 73.
3. Senate Regulations 29 (a).

Constituted under the Senate's regulations,[4] the Bar Council is stated to be autonomous and not subject to any directions from the Senate in the exercise of its powers and functions. The Senate gives the Council financial support and provides accommodation and secretarial services. Its membership is linked closely to the Senate and includes thirty-nine members of the Senate who are representatives of the Bar and a maximum of twelve Senate members who are barristers. Ex officio members are the Senate Treasurer, the Attorney General, the Solicitor General and each Circuit leader.

Each Circuit, to which practising barristers, with some exceptions, customarily belong, is a regional organisation based upon an administrative area of the court Circuits. There are six Circuits, namely the Northern, North Eastern, Midland and Oxford, South Eastern, Western and the Wales and Chester Circuits, each being responsible for its own affairs and managed by a Leader and committee. Originally of a social nature, they supervise and regulate on an informal basis the professional conduct and etiquette of members when working on the Circuit. They also discuss with court officials matters relating to the administrative aspects of court proceedings. Social contact between members of the Circuit and the Bench is maintained through dinners and other functions.

To establish chambers within a Circuit area outside Greater London the approval of the Circuit leader and committee is needed.[5] This effectively restricts the right of establishment and so restricts competition for the work available.

2. Finances of the Inns

It is the policy of the Inns not to publish annual accounts although it is understood that members may inspect them. A commissioned report upon the finances of the Inns, from which the following details were extracted, is contained in the Benson Commission Report.[6] This discloses the position in 1975 and 1976. Assuming that no radical changes in the nature of income received and expenditure have occurred since then, the figures quoted give a guide to the position at the present time. The present day amounts are undoubtedly greatly increased because of inflation but the nature of capital assets and the sources and disposition of income may well be unchanged.

Each Inn is in receipt of income, derived from extensive holdings of real property, in the form of rents for chambers, offices and residential lettings. Chambers is the term used to describe the office accommodation

4. *Ibid.* 11.
5. Code of Conduct p. 60 paras. 1 and 2.
6. Benson Commission Report, Vol. II Surveys and Studies p. 341–372.

let to practising barristers for the purposes of their occupation. Offices are let mainly to solicitors with a small number to other professional tenants. The residential parts are nearly all let to members of the Inn to which they belong.

Rents charged for chambers are usually two thirds of the full market rental. This represents an untaxed subsidy in favour of the tenant. Residential lettings are often at rentals below the full market rental but it is understood that in the Middle Temple a move is being made to charge an estimated registered rent in all instances. Offices are let at full market rentals. The total combined income from these sources for all of the Inns was in 1976, after the deduction of expenses including repair and maintenance costs, £1,442,000.

Income is also received from members and students for admission fees paid by students on entry and payments on being called to the Bar and the Inns Bench. The total under this heading for 1976 was £141,000. Income from investments and other sources amounted to £99,000.

The Inns are not registered as charities with the Charity Commission. Informal discussions with the Inland Revenue resulted in their being treated as charities for taxation purposes, excluding income or gains applied to what are considered to be non-charitable purposes. According to comments made by the Inns upon this question, the items assessed for tax were subscriptions to the Senate and any deficit arising upon catering expenditure for members other than students. This deficit does not take into account administration expenses or a charge for the use of premises and equipment.

Assets of the Inns are mainly freehold property of immense value. Auditors of the Inner Temple and Gray's Inn accounts qualified their report on the 1976 accounts on the grounds that certain fixed assets were not included and that the accounts of Gray's Inn included buildings only at a 1950 valuation of £2.5 million, excluding site value. The accounts of Lincoln's Inn and Middle Temple also omit real property but the accountants auditing these accounts did not qualify their report. Evidence of the value of the properties in 1976 is to be found in the insurance valuation of the buildings at £103 million. Other fixed assets not recorded are silver, pictures and chattels which were insured for £3 million. Fluid assets in the form of stocks of wine are shown in the accounts at cost or realisable value, whichever is the lower, the total for all Inns being £144,000. Investments held, at market value, were £1.1 million and consisted of loans, mainly to staff and members, of £130,000, the remainder being government and convertible stocks and quoted investments. Apart from the income and assets shown in the Inns' accounts, a number of scholarship and other funds are administered, the net value of these assets then being £894,000.

Expenditure for 1976 totalled £2,255,000 and the main items were estate expenses of £809,000, administration £685,000, education £221,000, a loss on catering of £199,000, library £202,000 and the remainder under miscellaneous items, including a subscription to the Senate of £80,000. The gross expenditure upon students in 1976 was estimated at £477,000 which includes £57,000 from trust funds and, after deducting revenue provided by students, the net expenditure amounted to £350,000, representing £350 per student.

It is clear that the institutions and groupings which constitute the professional and social organisation of the Bar would not exist in their present form without the considerable income derived from the Inn's property and the premises which they own and occupy. The Senate is supported to some extent by voluntary contributions but, without the Inns' financial support and provision of accommodation, these would not be adequate to support its present level of activity. Practising barristers also enjoy the untaxed benefit of subsidised accommodation from which to practise and subsidised meals. The Bar Council is financed by the Senate. The Council for Legal Education is provided with accommodation and its finances are the responsibility of the Senate and the Inns.

3. Education and Training

The educational and training requirements to qualify as a barrister and be called to the Bar are prescribed by the Consolidated Regulations of the Inns of Court.[7] To enter the profession, it is necessary to be admitted to one of the Inns as a student member. A solicitor is not eligible for admission and must be removed from the Roll of Solicitors and cease to have any financial interest in a solicitor's practice before joining an Inn. Admission is restricted to law graduates, non-law graduates and mature students. Under-graduates are allowed to enter provided they have passes at a prescribed standard and in subjects specified in the regulations. Mature students must usually have attained the age of twenty-five years, have similar passes and also have experience in an academic, professional, business or administrative field.

The education of students is divided into two parts, which are termed the academic stage and the vocational stage. The possession of an approved law degree passed at a standard acceptable to the Council for Legal Education and within the requisite time satisfies the requirements for the academic stage. For those with a non-law degree but who possess other legal qualifications, a certificate of eligibility is needed. This is issued by the Council and may stipulate conditions relating to further

7. Consolidated Regulations, Reg. 7–14.

courses of study and examinations which must be fulfilled by the student. These are intended to ensure that, taking into account previous academic qualifications, the student will have reached the standard required for an approved degree.

The vocational stage which follows consists of a course at the Inns of Court School of Law provided by the Council for Legal Education which leads to the Bar Examination.

This examination has the following six sections:

(i) General Paper 1—Common Law and Criminal Law;
(ii) General Paper 2—Equity and a special topic;
(iii) Civil and Criminal Procedure;
(iv) Evidence;

and two of the following: Revenue Law, Family Law, Landlord and Tenant, Sale of Goods and Hire Purchase, Local Government and Planning, Practical Conveyancing, Conflict of Laws and European Community Law, Labour Law and Social Security Law and Law of International Trade. A student who intends to practise at the Bar of England and Wales must include Revenue Law in the two optional subjects if not already taken as a degree subject. If, on taking the Bar Examination, a student fails in one section only, a conditional pass may be granted at the discretion of the Board of Examiners who take into account the standard reached in the failed paper. No student who is awarded a conditional pass is entitled to sit a fifth time for the section in which he or she failed unless permission to do so has been given. This is only granted in exceptional circumstances. There are further provisions under which the whole Bar Examination may be taken a fifth time and also for giving credit for passes which have reached a high standard. A student who intends to practise at the Bar of England and Wales must attend the full course provided at the Inns of Court School of Law and participate satisfactorily in Practical Exercises which include advocacy, drafting, court attendances and professional ethics.

A former solicitor wishing to transfer to the Bar is usually required to pass the examinations set in Civil and Criminal Procedure and Evidence for the Bar Examination, but is not required to attend any course provided by the Council for Legal Education. A transfer committee has power to grant exemptions from examinations and practical exercises. A solicitor, before having his or her name removed from the Roll of Solicitors, may apply to the transfer committee for information upon the conditions, including the keeping of terms, upon which transfer would be allowed.

As a member of an Inn, a student, before being called to the Bar, must dine in the Hall of the Inn on three separate days in each term for eight terms. There are a number of exceptions governing the frequency and timing of keeping terms. The purpose of this custom is for the student to be introduced to the collegiate life of the Bar and to take part in moots, mock trials and other activities of professional interest. Solicitors are not as a general rule allowed to participate in the social or educational functions of the Inns. Members of the Inns observe rituals and customs which are passed from one generation to another. These contribute to the maintenance of a group with a recognisable image and uniform standard of professional behaviour.

The handbook of one Inn gives an account of customs which are observed. As their piquancy would be lost if paraphrased, the following extract is given:[8]

"At dinner Masters of the Bench sit at the High Table. Other members are entitled to seats in order of precedence.

Members sit in Messes of four. The senior member, according to the date of his Call to the Bar or admission as a Student, is the Captain of the Mess. The Captain sits in the seat nearer to the wall and nearer to the High Table and the other members of the Mess sit clockwise in order of precedence. Each Mess is self-contained and no member should converse with anyone outside the Mess except that the Captain may speak to the Captain of the adjoining Mess for the purpose of passing the condiments or snuff.

The Ancients' Table below the Cupboard and High Table is reserved for the eight senior barristers in Hall who wish to dine there. In the 16th century the Ancients' Table was occupied by those barristers who had declined to accept the office of Reader and who were not therefore eligible to become Benchers.

When dinner is announced all stand, the Benchers enter the Hall in procession, the Head Porter strikes three blows with a gavel and Grace before Meat is said.

It is the ancient custom of Domus for members of a Mess to "take wine" together before any individual drinks wine. On the invitation of the Captain of the Mess each member "takes wine" with the other members by raising his glass in salute, first to the member of the Mess sitting opposite to him, then to the member sitting diagonally from him and lastly to the member sitting next to him. The salutation being returned by each member of the Mess in turn, the members drink. Those who do not drink alcohol take part by raising their glass of "soft" drink.

At the end of dinner the Head Porter gavels, all rise and Grace after Meat is said, after which the Benchers leave the Hall in procession. Members are then free to leave, but coffee is served and members are encouraged to linger and, if they wish, to mix with members of other Messes."

After being called to the Bar, a barrister must serve for a twelve month period as a pupil in the chambers of a junior barrister who is on a list of approved pupil-masters and has practised for not less than five years. The total period of pupillage need not be served with the same master. For the

8. *The Honourable Society of Middle Temple Handbook*, p. 20–1.

first six months, the pupil may not accept instructions to conduct a case in court. The pupil-master has a general obligation to instruct the pupil in all aspects of court proceedings, including the drafting of pleadings and other documents and giving opinions. The pupil should accompany the pupil-master in court and sit in on conferences. In the second six months, the pupil may accept briefs under the master's supervision. There is no system of monitoring progress either by certification, supervision of the Inns of Court or any other professional body or maintaining mandatory training records. Such control as there is consists only of guidelines laid down by the Senate,[9] which are reproduced in Appendix F.

After qualifying and serving the required period of pupillage, no further training is needed to practise. Unlike solicitors, no scheme for mandatory or voluntary post-qualification training exists. The barrister's expertise is gained from work experience. Some of those who specialise join specialist chambers and belong to specialist Bar associations. These are confined to practitioners who restrict their work to particular fields of law as distinct from being advocates undertaking work of a general nature. A specialist barrister acquires his or her professional status through experience and reputation and there is no provision for higher qualification by examination or formal training.

The total number of barristers practising at the Bar in October 1984 was 5203 (of these 641 were women). 1505 practised wholly or mainly in the provinces and the remainder in London. In the provinces there were 119 sets of chambers and in London 222 sets.[10]

4. Categories

Along with the rules and conventions which regulate the governance and work of barristers, rank and dress further emphasise their separateness. The English Bar has two ranks—Queen's Counsel, called variously leading counsel, silks (because of the silk gown they wear) or leaders; and junior counsel, usually referred to as juniors. Precedence or pre-audience among barristers reflects these groupings. In the Supreme Court, the Attorney General followed by the Solicitor General, when in office, take precedence over all. Queen's Counsel follow, ranking in order of seniority of appointment among themselves, and, finally, junior counsel, who determine precedence among themselves according to their date of call to the Bar.

The Queen, on the advice of the Lord Chancellor, appoints Queen's Counsel. No examination, either written or oral, is involved and any

---

9.   Code of Conduct, p. 4 para. 30, p. 42 Annex 5.
10.   Senate Annual Statement *op. cit.* 1984–5, p. 70.

junior barrister may apply for appointment. A list of the names put forward is prepared annually. A candidate's suitability is assessed through a process of consultation and upon the consideration of personal factors. In addition, the overall position within the profession so far as specialist skills and the number of specialists is taken into account in recommending those who are to be appointed. The distinction, considered to give higher status, is usually, but not always, accompanied by a rise in income. It can lead to a fall in the number of briefs received because of the presumption that greater expense may be incurred. However, financial considerations do not appear to be the only reason for seeking appointment. It is also a way of being relieved of written work in the form of pleadings and opinions. Some find this burdensome after a spell of twenty years or so as a junior. It is known for candidates to support their applications with medical certificates emphasising the need for a reduction in their work load.[11] About ten per cent of practising barristers are Queen's Counsel and in October 1984 there were 545.

At one time, it was a breach of professional etiquette for Queen's Counsel to conduct a case in court unless a junior was instructed to appear with him or her. This rule has been modified and Queen's Counsel may appear alone as an advocate. It is, however, assumed that a junior will also be instructed if the contrary is not stated when instructions are first given. A case may be refused if in the opinion of the Queen's Counsel it would not be possible to conduct it properly without a junior.[12] This overrides the cab-rank principle.

The wig worn with the court dress of barristers emphasises their separateness as a group from solicitors. The gown of today was first introduced on the death of Queen Mary in 1694. It was then adopted as being more convenient than an earlier style. Ede and Ravenscroft, robe makers since 1689, confirm that the style has not changed since that time. A solicitor's court dress is similar but without the wig and is worn only in the County Court. No robes are worn in the Magistrates' Court or before tribunals, enquiries or arbitrations. A barrister's court wear is carried in a blue bag and it is the custom for Queen's Counsel to present a red bag to a junior in recognition of creditable work in a case in which they have been jointly concerned.

Reasons for the use of court dress have been expressed from the bench as:[13]

"Robes are convenient in normal circumstances as an indication of the functions of those engaged in proceedings, and as enhancing the formality

11.   Benson Commission Report, p. 466 para. 33.72.
12.   Code of Conduct p. 7 para. 51, Annex 6, 1 (3) and (4).
13.   *St. Edmondsbury and Ipswich Diocesan Board of Finance v Clarke* [1973] 3 WLR 1042 p. 1048.

and dignity of a grave occasion: in their appearance they also lessen visual differences of age, sex and clothing and so aid concentration on the real issues without distraction, but they are not essential and the court may dispense with them where there is good reason."

5. Disciplinary Procedures

The professional discipline of barristers is initially exercised through the Professional Conduct Committee[14] consisting of fifteen members namely: the Vice Chairman, fourteen members of the Senate elected by the Bar Council (one being an employed or non-practising barrister) and the remainder being practising barristers. The Committee has power to co-opt up to three practising barristers who are Senate members and one or more lay representatives selected from a panel appointed by the Lord Chancellor's office. The Committee is appointed by the Bar Council.

A complaint about a barrister's conduct is first considered by the Committee. If the information given by the person complaining is thought to be adequate upon which to adjudicate then it will be decided whether there has been a breach of proper professional standards. If a prima facie breach of proper professional standards is established in which the facts of the matter are disputed and need to be resolved by evidence, the allegation must, in any event, be referred to a Disciplinary Tribunal constituted in the manner described below.

Where the facts given by the complainant are insufficient upon which to adjudicate, the matter is referred to an investigating officer. This official then ascertains the full facts of the complaint and, where possible, interviews the complainant. The case is then submitted to the Committee for a finding to be made. Where the facts are not disputed a barrister may appear before the Committee or be represented. The Committee has power to dismiss a complaint or decide that no action is needed. Alternatively, it can advise or admonish the barrister formally or informally. If a prima facie case of professional misconduct is disclosed, a charge on behalf of the Senate must be laid before a Disciplinary Tribunal of the Senate.[15]

A disciplinary Tribunal[16] is a committee of the Senate nominated by the President and consists of five persons—a judge as chairman, a lay person and three practising barristers. When the barrister charged is employed or non-practising, then one of the members may be in the same category. Charges brought before a Tribunal may relate either to professional misconduct or a breach of proper professional standards. A

14. The Senate Regulations r. 31 (2).
15. The Bar Council Bye-Laws s. 14 and 15.
16. The Senate Regulations r. 20.

Tribunal does not have power to subpoena witnesses or order the production of documents. The procedure at a hearing "is governed by the rules of natural justice" as interpreted by the Chairman who has power to regulate the proceedings. All costs and expenses incurred by a Tribunal or Professional Conduct Committee in preparing for and in connection with a hearing are paid by the Senate. If a charge of professional misconduct is not proved, the Tribunal may order the payment by the Senate of the costs and expenses of the barrister charged. Where professional misconduct is proved, the barrister may be disbarred, suspended (with or without conditions) for a definite period, ordered to repay or forgo fees, be reprimanded by the Treasurer of his or her Inn or, if an employed barrister, be removed from the Register of Employed Barristers. If the charge proved is that of a breach of proper professional standards, the sentencing powers are limited to admonishment and it may be ordered that the barrister be given advice upon his or her future conduct by the Tribunal or a person nominated.

6. Practising Arrangements

The nature of the work which barristers undertake in private practice is not unique to their branch of the legal profession. Solicitors perform similar tasks but at different levels and, in addition, they provide other legal services. Advocacy, drafting pleadings in court actions, the drafting of legal documents of all descriptions and advising upon the law are activities common to both branches of the profession. Other work which solicitors are trained to perform includes the initiation and conduct of proceedings in the courts, the administration of estates of deceased persons, the transfer of property and work of a legal nature generally. There are solicitor specialists both in advocacy and the law and judges who were solicitors. There are no restrictions upon the work a solicitor may choose to undertake apart from those resulting from the exclusive rights of audience which are reserved for barristers in the superior courts. These are in reality demarcation rules and are thought essential to preserve a divided profession. It is not a difference in the kind of work undertaken by the two branches of the profession which distinguishes them. The difference arises from the extent to which practitioners are allowed to practice their skills. It is this factor which provides the rationale for their separation.

A barrister has the exclusive right to appear and plead a case before the House of Lords when functioning as a Supreme Court of Appeal, the Judicial Committee of the Privy Council, the Court of Appeal and the High Court.[17] This monopoly extends to the Crown Court, subject to

17. Halsbury *op. cit.* 4th Ed. Vol. 3 1973, p. 633–6 paras. 1155–57.

directions, which the Lord Chancellor has power to give, allowing
solicitors to practise as advocates at sittings of the court held in places
which may be specified.[18] Two practice directions have been made, and
these represent an inroad into what would otherwise have been a clear-
cut demarcation rule. The first direction made in 1971, restored the rights
which existed before the Crown Court was constituted and which existed
in the courts of Quarter Sessions which they replaced. It allows solicitors
to appear before sittings held at a number of venues in England and
Wales but is restricted to all but the most serious cases. A second
direction in 1972 gave further rights at any sitting of the Crown Court
limited to civil and criminal appeals and committals of persons for
sentence or "to be dealt with" where, in each instance, the case originates
from a Magistrates' Court.[19] Solicitors and barristers have equal rights
of audience in all other courts and tribunals in England and Wales and
before the European Court of Justice.

Barristers practise as individuals and are strictly forbidden to practise
in partnership. They may agree to share professional expenses but not
professional receipts. Delegation of work is permitted to a limited extent
but this does not permit a brief to be handed over and the case conducted
in the name of the recipient unless the instructing solicitor consents. A
practice must be conducted from chambers which consist of offices
occupied by a group of barristers working on their own account but
sharing the use and cost of joint facilities in the form of clerical and
secretarial services. The consent of the appropriate Circuit must be
obtained to open a new set of chambers or a branch or annex of an
existing set anywhere outside Greater London. The permission of the Bar
Committee is required if chambers are to be opened in Greater London
in premises other than those managed by the four Inns of Court. In each
instance there is a right of appeal against refusal to the Bar Council.[20]
Among matters taken into account are the suitability of the applicant, the
premises and the clerk. The proximity of the courts and whether there are
other chambers nearby are also considered. The question of need is dealt
with in the following extract from the Code of Conduct.[21]

> ". . . The question of whether or not there is a need for a new set of
> chambers (or a branch or annex) in the proposed location shall be relevant
> only in support of an application. Lack of need shall not be a valid ground
> for refusing consent to an application."

A barrister is not permitted to practice without being insured against
claims for professional negligence. The cover must be for at least

---

18.   *Supra* p. 29–30.
19.   *Infra* Appendix E.
20.   Code of Conduct, p. 11, para. 74.
21.   *Ibid.*, p. 60, Annex 18 para. 7 (f).

£250,000 for each and every claim and upon minimum terms stipulated by the Bar Council from time to time.[22]

Supplementary occupations are not permitted unless they are considered to be compatible with practice at the Bar. A list of those which have been approved is contained in the Code of Conduct. They are divided into three categories namely: public appointments, legal services and commercial activities—all being of a part-time nature. Approval of the Bar Council can be sought if there is any doubt upon a particular occupation. During pupillage and the early years of practice the rule is relaxed and not applied strictly.[23]

A fundamental rule which acts to preserve the separateness of the Bar is the insistence that a solicitor must intervene when the services of a barrister are needed. This is laid down in the rule which states:[24]

> "Subject to such exceptions as may be authorised by custom or the Bar Council (including Annex 17), a barrister may not act in a professional capacity except upon the instructions of a solicitor, or in appropriate cases of a Parliamentary Agent or Patent Agent or Trade Mark Agent. Notwithstanding that he does so for no fee, a barrister who appears in or drafts a formal document for the purpose of a contentious matter is acting in a professional capacity. There is however, no objection to a barrister giving advice free on legal matters to a friend or relative or on a charitable basis."

Customary exceptions to the rule include instructions from: a lay client for advice upon libel or contempt when material is to be published; a prisoner in the dock at the Crown Court; the Chief Land Registrar for advice on titles; the joint registrars of the Synod to draft General Synod Measures; and a local authority clerk but only in non-contentious matters and for representation at local enquiries. The exception in Annex 17 relates to barristers who are in employment. The separation of the barrister from the lay client also extends to witnesses in a case and is dealt with in detail in a further rule which stipulates that:[25]

> ."(a) a barrister may not appear in Court, or discuss a case with or take instructions from or give advice to, his lay client unless the instructing solicitor or his representative is present;
> (b) a barrister may not discuss a case with or in the presence of potential witnesses, save for his lay client (or where his lay client is a corporate body, the person or persons in charge of the case) and expert or professional witnesses, save in exceptional circumstances when counsel must exercise his own judgement and discretion. Different considerations apply to prosecution counsel and general guidance is set out in Annex 12."

22. *Ibid.* p. 4, para. 28A.
23. *Ibid.* p. 5, para. 35 and p. 40 Annex 4.
24. *Ibid.*, p. 7 para. 50.
25. *Ibid.*, p. 18–9 para. 142.

Arrangements to engage a barrister are made by the instructing solicitor with the chambers clerk. The functions of the clerk resemble those of a theatrical agent and the clerk is not responsible to the lay client for the suitability or competence of his or her principal. The Bar Council does not claim any jurisdiction over a clerk's activities and these are considered to be the responsibility and concern of the barrister.[26]

Special rules apply to barristers who work in Law Centres. Without them the Bar would be unable to participate effectively in the work of Centres which provide legal services in socially deprived areas. Solicitors and barristers work together and for the latter there is almost complete fusion. In addition to having a right of audience before all courts, a barrister is allowed to do all the work which a solicitor is permitted to perform with the exception of conveyancing, instructing counsel and issuing any writ or process.[27]

The Barristers' Clerks Association represents the collective interests of barristers' clerks. Its members are expected to attain prescribed educational standards, undergo a short course and pass an examination. Membership of the association is not compulsory. Barristers are free to employ clerks who have not passed the Association's examination. It is usual to refer to clerks by the grades of senior and junior. A senior clerk, employed by the barrister members of a set of chambers, acts as office administrator, accountant, business manager and agent. By establishing personal contact with solicitors a flow of work is introduced to the chambers. Where a solicitor does not know individual barristers, the clerk's advice will often be relied upon in making a selection. When a brief is returned the clerk will usually be ready with a substitute. The effectiveness of the clerk is often a major factor in making a set of chambers viable and successful. A junior clerk is responsible for clerical work and routine tasks.

A fee upon a brief is normally fixed by agreement between the instructing solicitor and the clerk and must be marked upon the brief before the hearing. There are exceptions to this requirement which include prosecution briefs, briefs on behalf of the Crown and briefs in interlocutory matters of uncertain length and complexity or which are short in duration or urgent. In appropriate cases 'no Fee' or 'Legal Aid' is marked instead of the fee. A barrister may discuss the amount to be charged direct with the solicitor. If no written brief is provided, a back-sheet (which is the outside cover of a brief) must be delivered to the barrister showing, among other details, the fee, if known. Payment of the barrister's fee is the personal responsibility of the instructing solicitor and not of the lay client except in legal aid cases where a fee is paid direct from the Legal Aid Fund.

A barrister cannot sue in the courts for the payment of a fee but, in privately funded cases, the Law Society will assist in collection. Where appropriate, non-payment can be treated as professional misconduct and lead to disciplinary proceedings against the solicitor.

PART 3—THE JUDICIARY AND THE COURTS

1. General

The manning of the judiciary reflects the division of the profession. In Magistrates' Courts, where solicitors and barristers have equal rights of audience, stipendiary magistrates are drawn from both branches of the profession.[1] The only stipulation is that a candidate must have practised for at least seven years. At present there are solicitor and barrister stipendiary magistrates.[2] Without the trappings and formalities of the higher courts, proceedings before magistrates are usually shorter and more comprehensible to the lay person. Advocates have a direct and concise style, lengthy addresses to the court being rare. This may be due in part to the relative unimportance of some cases. Trials in the higher courts are conducted more slowly and an element of contrived drama is introduced. A stylised technique of advocacy prevails. To some extent this may be due to the serious nature of many cases. This cannot, however, be an influence when, for example, relatively simple issues are being tried. The court environment is, in the main, created by the dress, manners and conventions observed by the bench, barristers and officials. There is little opportunity for non-conformity.

Proceedings before County Courts, although more formal, have something of the quality of Magistrates' Courts. Hearings before a judge do not have the dramatic and sometimes intimidating effect of a High Court or Crown Court hearing. Solicitors and barristers appear on the same terms and the relationships between them are not inhibited by demarcation rules. Hearings before a registrar are even more relaxed. This does not detract from their authority or effectiveness.

It is in the Crown Court and superior courts that the roles and functions of the two branches of the profession are more clearly defined. The solicitor, burdened with the case papers and constantly with the client and witnesses, organises and communicates but does not take part in the actual hearing. When a solicitor is entitled to appear as an advocate the distinction is maintained by differing court dress. The barrister and judge on the other hand clearly belong to a separate group from which the solicitor is excluded. The higher judiciary originates only from the ranks of practising barristers.

2. Appointments reserved for Barristers

The offices at present reserved solely for those who are or have been members of the Bar are Lord of Appeal in Ordinary, Lord Justice of

---

1. *Supra.* p. 8.
2. Source: Lord Chancellor's Department Letter 4th September 1985.

Appeal, Lord Chief Justice, Master of the Rolls, President of the Family Division and a judge of the High Court.[3] Circuit judges and recorders appointed under the Courts Act 1971 may sit as judges in the High Court but only on a temporary basis and at the request of the Lord Chancellor. A number of other posts of a judicial or legal nature are, by statute, reserved for barristers and these include Judge Advocate General, Chief National Insurance Commissioner, the permanent secretary to the Lord Chancellor and the Clerk of the Crown, a Master of the Queen's Bench Division of the Supreme Court, a Master of the Court of Protection and conveyancing counsel to the court.

A number of ecclesiastical appointments are also reserved for barristers and these include the Chancellor of a diocese, the Dean of the Arches and Auditor. Persons who have held high judicial office are also eligible for some of these posts. It has become the custom to appoint barristers to some offices although there is no statutory requirement to do so. These are the Attorney General, Solicitor General, Lord Chancellor and the Attorney General to the Duchy of Lancaster and of Cornwall.

3. Appointments open to Solicitors and Barristers

There are other posts open to the whole profession. They include a deputy Circuit judge, Recorder, Stipendiary Magistrate and Circuit judge. For a solicitor to be appointed a Circuit judge, at least three years service as a Recorder beforehand is required. Judges in the County Court are drawn from Circuit judges.[4] A judge of the Court of Justice of the European Economic Community must be either a judge or professor of a member state. No distinction is made in respect of the two branches of the profession.

In the Crown Court anomalies over rights of audience have arisen to some degree. With judges, an even more fundamental contradiction has emerged. A solicitor Circuit judge is not entitled, as is his barrister counterpart, to be appointed to the High Court Bench. The duties they perform are identical and no convincing reason has been given to justify this discrimination. In 1982, an attempt to make solicitor Circuit judges eligible for appointment to the High Court was successfully resisted. With their background and experience in judicial office, they would be suitable candidates.[5] This has been recognised by the fact that they preside regularly in the High Court on a temporary basis and has great

3. For a detailed account see *Halsbury's Laws of England* 1973 4th Ed., Vol. 3 p. 605 7 paras. 1122 3.
4. Courts Act 1971, s. 20 (1).
5. A. Samuels, 'Solicitor Circuit Judges as High Court Judges' 126 *Solicitors Journal* 843.

significance for it means that the competence and suitability of solicitors for judicial office at all levels is no longer questioned. It will become more difficult to justify a two tier system in this situation as the number of solicitors who become Circuit judges increases. A distinguished legal writer views the exclusion of solicitors from high judicial office as:[6]

". . . a restrictive practice rooted in history, the product of a divided profession. It is not in the public interest."

4. Selecting Judges

The process of selecting judges is closely linked with the Bar. The Central figure is the Lord Chancellor who, with the Prime Minister, advises the sovereign upon appointments. His departmental staff is responsible for seeking out candidates and making confidential enquiries to establish whether they are suitable to become members of the higher judiciary. This is a highly responsible task as appointments are made by invitation and are virtually for life with no probationary period. The advice of the judges and particularly the heads of divisions, and also the members of the Bar, is sought. The head of the Lord Chancellor's Department is also a barrister and will have met a number of candidates at the social functions of his Inn.[7] Lord Hailsham has observed that, with a large number of deputy judges and assistant Recorders appointed only temporarily, the opportunity now exists to observe likely candidates who display the qualitities needed in an effective judge.[8] There does not seem to be any reason why this should not become the normal way of assessing the work of all potential judges. With the increase in the number of solicitor Recorders and Circuit judges, the principle of reserving judicial offices above the rank of a stipendiary magistrate for the Bar has been breached. New methods are now needed to make selections from the considerably larger group of candidates available. Justice has put forward the suggestion that an Advisory Appointments Committee or a Judicial Commission should be constituted to advise and recommend upon all judicial appointments. Members of this body would be drawn from the legal profession, academic lawyers and lay people with special skills in personnel selection.[9] Under the scheme, solicitors would be eligible for promotion to the High Court bench and academic lawyers to the Court of Appeal and House of Lords.

---

6. *Ibid.* p. 843.
7. A. Samuels, 'Appointing Judges' 1984 *New Law Journal* 85-7
8. Lord Hailsham, 'Appointment to Silk and the Judiciary' 82 *Gazette* 2335 (1985).
9. Justice, *The Judiciary* 1972 p. 29-31 paras. 40-3.

CHAPTER 4

Fusion—an Account of the Controversy

PART 1—MODERN ARGUMENTS

1. The Scene

The proposal that the two branches of the legal profession in England and Wales should amalgamate is not, as already described, a new one. Fusion, the term used for this restructuring, is understood by lawyers but means little to the general public. The topic, however, is not merely one of self-interest. If implemented, the reform proposed would have a profound effect upon legal services. Some believe that great improvements would follow its introduction and others take the opposite view. A striking feature of all discussion and debate upon the subject is the complete absence of any indication that a compromise will be reached by general agreement. Opinion and argument have become polarised and no meeting point between the opposing factions is in sight.

Some lawyers see fusion as a threat to the established system, to be opposed with the utmost vigour. The persistence of this controversy over a long period invites a study of the arguments put forward against any change in the status quo. These can be found in the evidence submitted to the Benson Commission by the Senate of the Inns of Court and the Bar[1] and in the Commission's final report.[2] The importance of these sources as an authoritative and modern account of the official view of the Bar and its associated institutions is acknowledged in comments made on behalf of the Bar Council. These arose from an announcement by the Law Society of a campaign to secure the right of audience for solicitors before all of the courts in England and Wales.[3] In response, a statement issued on behalf of the Bar Council opposed the move and indicated that the question had already been debated exhaustively and rejected by the Benson Commission.[4] It can, therefore, be assumed that the evidence submitted to the Commission on behalf of the Bar represents current thinking upon the problem. The decision recommending that there should be no extension of solicitor's rights of audience was undoub-

1. Senate Evidence Sect. IV Fusion.
2. Benson Commission Report, p. 187–202.
3. The Law Society, Press Release 27th March 1984.
4. *The Times*, 3 April 1984.

ATLP–E

51

tedly influnenced by this evidence. It is generally accepted that should solicitors and barristers have equal rights in every court, fusion will inevitably follow. Consequently, arguments used to oppose any increase in rights of audience are with equal force applicable against the case for fusion. The two questions are inextricably bound to each other.

In the past a belief was often held that solicitors, because of the nature of their training and experience, were not suitable or capable of performing the work undertaken by barristers. Happily, this outdated view is no longer expressed openly. It lingered on until quite recently and probably accounted for the deferential attitude which solicitors, both collectively and individually, have shown towards the Bar. Since the announcement by the Law Society of the campaign to secure an extension of solicitors' rights of audience a more realistic and frank approach to problems affecting the relationship between the two branches of the profession is discernible. In this spirit, the following discussion is advanced. Criticism is made of the effects of the existing division but this is not intended to be destructive. Unless defects are diagnosed and possible remedies discussed openly, progress will be hindered.

To assess and appreciate the arguments of the present time in favour of a single legal profession there is no need to go back in time beyond 1975. In November of that year an attempt was made to still criticism of the profession coming from within and without which was considered to be "ill informed". Representatives of the Council of The Law Society and the Bar Council met in Bath to discuss issues affecting the profession. No announcement of the meeting was made beforehand or names of the participants disclosed. At its conclusion a statement of policy was issued entitled *The Declaration of Bath*. Beginning with a recital about the importance of maintaining the rule of law, it went on to state that:[5]

> "the interests of the public are best served by a legal profession divided into two branches—barristers and solicitors, of equal status but with different and complementary functions."

Despite this assertion there was and always has been disagreement among lawyers with that view. Ten years after the statement was made dissent has become more widespread.

The Benson Commission was appointed under the chairmanship of Sir Henry Benson, now Lord Benson, in February 1976. The terms of reference were broad enough to include the question of fusion, the relevant words being:[6]

5.   72 *Gazette* 1245 (1975).
6.   Benson Commission Report, p. vi.

". . . to inquire into the law and practice relating to the provision of legal services in England and Wales and Northern Ireland, and to consider whether any, and if so what, changes are desirable in the public interest in the structure, organisation, training, regulation of and entry to the legal profession. . ."

Immediately after the Commission's appointment, the then chairman of the Bar Council addressed a circular letter to all practising barristers emphasising the need to present evidence to the Benson Commission collectively to establish above all the principle "that the legal profession should remain independent, serving the public through two separate and equal branches."[7] No change has been made to this policy which can, therefore, be taken as representing the official view of the Bar at the present time. The submissions on behalf of the Bar and the report of the Commission supported and confirmed this stand, without reservation.

Fusion, in effect, means the abolition of the distinction between a solicitor and barrister. The definition put forward by the Bar is more explicit but amounts to the same thing. It is the creation of [8]

"one undivided legal profession of 'lawyers' in which all members would share the same rights of audience in all courts and tribunals and the same right to perform for clients other work e.g. conveyancing and would be able to and would in fact accept instructions directly from lay clients."

In other words, all lawyers would be free to undertake any task normally performed by a legal practitioner without restriction. Under these circumstances, they would be at liberty to accept instructions exclusively or occasionally from other lawyers as well as from the lay client. For reasons which are not stated in the fuller definition given above it is maintained that[9]

"a profession some of whose members were able to and did practise on the basis that they would accept instructions only from other lawyers and not directly from clients would not be a 'fused' profession . . ."

This qualification is difficult to understand. In a single unified profession no restrictions would be imposed upon lawyers. They would be entitled to respond to the demand for legal services in the most effective way possible. Instructions would be accepted from other lawyers or direct from clients. The method used would depend upon choice and not compulsion. It would not be permissible to indulge in a restrictive practice intended to prevent a lawyer practising in a manner most appropriate to the client's interests. Any restriction of this nature would

7. P. Rawlinson, 'A Royal Commission to Inquire Into the Legal Profession' 73 *Gazette* 341 (1976).
8. Senate Evidence, Sect. IV.1 Introduction.
9. *Ibid.* IV. 1.

be contrary to the true concept of one legal profession free to provide legal services in the best possible way. The definition of fusion already quoted recognises the change which this would bring by saying that lawyers "would be able to and would in fact accept instructions directly from lay clients." This does not, however, mean that they would be forced, always, to accept instructions in this way.

2.   Availability of Barristers

Probably the most persuasive argument in favour of a divided profession is that barristers are available to serve all solicitors in private practice. It is put this way in the Bar submission:[10]

> "The disadvantage of fusion from the public's point of view would be the loss of the following advantages of a separate profession:
>
> (a) The availability in principle to every solicitor, and therefore to each lay client, of the services of every member of the Bar on equal terms.
> (b) A higher degree of competence, particularly in specialist matters.
> (c) A better overall cost effectiveness.
> (d) A corps of specially independent advocates and advisers.
>
> Moreover few, if any, sole practitioners would be able to survive in a fused profession, and advantages of individual practice would therefore be lost, in particular those of detachment, independence and undiluted commitment. . ."

The Benson Commission accepted the validity of this view and considered it to be:[11]

> ". . . an important advantage of the present system that it enabled small firms to operate in the confidence that they could, at need, command the services of able and experienced advocates and specialists in remote branches of the law."

This conclusion does not rule out the possibility that an undivided profession may be in a position to provide an even larger supply of skilled advocates of integrity and a more diverse source of expert advisers. However, before considering this question, an examination of the workings of the present system in the light of the Bar's submission is necessary to judge whether the assertions made are supported in practice.

Barristers' services are used extensively throughout the country. Their existence as a separate group stems from the exclusive right of audience which they enjoy in the superior courts as already described.[12] Strict demarcation rules make it obligatory to engage a barrister in these courts. Where solicitors enjoy equal rights, the choice of a barrister to

---

10.   Senate Evidence, Sect. IV, A 2.1.
11.   Legal Services and Lawyers 1979 H.M.S.O., p. 7 para. 20.
12.   *Supra*. p. 43–44.

represent a client is optional. Where no court proceedings are involved, a specialist Bar is available to advise and draft documents in specific areas of the law e.g. planning, landlord and tenant, taxation etc. There is another use made of barristers which does not depend upon their expertise either in advocacy or law. Frequently a solicitor, faced with a problem which he or she should be capable of dealing with, may lack the time or confidence to give clear and unequivocal advice to a client. By taking 'counsel's opinion' the responsibility for making a decision can be shared with the barrister. Sometimes the solicitor makes no contribution to the case at all as, for instance, where an accountant prepares instructions. The papers are merely sent to the barrister and the advice received forwarded to the client. Although the solicitor cannot always avoid responsibility if the advice given is faulty,[13] the relief obtained from the worry of a heavy or onerous work load makes the risk worthwhile.

The profession, because of its rigid structure, is limited in the extent to which it can adjust to meet changing demands. As a consequence, the client's freedom of choice is restricted. Where it is compulsory to instruct a barrister or for a solicitor to intervene, the client's wishes become secondary to the observance of established practices. In short, the consumer must adapt to the system. For this to be acceptable it must be shown that the services provided would not be improved by changes which would meet the demands and convenience of the public. It has already been described how a single profession can provide a full range of legal services in countries with comparable legal systems.[14] The question to be answered, therefore, is whether a unified profession is likely to provide a better service than a divided one.

A separate Bar is not essential for the provision of specialist legal services in advocacy and law. Under existing arrangements, situations comparable to fusion already exist, and these give a guide to the form a single legal profession might take. There are firms of solicitors among whose members are specialists with considerable experience both in advocacy and in specific areas of the law. Their services are sometimes used by other firms of solicitors who do not possess this expertise. In the case of advocacy, agency work is not uncommon in the County Court and Magistrates' Court and, if it were permitted in the Crown Court, would no doubt be frequently undertaken there. The London agent has long been used by the provincial solicitor's practice, conducting actions in the High Court and dealing with interlocutory matters in Chambers. Specialist solicitors' firms are available who concentrate upon individual aspects of the law, e.g. company law, shipping, air law, etc.

---

13. *Davy-Chiesman v Davy-Chiesman and another* [1984] 1 All ER 334.
14. *Supra.* p. 16 et seq.

Other firms consult them when faced with unfamiliar work of this nature. Convenience and accessibility are factors accounting for the use made of these services.

It is suggested that a disadvantage which would accompany the development of specialist services in the way described above would be the risk of losing clients to other firms.[15] This is not a significant problem at present. If it were so, agency or other consultative facilities provided by solicitors would not be offered or utilised. In a single profession, lawyers, free to offer advocacy services in all courts, would be in a position to provide an extension of the services already available.

The services of the Bar are said to be available for all solicitors on 'the cab-rank principle'.[16] This metaphor may be thought to oversimplify what happens in practice. In theory a barrister must not arbitrarily refuse to accept instructions. This is compared with the position of a cab-driver who should not refuse to accept a passenger when plying for hire. It is maintained that this rule gives the client the opportunity to engage a barrister of his or her choice, no matter how unpopular or unsavoury the case may be, knowing that it will not be rejected on this account. The rule does not apply to paperwork as distinct from representation before a court or tribunal. Neither does it apply where the two-counsel rule is invoked.[17] Fortunately, in this country, the inability to find a lawyer to defend the most unpopular cause, whether a solicitor or barrister, has never within living memory been a problem. There are a number of reasons which make it a duty to decline instructions but this is not one of them. Conflict of interest, unfamiliarity with or lack of competence in the relevant area of law are the main examples. The creation of a single legal profession would not in any way affect these fundamental principles. They are already observed by all lawyers worthy of the name.

The number of cases with which a barrister may not wish to be associated because of their nature must, in any event, be infinitesimal. Set against the very real and tangible obstacles which prevent people from engaging suitable representation they are insignificant. Where outside funding is not available in the form of Legal Aid or other financial assistance the ability to pay may be and often is the sole and deciding factor. The cab-rank principle is of no assistance if the fare to be charged is beyond the hirer's means.

There is another factor which affects not only the choice of a particular barrister but the availability of barristers generally. It is the frequency with which briefs are accepted to represent a client and then returned

---

15. Senate Evidence, Sect. IV A 2.2.
16. *Supra.* p. 41.
17. *Supra.* p. 41.

shortly before the hearing because of other commitments. The reasons for and extent of this problem are important because they undoubtedly arise from the way in which the profession is structured. The practice of returning briefs was regarded as 'a serious matter' by the Benson Commission.[18] Its implications are not, however, fully explained. In evidence submitted by the United Lawyers' Association, a survey in Oxford showed that 58 % of barristers who accepted briefs were replaced by substitutes before the hearing.[19] That was in 1974 and recent enquiries indicate that the situation still persists. A barrister of considerable experience in the criminal courts explains the problem as he sees it:[20]

"The listing system currently operates in such a way that the middle ranked practitioner, the man upon whom the system actually depends, the engine room of the criminal Bar, is faced with the proposition that of the work which he receives he is unlikely actually to do more than 50 or 60 %. Not because he doesn't want to do the other 50 or 40 % but simply because the listing system works in such a way that he isn't available to do it."

Where the sole cause of a returned brief is the clash of engagements this could indicate unrealistic planning of a barrister's work-load combined with an inflexible attitude on the part of court officials in fixing lists. Overbooking is another possible cause which may explain the need to arrange a substitute at very short and often inadequate notice. A chamber's clerk has the task of ensuring that the barristers who employ him or her have an adequate supply of work. This is an overriding consideration if the group is to remain viable. Briefs may be offered to a senior and experienced member of the chambers and more accepted than the individual can be expected to undertake. The clerk will have full knowledge of the situation and of the vagaries of the listing arrangements. Without difficulty, a substitute is found, often in the same chambers, on the afternoon of the day before the hearing. Court officials will rarely agree on adjournment on the grounds of a prior engagement so placing the client and solicitor in a vulnerable position. This leaves no alternative but to accept the substitute barrister. The Benson Commission mentions the existence of this practice and comments:[21]

"In its evidence the Senate agreed that clerks sometimes overbook, but it is said that this is rarely if ever deliberately done. We accept that overbooking occurs because of the many uncertainties and varying factors which apply in all litigation. . ."

Another aspect of the problem is the suggestion that:[22]

18. Benson Commission Report, p. 300 para. 22.47.
19. United Lawyers' Association, Evidence to the Benson Commission EV.
20. R. Johnson and M. Hill, 'Legal Aid Comment' 82 *Gazette* 580 (1985).
21. Benson Commission Report, p. 492 para. 34.34.
22. *Ibid.* p. 492 para. 34.35.

". . . in certain classes of case, in particular minor criminal cases, clerks receive briefs which are not marked with a barrister's name and do not allocate them until the evening before the trial. . ."

The Howard League for Penal Reform expressed concern over the return of briefs at a late stage.[23] An example was cited of a case where the barrister, who had been working upon a case involving a grave charge, was unable to appear and another one took over only twenty-four hours before the hearing. The client received a life sentence. A lay client is bound to feel that the case was not properly attended to under such circumstances.

It would be utopian to imagine that a client could always be represented by a chosen barrister. Clashes of engagement must happen occasionally. If they, or other factors, result in the very frequent return of briefs, at least a detailed and searching investigation needs to be made into the precise circumstances which lead to this situation. To bring a strange advocate into a case at a late stage can have a deleterious effect upon solicitor and client relations. This is particularly so where family matters are in dispute or a custodial sentence possible. A parent likely to be deprived of a child or an accused in fear of going to prison may be disturbed by the questioning of a substitute advocate seeking to get the grasp of a case just before going into the court. The Benson Commission stated:[24]

> "The propriety of returning a brief and the time at which to do so depends on the nature of the case and the circumstances of the client. There are a number of minor criminal cases in which the client can be adequately represented without a conference before the day of trial and without lengthy preparation by the barrister. We can see no objection to transferring the brief in such a case shortly before trial provided there is sufficient time for preparation."

If this guidance were followed, the position would probably be acceptable, even if not desirable. Unfortunately, experience shows that the pattern which has existed for at least thirty years is not changing and briefs are being returned even more frequently without adequate notice.

The disquiet which can result from a brief being returned shortly before a hearing has now been recognised and commented upon judicially in relation to child care cases. This is a new development for, in the past, neither the client nor the public have been informed or made aware of the practice and its frequency. Instead, it has been regarded as an acceptable method of organising representation. Problems arising are left to be resolved by the solicitor responsible to the client, and the barrister's clerk, an intermediary accountable only to his or her principal.

23.　Howard League for Penal Reform, Evidence to Benson Commission EV.
24.　Benson Commission Report, p. 300 para. 22.48.

The Court of Appeal, in July 1984, after consultation with the President of the Family Division, directed that any appeal from an order transferring the care of a child either from one parent to another or from the local authority to a parent must be heard within twenty-eight days of the order. Lord Justice Cumming-Bruce when stating that counsel's convenience would not be an acceptable reason for delaying the hearing of an appeal involving the transfer of a child said:[25]

> "If counsel accepted a retainer to appear in such a case counsel must make it plain to the instructing solicitor that they would follow the case to appeal, if there was one, in spite of other commitments. If counsel could not give that assurance counsel's clerk should tell the solicitor, so that the client would know that in the event of an appeal it would not be conducted by the counsel who conducted the case at trial."

This does not, however, affect the probability that the barrister instructed at the original hearing will not, in a considerable number of cases, take the appeal. The only improvement is that an obligation is imposed upon counsel to warn the solicitor that a last minute change may be likely. As the liberty and welfare of a child can be at stake, it is an advance to have this inherent defect in the system acknowledged. It will at least prevent the period of suspense and uncertainty being prolonged because of a postponed hearing.

The returned brief is a situation which is suitable for a comparative study. An increasing amount of advocacy is being undertaken in the lower courts by solicitors. It is rare for them to experience the problems which barristers encounter arising from the clash of engagements. This may be due to the fact that most solicitors work in local courts and are able to plan their work schedules with more certainty. Only in a situation of dire emergency would a case be passed to another solicitor to deal with a few hours before the hearing. In the Crown Court the position is even more closely comparable. Where, in these courts, solicitors have a right of audience there is a direct and continuing relationship with the client throughout the case. This makes it unlikely that a change of advocate would occur without adequate notice being given to the client.

3. Competence of Practitioners

Fusion, it is maintained, would result in the loss of:

> "a higher degree of competence, particularly in specialist matters"[26]

which is possessed by barristers. All practitioners would probably regard this vague comparison as invidious. It is unlikely that an incompetent

---

25. *In re W. and Another*, The Times 6th July 1984 (unreported).
26. Senate Evidence, Sect. IV A 2.6.

specialist, whichever branch of the profession he or she belonged to, would survive. The problem is rather how to utilise the expertise of all specialists. Existing restrictions may well be hindering the practitioner with special ability. Despite this, the number of solicitor specialists is increasing. Many firms have become recognised as possessing expertise in particular areas of practice. The increasing number of legal text books written by solicitors testifies to their growing influence in specialist matters. It is conceivable that before the end of the next decade they will outstrip the Bar as a source of legal authorship. There is nothing unusual or surprising in this trend. It would be unrealistic to expect a relatively small Bar, with only a proportion of its members specialising in specific areas of the law, to cover the whole spectrum of legal activity.

It would need a comparative evaluation of the performance of solicitor and barrister specialists to see where the greater competence lay. This would be an impracticable task. Consequently, observations upon the relative merits and effectiveness of practitioners in a profession which imposes restrictions upon the right to practice are of no value. Possibly the official view of the Bar, as expressed in its submission to the Benson Commission, is coloured by memories of two decades ago when the profession was much smaller and the need for specialists less. It is true that there was far less specialism among solicitors in those days.

4.   A Corps of Advocates

The Bar, in evidence to the Benson Commission, put forward the view that:[27]

> "The existence of a separate corps of advocates, who alone may appear in important cases, tends to improve the speed and efficiency of trials. Time and costs are saved because (a) skill in pleading and in advising on evidence for trial can significantly limit the issue: (b) skilled oral advocacy confines itself to good points and avoids the bad."

This is said to be the product of a number of factors, two of which are explained. The first is the experience which the barrister advocate gains from continuous practice in the courts—rather inelegantly expressed in this way:[28]

> "the more you do it and see others doing it the better you become."

This, though, is a truism which applies to all advocates. The exclusion of solicitor advocates from the higher courts deprives them of the opportunity to develop their skills. It does not follow that their performance would be less effective than that of their barrister colleagues

---

27. *Ibid.* Sect. IV A 2.9.
28. *Ibid.* Sect. IV A 2.9 (a).

if they were allowed to practice in those courts. The argument is similar to the one used in the past against the appointment of solicitor judges. It has always been maintained that a judge should have long experience as an advocate in the courts over which he or she was to preside. Lord Devlin expressed the belief by stating:[29]

> "I think that under our existing system of oral trial and the extempore judgement, a man could not successfully preside as a judge in a class of court in which he had not experience as an advocate. I can see no objection at all to a solicitor who has built up a good practice in a magistrates' court or a county court being made a magistrate or county judge."

The weakness of this contention has been shown by the appointment of solicitors to the Circuit bench. When the Courts Act 1971 was passing through Parliament, there were reservations over the provision making solicitors eligible to serve as Recorders, and Recorders as Circuit judges. These doubts proved to be totally unfounded and the competence and efficiency of solicitor Circuit judges who have since been appointed has never been questioned.

A second reason given in support of the contribution which barristers make towards effective trials is stated to be the likelihood that an advocate's shortcomings:[30]

> "whether of competence or of ethics will be noticed both by the judge and his opponents each of whom will know him or of him. . ."

The advantages thought to exist in this situation are left to be imagined as no examples are given. In an endeavour to understand the practical implications, it is necessary to consider hypothetical cases. Imagine, for instance, that a judge is aware that an advocate is inclined to leave important connecting facts or circumstances unsaid, assuming they are understood by those listening. Presumably, allowance will be made for this defect and a gentle rebuke or subtle reminder conveyed to the advocate. Then there is the beginner who makes the unpardonable error of failing to know his or her brief adequately. As a consequence, a client's case may be prejudiced, not through lack of merit but because of poor presentation. A judge may, in these circumstances, help the erring advocate without making critical remarks in public.

An observer can be forgiven for suspecting that the obviously close relationship between the judiciary and the Bar has disadvantages. The suspicion may be invited that slipshod work is concealed or matters understood between the judge and advocate which remain unknown to the other parties to the trial or the public. It is appreciated that this may be an effective way of maintaining discipline and conformity with set

29. Unpublished letter 4th November 1966.
30. Senate Evidence. Sect. IV A 2.9 (b).

standards among barristers. There is, however, evidence to show that a similar degree of understanding does not always exist between the judiciary and solicitors and this is discussed later.[31] Some may be prompted to suggest that the greater the separation between judges and those who appear before them the less likelihood there is of influence being exerted in a hidden and undeclared way. In a unified profession the existing close professional and social relationships between the Bar and Bench would be unlikely to continue. The Inns of Court, through which this contact is maintained, would need to surrender their powers to a single governing body. A feeling of regret over the passing of these venerable institutions would be understandable. This should, however, be tempered by thoughts of corresponding benefits which would accrue to society as a whole. There could then be no doubt whatsoever that the judiciary was completely independent and separate from the lawyers appearing before the courts. This crucial principle is discussed in greater depth later in relation to our changing industrial society and the prevalence of civil disorder.[32]

5. The Cost of Litigation

The cost of legal services, particularly for litigation, is a source of persistent criticism. The Benson Commission devoted a great deal of effort to an investigation of the subject but little emerged to affect or change the situation. The cost of bringing or defending proceedings in the courts is a daunting prospect for those who do not qualify for legal aid and yet are not wealthy.

There are cases in which costs are inflated by the need to employ two lawyers where one would suffice. This is of no consequence to the litigant whose costs are paid out of the Legal Aid fund. For the unfortunate individual who must foot the bill personally it can become an unfair burden. The effect of double manning is evident in the Crown Court. The insistence that both a solicitor and barrister must be employed to conduct any case, with limited exceptions, inevitably leads to an increase in the total charge for representation. No account is taken of the complexity of the proceedings in imposing this rule. A single experienced lawyer, with adequate supporting services, would be perfectly capable of dealing with the majority of cases which come before the Crown Court. Sometimes the anomalous situation arises where the instructing solicitor who is not allowed to appear is more experienced as an advocate than the barrister instructed. This often happens when a brief is returned.

The Bar's submission to the Benson Commission gives views upon the

31.   *Infra.* p. 83 et seq.
32.   *Infra.* p. 116–117.

cost effectiveness of services provided by barristers. The present system, it is averred, enables legal resources to be used efficiently and that this would not be the case in a single profession because:[33]

> "A solicitor's secretarial staff, compared with that of the ordinary barrister, needs to be large; and a solicitor needs the services of legal executives. For these reasons, a solicitor's overheads are probably at least twice as high as those of a barrister (expressed as a percentage of his or his firm's gross professional receipts, and excluding a barrister's travelling expenses). In principle, therefore, a barrister's time tends to cost less than that of a solicitor."

There are, however, other factors which need to be taken into account when assessing whether fees charged are applied in the most economical and productive manner. The comparison quoted above is an over-simplification of the true position. No explanation is given of the precise functions of a solicitor and barrister, the amount of work performed and the facilities provided for the client. The solicitor actually supplies extensive services incidental to the limited function undertaken by the barrister. The cost of providing these and the ratio of profit they attract are in a different category from the charges made for advising, settling documents and advocacy. The charges of a solicitor conducting a case alone will include items for advocacy and all work ancillary to the proceedings. By eliminating the need for two people to sit in court, duplication and unnecessary work is avoided. The total fee paid by the client will, in most instances, be less than if a barrister were employed. This is the true test of cost effectiveness. It is also probable that by employing a solicitor advocate the client will enjoy the additional benefit of direct access, adequate pre-hearing conferences and constant accessibility. These advantages would be gained in a fused profession. A solicitor who, for instance, conducts a case in the Magistrates' Court will interview witnesses, prepare the case and appear in court for a fee which will often be less that that charged by a barrister. If the solicitor employs a barrister the total charge to the client will almost invariably be higher than if the solicitor acted alone. The same situation would prevail for a considerable proportion of the work available in the Crown Court.

Double manning undoubtedly adds to the cost of proceedings. This cannot be justified where unnecessary duplication of effort occurs. There are instances where the preparation of a brief is a mere formality as the material needed in a case is to be found in the statements and documents supplied to the barrister. Yet, it is not unknown for a lengthy repetition of the facts taken from the statements provided, without the addition of any new material, to be prepared and charged for as a brief. An even more striking example of wasted manpower is the insistence that a

---

33. Senate Evidence, Sect. IV A 2.13.

solicitor should accompany a barrister whilst a case is in progress. There may be instances where this is of benefit to the client or necessary if the matter is complex. Frequently, though, the solicitor's presence is that of a supernumery without a task to perform commensurate with his or her qualification. The indiscriminate application of this rule results in a waste of time and effort. The attendant solicitor's duties are often reduced to those of maintaining contact with witnesses and controlling the case papers and documents.

6. Independence of Practitioners

The conviction that the Bar, because it is separate, provides:[34]

> "a corps of specially independent advocates and advisers. . ."

is strongly held and believed to be of great advantage to the public. Independence, it is said, arises because the barrister only acts for the lay client, through the intervention of a solicitor, for a specific purpose and not generally. This may be as an advocate before a court or tribunal, to advise or to draft documents and pleadings. The solicitor has a direct and contractual relationship with the lay client and is personally responsible for the payment of the barrister's fee.[35]

It is this differing relationship which it is thought enables a barrister to view a case more objectively and with greater detachment. The Bar submission to the Benson Commission gives the following reasons:[36]

> "Many cases are settled before they ever reach counsel, because of the advice given to their respective clients by the solicitors on each side. But often fresh, and even more detached, advice is needed. This is given by each of the barristers involved, who scrutinises his client's case with a fresh mind and with extra detachment, because he has not been involved at the beginning of the issue. It is his duty to test his client's case and to tell him when, or to what extent, it is bad and for what reasons. Often the client does not like being told: he may never want to see the barrister again. But it is easier for the barrister to do this than for the client's solicitor. The client may be one of long standing, possibly a friend. The good solicitor, preparing his client's case enthusiastically and efficiently, will to some extent identify himself with it."

Presumably, this 'identification' is thought to diminish the solicitor's power of objective judgement. This, however, is a difficult quality to assess. There will always be occasions when a lawyer becomes personally concerned and affected by the merits of a case, but they are rare. Some judges are not immune from this failing when trying issues upon which

34. *Ibid.* Sect. IV A 2.18.
35. *A Guide to the Professional Conduct of Solicitors,* The Law Society 1974, pp. 74–6.
36. Senate Evidence, Sect. IV A 2.18.

they have strong personal views. With advocates a crusading spirit, for example, may be aroused when an infringement of civil liberties is alleged or if racial discrimination is an issue. Most lawyers will have experienced feelings of this kind early in their careers but they fast disappear as their work load increases. Provided involvement does not exceed reasonable concern for the welfare of a client, it can provide the motivation for a vigorous and fearless stand against injustice. To suggest that solicitors are likely, as a general rule, to suffer from impaired judgement because they are familiar with issues from the beginning to the end attacks the very essence of their professional integrity. The vast amount of contentious work undertaken by them without the assistance of barristers shows that this failing is of no significance. In the Magistrates' Court alone approximately 95% of all criminal cases are conducted by solicitors. There is no evidence to indicate that the advice or representation they provide lacks objectivity.

In civil cases, the advice of a barrister is often confirmatory and obtained to shield the solicitor against accusations of weakness in making concessions when settling a claim. This is particularly so with claims for personal injuries suffered in road accidents or at work which are settled before trial. A writ is issued as a formality to ensure that the limitation period for taking action in the court does not expire during the course of negotiations. An opinion of a barrister upon the amount to be claimed will then be taken and used by the solicitor in negotiating a settlement. Experienced solicitors, however, rely less upon outside opinion. They will have acquired a fund of knowledge over long periods involving a substantial number of cases both large and small. They accept the responsibility of advising upon the terms of settlement. Others, perhaps not so certain of their judgement through inexperience, caution or lack of time, will protect themselves by relying upon a barrister's opinion. The experienced and confident solicitor, being totally responsible to the client, is unlikely to pursue a claim which has no merit or substance. The thought of failure with the ruinous financial obligations which may follow, is an adequate deterrent in the overwhelming number of doubtful cases. Where legal aid is involved the certifying committee will, in any event, need to be satisfied that there is a reasonable prospect of success.

The detachment of the barrister is not always of benefit to the client. It can lead to a superficial knowledge of the case. Where incomplete or badly drawn instructions are given, this may be reflected in the advice tendered. Unfamiliarity with the background to a case or the personality of the client can be extremely damaging where personal relationships are involved. This is particularly so in matrimonial and child welfare matters. A fleeting glimpse of a marriage or history of a child's treatment over a number of years is rarely a sufficient basis for advice which may affect the future course of a person's life.

In criminal cases it is often necessary to advise a client to admit a charge and plead guilty. The Senate's evidence explains how difficult it can be to do this and also to give firm and unpalatable advice in appropriate cases, and continues:[37]

> "This is rarely easy but the divided profession enables the difficulties to be overcome in the vast majority of cases. If, however, one person had to fulfil both functions in serious cases, the frequent result will be the prolonging of criminal trials because he would have, in the last resort, either to accede to the lay client's instructions or to withdraw from the case; he would not have the assistance of the independent advocate to help him resist or guide the client in the necessary way. Without the dual system defendants would dismiss their lawyers or lawyers would withdraw from cases much more often, trials would be prolonged and the task of the judge and jury would be more complicated."

This problem is not confined to barrister advocates. Any solicitor who practices regularly in the Magistrates' Court will have experienced the same difficulty. No doubt the combined efforts of two lawyers, the barrister and solicitor, does make it more difficult for a client to ignore advice. This may not, however, be the result of the barrister's independence but rather the psychological pressure that can be exerted. It will be observed that the situation is, in the Senate's evidence, confined to 'serious cases'. Where solicitors, acting alone in the lower courts, are in a similar position, they often have to give advice which the client finds hard to accept. It may take longer to convince the client without the support of another lawyer but the problem is identical. Not all cases in the Magistrates' Court, for instance, can be considered trivial or lacking in seriousness. If advice is ignored, the consequences in the long term upon an individual's life and reputation may be damaging. Should a client insist upon a case being conducted in a manner which is unwise or against ethical principles, the duty of a solicitor advocate is the same as that of a barrister. The client must be told that it is not possible to act in the manner suggested. There is no evidence to show that there is any greater likelihood of solicitors being dismissed or withdrawing from cases for these reasons than their colleagues at the Bar.

---

37.   Senate Evidence Sect. IV 2.19.

PART 2—ROYAL COMMISSION ON LEGAL SERVICES, FINAL REPORT

1. Retention of a Divided Profession

It is in the Report of the Benson Commission that the arguments against fusion are summarised. Unequivocally it recommended that:[38]

"The legal profession should continue to be organised in two branches, barristers and solicitors."

Two main reasons are put forward in support of this conclusion. They are described in this way:[39]

"We consider it likely that in a fused profession there would be an unacceptable reduction in the number and spread of the smaller firms of solicitors and an increase in the proportion of larger city firms. This would accentuate the present uneven distribution of solicitors and reduce the choice and availability of legal services. We are satisfied that in the future there will be a greater need for specialisation. Fusion would disperse the specialist service now provided by the Bar and we consider that this would operate against the public interest."

Following the Senate's view, the Commission does not, in the context of fusion, envisage a single profession in which practitioners would be free to decide upon the way in which they wished to practise. If lawyers were at liberty to accept instructions only from other lawyers, act as agents or deal direct with the lay client, then this, according to the Senate's evidence, would not constitute fusion in the sense previously defined.[40] The profession, it is maintained, would still be divided. It is not, however, explained that any division under such circumstances would be entirely one of function and method of practising within a single profession, without compulsion. The practitioner would have the right to become established wherever the need existed. The failure to examine in depth the options open to lawyers in a single profession limited the Commission's assessment of alternative ways of providing legal services. Consequently, a restricted view of the definition of fusion may have lead to undue importance being attached to the number and location of smaller firms of solicitors. No survey was undertaken to reveal the geographical distribution of solicitor's firms and the type of work they undertake. The Users' Survey carried out by the Benson Commission,[41] however, shows that in only ten per cent of first consultations was a solicitor chosen because his or her office was conveniently situated. The main source of

---

38. Benson Commission Report p. 202 para. R 17.1.
39. *Ibid.* p. 201 para. 17.45.
40. Senate Evidence, Sect. IV introduction.
41. Benson Commission Report, Vol. 2 Surveys and Studies Oct. 1979, Cmnd. 7648-1, p. 212 Table 8.23.

introduction was through the recommendation of other organisations or relatives and friends. There is no direct information relating population to the siting of offices.

Another factor, more important than ease of access, is the nature and quality of the services available. Although a client may be able to consult a small firm close at hand, the advice given or representation arranged may be inferior to that which a larger firm some distance away can offer. A sole practitioner may, for instance, be an excellent conveyancer but totally out of his or her depth in conducting a court action, even with the assistance of a barrister. The availability of counsel under these circumstances may even be damaging because it enables solicitors to become involved in work which is beyond their experience and capacity. Where barristers are used in this way the solicitor is often merely the means of communication and contributes no special skill to the case. In substantial actions, London agents are often employed by provincial solicitors and they assist and advise upon the running of actions. This, however, is hardly an efficient division of labour when it is considered that two solicitors and one barrister all with their supporting staffs are involved in a single case.

A tendency in most spheres of activity is the creation of larger groupings to concentrate resources. This is a different process from the creation of monopolistic units in commerce and industry. It is more comparable to the situation in the medical profession where group practices are able to provide a greater range of services than the sole practitioner. Similarly in the legal profession, a moderately sized partnership will have at its disposal a much greater range of expertise than the very small practice. From within, it will probably have litigation, advocacy, tax, conveyancing, landlord and tenant and probate departments at the service of clients. By enabling practitioners to become expert in particular areas of the law, the public will benefit from a more comprehensive and efficient service.

Concern was expressed by the Benson Commission, not only over the possible loss of smaller firms, but also because of the expected growth of larger ones. The grounds for this fear are not investigated in any depth. A profile of the size of existing firms of solicitors shows, according to the Law Society,[42] that in December 1984 45.5% were sole practitioners (not all in full-time practice), 51.5% belonged to partnerships with 2–10 members, 1.8% with 11–15 members and 1.2% with 16–20 members and over.[42] If, in a single profession, there were to be an increase in the number of 2–10 partner groups, this may, in fact, improve the extent and quality of legal services offered to the public. Firms of this size are in a

42. *Supra*, p. 28.

vastly superior position in terms of resources to meet the demands of clients and sustain their own advocates.

A new trend adds to the probability that the number of medium sized partnerships will grow and at the same time cover a wider geographical area. Larger firms in towns and cities of a modest size have found that there is both a need and necessity to open branch offices in outlying districts. At least two factors may account for this development. Clients are often reluctant to go into a city centre because of travel and parking problems. As the convenience of suburban and out of town offices becomes appreciated, work is attracted to those firms with offices in these locations. Branches are being established at an increasing rate either by opening new offices or taking over an existing small practice. The replacement of very small practices in this way brings to the public the advantages, already described, which a larger firm possesses.

A pilot survey of branch offices belonging to firms in three centres of population confirms this trend. Brighton and Hove, Bristol and Oxford were selected. The principal offices of firms grouped according to the number of partners and the branch offices which they control were noted. Branch offices of firms outside the area being considered were ignored. The table in Appendix G shows the results. Firms in the 2–5 and 6–10 partner groups together provided the greatest number of branches representing 65% of the total. Those with 11–15 had 21%, sole practitioners 6.5% and the largest firms with over 16 partners only 5.6%.

It does not seem that the fear of extensive monopolies emerging from this process is justified. As has been demonstrated it is the small and medium sized firms which sustain the majority of branches. In the larger urban areas, these firms compete with each other, as do the offices they control. This competition is encouraging the spread of branch offices in the catchment areas. It can, therefore, be argued that by a natural process of decentralisation solicitors are responding to the demands of the public. Should fusion hasten this process, a higher grade of legal service will become more generally available. Single practitioners, as they do now, may require the assistance of specialists in law or advocacy. Where this need exists it can be met either by larger firms or by lawyers who choose to practise as consultants, alone or in partnership, taking their instructions only from other solicitors. The consultants as envisaged, not being subject to restrictions, could provide a complete litigation service. This would include all of the functions which a solicitor now performs. The range of expertise at their disposal would be wider and working arrangements more flexible. Risk of delay and error, present when a sole general practitioner endeavours to handle substantial litigation without an adequate knowledge of procedure, would be lessened.

The Benson Commission deplored the possible loss of small firms of solicitors in areas outside larger cities. No positive evidence, as distinct from expressions of opinion, was referred to which would explain why this possibility was considered likely with a fused profession. Countries which have a single profession do not suffer from the problem. None of the legal journals of Australia, Canada and New Zealand reveal complaints about the lack of adequate legal services in remote districts. By failing to explain why the situation would be different in England and Wales, a major conclusion is shown to be based upon a weak foundation. As an argument against fusion it can hardly be regarded as conclusive.

2.   Costs

The cost of legal services is one of the chief sources of dissatisfaction. Although the Benson Commission dealt extensively with this topic, little attention was given to the possible effect of fusion in reducing the cost of representation in the courts. The absence of factual evidence or comparisons is striking. A considerable amount of material taken into account by the Commission is anecdotal. Yet the only actual survey made upon the possible cost of litigation was rejected in these terms:[43]

> "The taxing masters of the Supreme Court at our request made comparative estimates of the costs of a sample of cases, on the basis of a fused and a two-branch profession. They found they could do this only if they made a number of assumptions about the conduct of litigation in a fused profession which, they warned us, were speculative, and about which both the Senate and Law Society expressed strong reservations. In the light of the views expressed, we consider that no firm conclusion could be drawn from this exercise."

The taxing masters' memorandum in fact showed estimated savings in cases assessed varying from 5% to 31%. The greatest reduction appeared to be likely where judgement is obtained by consent.

There are a number of other sources from which data of a factual nature could have been obtained and used to assist in a realistic assessment of the position. The taxing masters referred to one of them and suggested that:[44]

> "An investigation in County Court cases where both barrister and solicitor would enjoy similar rights of audience would give a more direct comparison..."

Also, in the Crown Court cases are conducted by solicitors in those sessions of the court which are open to them.[45] A comparison of the total

43.   Benson Commission Report, p. 195 para. 17.25.
44.   Taxing Masters Evidence to the Benson Commission, EV 884.
45.   *Supra.* p. 29–30.

cost of representation with and without a barrister would be easy to obtain by those with access to official sources of information. This would, to a limited degree, give an indication of the effect of double manning. From enquiries made, when employing a solicitor alone a reduction of about 20 % in the total cost of representation is possible. According to an estimate about 50 % of all business in the Crown Court consists of guilty pleas.[46] In a fused profession only one lawyer would be needed to undertake this work. The saving upon these cases would be an immediate and substantial benefit both to the Legal Aid fund and to clients who pay their own costs.

As the taxing masters pointed out, the County Courts provide another area suitable for a comparative study of costs. There, a client has the opportunity of engaging a solicitor advocate alone or a barrister through the solicitor. This is a situation which can be envisaged in a single profession where some lawyers choose to accept instructions only from other solicitors. Similarly, in the Magistrates' Courts this choice exists. A vast amount of advocacy is performed in these courts by solicitors. Generally speaking and in the majority of cases the total costs charged are less than they would be if a barrister were employed.

It is unfortunate that the Benson Commission did not commission studies upon comparative costings. The efficient and effective use of resources has a direct connection with the quality of service given. This factor was recognised by the fact that consultants Coopers and Lybrand were engaged to unravel the complicated accounts of the Inns of Court and their report runs to 32 pages.[47] If the information originally provided by the Senate did not enable a proper assessment of the Inns of Court finances to be made, further details could have been called for. It does appear that the expense of this consultant's report would have been more usefully spent upon the conduct of a searching examination of the effect of double manning upon costs on the lines suggested.

3. Rejection of Arguments in Favour of Fusion

The main criticisms of the two-branch profession which the Benson Commission noted are described in the following paragraph:[48]

> "Of the many witnesses who submitted evidence on the structure of the profession, a small minority advocated fusion. These witnesses put forward three main criticisms of the two-branch profession, that it was inefficient, harmed the confidence of clients and was more expensive. It was argued that these defects could be cured by the creation of a fused profession."

46. Benson Commission Report. p. 218 para. 18.58.
47. *Ibid.* Vol 2. Surveys and Studies, pp. 341–373.
48. *Ibid.* p. 191 para. 17.14.

Evidence submitted in favour of fusion or of reforms which would eventually lead to this end, in fact included that of substantial and influential bodies. The Society of Labour Lawyers[49] took the view that clients should not be forced to employ a barrister and supported the extension of solicitors' right of audience to all courts. The comment was added that should this result in the loss of a separate Bar then the Bar's claim to a separate existence could no longer be justified. The Labour Party,[50] although not using the word 'fusion', made proposals which, it is generally accepted, would lead to a single profession. They were that:

> "Monopolies over rights of audience in the higher courts that favour barristers over solicitors should be abolished. There should be a prohibition on any professional rule requiring lawyers to take cases only from other lawyers—though individual lawyers should be allowed to practise in this way if they choose. . ."

The National Council for Civil Liberties[51] expressed total support for fusion stating that the benefits would include:

> ". . . an increased range of people from whom the judiciary is chosen . . .
> It would help ensure that clients' instructions were followed . . .
> It would involve the direct responsibility of the advocate to the client . . .
> It would help de-mystify the legal process as far as lay people are concerned
> . . ."

Other bodies who gave outright support to fusion were the Haldane Society of Socialist Lawyers,[52] the United Lawyers Association[53] (a group of solicitors and barristers pledged to a unified profession) and the Legal Action Group.[54] Professor Michael Zander submitted a detailed and scholarly submission upon the advantages of fusion.[55]

Evidence was given by the General Council of the Trades Union Congress firmly in favour of ending the division in the profession. This fact was not specifically referred to in the Benson Commission Report. Its importance must be considerable—not only because it represents the collective view of a vast section of the country's workforce but also because of the experience of affiliated unions in their dealings with the law and lawyers. In referring to advocacy, the Council observed:[56]

> "the simple distinction between representation and all other aspects of a case is an artificial one and, in the experience of affiliated unions, leads too often to the situation where he [counsel] is only briefed at the last minute or because there is a late change of counsel for the case."

49.   The Society of Labour Lawyers, Evidence to the Benson Commission, EV 438 p. 7–8 para. 18.
50.   The Labour Party, *Ibid.*, EV 343 p. 45.
51.   The National Council for Civil Liberties, *Ibid.*, EV 389 pp. 30–1 para. 71.
52.   Haldane Society of Socialist Lawyers, *Ibid.* EV 476 p. 7.
53.   United Lawyers' Association, *Ibid.*. EV 673.
54.   Legal Action Group, *Ibid.*, EV 469 p. 10.
55.   Prof. Michael Zander, *Ibid.*, EV 1.
56.   General Council of the Trade Union Council *Ibid.* EV 622, pp. 15–16.

The submission also points out that specialists could be provided in a unified profession, that clients would have direct access to all lawyers and that there would be a saving in costs because of the elimination of the need for a second lawyer to intervene as does a solicitor at present.

The Commission's report gave a summary of the arguments put forward by some of the witnesses who were in favour of abolishing the divided profession. Each and every point made is rebutted either by contrary statements of other witnesses or conclusions expressed collectively by the Commission. No support is given to the belief that fusion would contribute towards the elimination of the faults inherent in the present system. Unfortunately, the impression is conveyed that the evidence referred to in the report is not presented in a balanced manner. A sociologist, reviewing the report, goes further and writes of the selective use of evidence as one of its most distressing features. He instances the rejection of comparative costings by the taxing masters of the Supreme Court on the basis of a two-branch and fused profession and notes that, in contrast:[57]

> ". . . off-hand comments by legal luminaries from other countries are thrown in, for example, to support claims that the British advocates in a divided profession provide a superior service."

The following example of the kind of remark selected and used as 'evidence' is quoted:[57]

> "The Commission apparently endorses the view of a barrister with knowledge of practice in California that fusion has stratified the profession between large firms and marginal one-man 'street front' practices serving the poorer areas."

These sweeping statements are unverified and their choice also illustrates the reliance placed upon anecdotal evidence.

Many of the criticisms of the quality of service are, the report states, directed towards the return of briefs by barristers shortly before a hearing. The Commission regarded it as a serious matter. The question to be asked is whether the situation would be improved with fusion. Again it is, unfortunately, necessary to note the paucity of factual evidence. The prevalence of the complaint justifies a full investigation of its extent and frequency. If a group of solicitors were selected according to established statistical principles they could be asked to report upon cases in which a brief was returned giving the reason stated. The barristers involved could then be requested to record the exact events which led to the return e.g. the date when instructions were received for the case actually taken and the one returned and the precise reasons for the return. It does not appear

---

57. R. Luckham, 'The Final Report of the Royal Commission on Legal Services—a Sociologist's View.' 43 MLR 543 (1980).

that a methodical study has ever been made to ascertain the causes of the problem. As a consequence the Commission's proposals[58] on ways in which this situation can be improved do not indicate that the extent of the problem was appreciated. The Commission maintained that in some minor criminal cases the transfer of a brief shortly before trial was acceptable. Only minor administrative reforms were proposed. One suggestion was that a list of barristers be compiled, with the agreement of solicitors, the transfer of briefs among those on the list being permitted without further reference to the instructing solicitor or, presumably, the client. The other was to allow barristers' clerks the freedom to allocate briefs to ensure, as far as possible, that individual barristers were in one court only on a particular day.

It is clear from the evidence presented to the Commission that many believed a client's confidence in the quality of representation to be damaged because of the divided profession. The constant exchange of briefs between barristers is a contributory factor. Solicitors have the invidious task of explaining the substitution of a stranger for the barrister first instructed. Justice, a legal reform group, condemned the practice by remarking:[59]

> "Nothing is more calculated to shake the lay client's confidence in the legal system than to be told at the last minute that X cannot take the case and it will have to be done by Y, who has not previously been involved and indeed may belong to a different set of chambers."

This happens with great regularity in the Crown Court. By allowing solicitors to plead at any session of this court the position could be relieved. However, in deciding that a divided profession should remain, the Commission ruled against this proposal. To surrender any of the work exclusively reserved for barristers would, it was felt, weaken the Bar and so jeopardise its separate existence.

In discussing the possibility of allowing solicitors to conduct guilty pleas in the Crown Court it is maintained that:[60]

> "... the convicted offender requires the highest possible standard of representation which can only be provided by a specialist advocate."

As an ideal this statement is laudable. In reality the present system does not even ensure that the advocate chosen or an acceptable and experienced substitute will take the case.

Having selected and rejected some of the arguments put forward in support of fusion the latter part of the Commission's report turns to 'Arguments against Fusion'.[61] The tenor of this section is, in approach,

58. Benson Commission Report, pp. 300–1 para. 22.48.
59. *Ibid.* pp. 193–4, para. 17.21.
60. *Ibid.* p. 218 para. 18.58.
61. *Ibid.* pp. 196–202 paras. 17.27–45.

similar to that of the Bar's evidence to the Commission which states categorically that there are no advantages to the public to be found in fusion. A number of suggested benefits are then listed and rejected. These do not include many improvements which those who favour reform believe likely. The Commission's report, in dealing with the arguments against fusion, makes no concession to those who believe that a unified profession would be beneficial and improve legal services.

The whole question is ultimately one of justifying the restrictive practices which effectively split the legal profession into its two branches. The Benson Report describes the rules which achieve this end as having a direct and also an indirect object. Although this may be their effect at the present time, they were never devised as part of a coherent plan for the provision of legal services. As described in Chapter 1, their evolution is a product of competing interests between various functionaries over a long period. It is probably more correct to say that the ultimate reason for the rules is the preservation of the Bar as an entity together with the privileges its members enjoy.

The purposes of the rules which restrict the right of audience of solicitors and prohibit access to the lay client are explained in this way:[62]

> "The direct object of the rule governing rights of audience is to ensure, so far as possible, that advocacy in matters of substance is performed only by practitioners who specialise in it, and who have the time and facilities to do so. The direct object of the rule which prevents access save through a solicitor by the client to a barrister is to ensure that barristers are free from hour-to-hour distractions and that specialist matters with which they deal are presented to them by a lawyer who has already identified the issues and sifted out the relevant facts, rather than by the lay client himself who can only present his problem as a whole. The object is not to put the barrister at a distance from his client, but to ensure, so far as possible, that his specialist skills are efficiently used, that he is ensured, so far as possible, the time necessary to concentrate on them and—this is put forward very much as a secondary objective—that he remains sufficiently detached from his client to be able to give him advice which is wholly objective. The indirect object of both these rules is to prevent the fusion and blurring to two categories of practitioner, by ensuring that the solicitor does not undertake work for which a barrister is required and by ensuring that the barrister is not diverted to functions outside his speciality functions which can be better performed by the solicitor."

This detailed explanation of the roles of the two branches of the profession leaves the most important question unanswered. Is it in the public interest for a separate Bar to be maintained for the purpose of providing specialist advocates who can handle 'matters of substance' without distraction? Throughout the report and in the evidence submitted by opponents of fusion, the freedom which lawyers in a unified

---

62. *Ibid.* p. 196, para. 17.27.

profession would have to provide specialist services is not appreciated.

The 'detachment' which is said to be very much a secondary object does not seem to be regarded as an important feature of separation. This quality, which is reputed to exist in the barrister–client relationship, has in the past always been stressed as being of primary importance. Difficult to define and impossible to quantify, it should in fact be the mark of all true professionals. The vast majority of solicitors and barristers are, as their careers progress, faced with a continuous stream of problems. So far as solicitors are concerned, it would not be possible to cope with even a modest work load if there were any personal involvement in the problems arising from day-to-day. There is detachment of another kind which can be detrimental to a client's interests. This can happen when, because of the system, a barrister receives instructions only a short time before a hearing. There is no substitute for adequate preparation and the mastery of facts. Here, the solicitor is often in an advantageous position, having more time to reflect upon a situation.

The division of function between the two branches of the profession is maintained by the general rule that a witness must not be interviewed by the barrister or be present at a conference with the client. There are exceptions to this stipulation in the case of an expert or professional witness or in exceptional circumstances at the Barrister's discretion.[63] Sir David Napley advocates the abolition of the rule and comments:[64]

> "In fact the bulk of contentious legal business is conducted in the county and magistrates' courts by solicitors who both interview the witnesses and conduct the advocacy without the dire consequences which it is said would flow from the removal of this rule affecting Barristers. In my view, it is outmoded and should be abolished, so that every advocate can see and assess his client's witnesses as he does the client himself."

Differing reasons have been advanced over the years to justify the barrier placed between the barrister and those concerned with a case. Another objection sometimes put forward is that an advocate might deliberately or by a hint, suggest to a witness how evidence should be given. If this were a real danger all advocates both solicitors and barristers should be forbidden to interview witnesses. The fact that this has never been suggested indicates that the true reason for the rule is that given by the Commission, namely:[65]

63. *Supra* p. 4 and 45.
64. Sir David Napley *The Technique of Persuasion* 3rd ed. 1983 Sweet & Maxwell, London p. 53.
65. Benson Commission Report, p. 196, para. 17.27.

"to prevent the fusion and blurring of two categories of practitioner, by ensuring that the solicitor does not undertake work for which a barrister is required and by ensuring that the barrister is not diverted to functions outside his speciality—functions which can be better performed by the solicitor."

Here is revealed what appears to be the primary object of the rules governing a barrister's contact with the lay client and witnesses. It is to keep the two branches of the profession apart and so ensure that the identity of the Bar as a separate group remains intact. Standing alone these rules do not have any particular merit apart from the mere organisational one of defining the functions of those involved in a case. There are many instances where it would be more convenient for the client and lawyer to dispense with them. If abandoned it is unlikely that barrister advocates would suddenly abandon their ethical principles and attempt to influence witnesses. On the contrary this would assist barristers to obtain fuller details where needed to supplement inadequate proofs of evidence.

4. Quality of Service

A separate Bar with limited functions has, according to the Commission, advantages over a fused system. A reason given by nearly all witnesses, including judges, in support of their opposition to fusion was that:[66]

". . . it would lead to a serious fall in the quality of advocacy and hence also, because of the nature of court proceedings, in the quality of judicial decisions. They argued that this would damage not merely the interests of individual litigants, but the administration of justice itself . . ."

Repeating the argument of availability, it is explained that the services of the most highly skilled members of the Bar are at the disposal of the small firms of solicitors. In predicting the effects of fusion it is thought likely that the most experienced barristers would join larger firms of solicitors. In support of this belief the observations of a young solicitors group and two law societies were adduced. In this part of the report, evidence used to justify conclusions consists only of the views and opinions of witnesses. Facts and statistical data have not been tendered or obtained by specific research. With the question now discussed, for instance, mention is made of the number and size of solicitors firms:[67]

"It will be observed from Table 17.1 that, in April 1979, 58.4 per cent of all firms of solicitors had one or two partners and that a further 23.6 per cent had three or four partners."

66. *Ibid.* pp. 196–7, para. 17.29.
67. *Ibid.* p. 197, para. 17.30.

This is sparse information upon which to base any conclusion about the need for these firms to have the services of the Bar in its present form. There would be no great difficulty in ascertaining, on a sample basis, how many qualified and unqualified employees each firm had. This is relevant in assessing the size of the firm. In any event the figure of 58.4% for one or two partner firms is misleading. The number of sole practitioners included those who did only part-time or occasional legal work.[68] Then there is the nature of the work undertaken. A survey could show which firms utilise the services of barristers, the kind of cases in which they become involved and the frequency of consultation. The growth of branch offices and the improved and more comprehensive service they are able to provide has been described.[69] The existence of a large number of small firms with access to the Bar does not necessarily mean that the service they provide is the best obtainable. An attempt needs to be made to compare the service given by sole practitioners with that of the branch offices of partnerships. Representation is a crucial area for study as the provision of advocacy is one of the most important and truly legal functions of a solicitor. By far the most frequent need for advocacy is in the Magistrates' Court and County Court. The very small firm may engage in such work as incidental to more lucrative activities. If this results in the undue use of barristers it is the client who suffers through having to pay higher fees. Also it is by no means certain that a barrister employed under these circumstances will be as skilled as a solicitor advocate employed by a larger firm.

The creation of a single unified legal profession would, the Commission concluded with some certainty, bring about a decline in the standard of advocacy. Once more, the probability of some practitioners offering their services solely to other lawyers is not discussed or contemplated. There is only a passing reference to this likely development in an earlier paragraph which, when discussing access to advocates, mentions:[70]

> "In the event, many firms would not be able to recruit barristers because there would be too few to go around. This difficulty would be exacerbated if a large number of barristers decided to set up their own firms which they are not at present permitted to do."

The implications of this possibility are not elaborated upon. This is an admission that advocates in a fused profession could, if they wished, associate and practice in a way similar to that of barristers. The advantage would be the absence of any compulsion and the freedom to adjust working practices to meet the client's convenience. As to a possible shortage of advocates, this is unlikely. The question to be considered is

68. *Supra.* p. 28 gives current profile of profession.
69. *Supra.* pp. 68–9.
70. Benson Commission Report. p. 197. para. 17.31.

how they are to be deployed; whatever the structure of the profession, the same number of advocates will be available for a similar amount of work.

The concern of the Commission that in a fused profession advocates may not have the opportunity to appear regularly and so will lose their skill is illustrated by a quotation from the evidence of Lord Justice Roskill, in which he says:[71]

"I have known of one firm of solicitors who wished to specialise in a particular field having sought to secure the services as a partner of a barrister specialising in that field. They were disappointed in the result because that former barrister's skills began to diminish in quality once only a limited source of supply of work—the clients of that particular firm—was available to him."

Without a great deal more detail this comment is not very illuminating. The nature of the speciality and the particular skill which diminished are not described. If the particular firm did not have sufficient work to keep the specialist fully occupied then the situation can hardly be considered typical. In any occupation, constant application to a limited field of activity is the mark of a specialist. There are many solicitor specialists both in advocacy and law. Their skills do not appear to have been affected through working for one firm. There would be few solicitor specialists if this happened frequently. If the main argument against fusion is a diminishment of skill through lack of practice then this is equally a reason for removing restrictions to enable all practitioners to use their talents effectively.

5. Selection of Judges

It is impossible to exaggerate the importance of ensuring that only the most suitable lawyers are appointed to judicial office. In a single profession there would be a larger pool of candidates eligible to serve as judges. Those responsible for advising the Lord Chancellor upon appointments do not apparently see any merit in this. With a restricted number of candidates it is suggested that the talents of candidates can be observed and noted more easily. In many instances, the Lord Chancellor and his advisers are likely to have personal knowledge of potential judges. The argument is put in this way:[72]

"Fusion would increase the numbers available for consideration but might increase the possibility of making an unsuitable choice."

This may be so because existing staffing arrangements and methods of assessment make it difficult to investigate a great number of candidates.

---

71. *Ibid.*, p. 200 para. 17.40.
72. *Ibid.*, p. 200 para. 17.41.

It could equally be maintained that by artificially restricting the supply of candidates the range of talent from diverse social and educational backgrounds is reduced. However, the concern of the Lord Chancellor's Department does not seem to have been regarded seriously. By July 1985, Lord Hailsham announced that 41 solicitor recorders had been appointed. This has increased the number of practitioners from whom to select Circuit judges. At the time of the Commission's report only nine solicitors had been appointed as Circuit judges. Now there are approximately 31. No complaint has been made of the difficulty of selection because of the numbers involved or the quality of those appointed.

A glaring anomaly is revealed when demarcation rules governing rights of audience and appointments to the bench are compared. It is the orthodox view that judges should be drawn from the ranks of practising advocates. Some may feel that this overstates the position if experience is taken to mean an inordinately long spell as an advocate in a particular type of court. Nevertheless, it does seem essential that, before appointment, a judge should, at least, have worked on some occasions in the court concerned. This view is inconsistent with the Commission's justification of the anomaly which results in solicitors being appointed Circuit judges and yet denies them the right to practise in the Crown Court without restriction. It is stated:[73]

> ". . . a solicitor may well be fitted for judicial office and it would be wasteful if there were no means by which he could achieve it. It does not follow that all solicitors should be regarded as qualified to practice advocacy in courts in which former solicitors may sit as judges."

It follows that the talents of a solicitor, well fitted to perform advocacy at all levels, are wasted if he or she is not permitted to conduct cases in the superior courts. The wastage in this instance is, presumably, acceptable as the price to be paid for a separate Bar.

6. Trends

In closing the arguments against fusion, there is a short account of the effect of what are seen to be present trends towards specialisation and the need for effective advocacy at all levels. This, it is pointed out, makes it likely that in a fused profession there would be a demand for services of the kind now supplied by the Bar. It is, therefore, difficult to understand why the possibility of lawyer specialists and advocates becoming established, free from the restrictions which exist in a two-branch profession, where they are needed has not been considered in greater

73. *Ibid.*, pp. 214–5, para. 18.48.

detail. There is only a passing reference to this probable development, apart from the one previously referred to. It is made in a quotation from the evidence of a supporter of fusion who said:[74]

> ". . . in my submission there must be, even if one has fusion, a rump of the Bar. Call it what you will, there will be some kind of lump advocacy labour, in other words, a pool on which one can draw for a particular case. That has to exist even under a fused system."

This arrangement would have distinct advantages. Public needs and convenience would be met by lawyers free of restrictive practices. Instead of a rigid and unchanging system, they would be at liberty to serve the public in the most efficient and least expensive way possible. The Commission does not indicate why this concept should be regarded as an argument against fusion. Two observations from other jurisdictions are put forward to support the view that this development would take place. One is that of the Chief Justice of Australia who said that specialist Bars had arisen in some states of Australia to meet a demand and they had resulted in an improvement of the standard of advocacy. That country has an untypical structure, having a divided profession in three states and a fused one in the other three.[75] The other is the praise which a judge of the New Zealand Court of Appeal gives to the concept of a separate Bar as it exists in England and Wales. A former Chief Justice, the late Sir Richard Wild, made this observation but added that formal division in New Zealand on the British pattern was unlikely. He did, on the other hand, agree that the single profession in his country works well. These comments do not give any indication of a significant trend towards the separation of legal practitioners as in England and Wales.

7. Summary of Recommendations

The Commission's eventual recommendation that the structure of the legal profession should not be changed was in accord with what Professor Galbraith has termed conventional wisdom. Throughout the report a sustained belief prevails that every advantage seen to be likely in a fused profession is illusory. Broader questions such as the freedom to practice and right of establishment in a democratic society are not considered in depth. The gradual and inexorable advance of solicitors into work at one time almost exclusively reserved for the Bar has not been taken into account. It would be contrary to human nature for the organisation of the profession to remain fixed and unchanging for any great length of time. Altered circumstances call for new methods to meet

---

74. *Ibid.*, p. 200, para. 17.42.
75. *Supra.* p. 16.

them. It is disappointing to find the Commission's ultimate conclusions so categorical, based as they are upon highly speculative and, in some instances, vague anecdotal evidence.

Fusion would bring, it is asserted, an unacceptable reduction in the number of smaller firms of solicitors and concentrate business in the larger ones. This, it is thought, would result in an uneven distribution of lawyers throughout the country. There is, however, another view that can be taken, which is backed by present trends in England and Wales. It is the establishment of branch offices by firms, large and small. This process of decentralisation brings advantages to the public in the form of a greater range of expertise. Fusion may well accelerate the process.

As noted, the Commission has not analysed by survey the quality and range of services offered by sole practitioners. It is taken for granted that their deficiencies can be made up by using barristers' services. The number of cases which require the services of the Bar have, however, been shown to represent only a small fraction of the total work of a general practice. The remaining work requires the skills and resources which a larger firm is better placed to provide.

Fusion, it is claimed, would disperse the specialist service which is now provided by the Bar. Larger firms with advocate partners may, it is conceded, improve communication between advocate and client. This would not be so, it is suggested, where a smaller firm refers a client to a larger one for representation in court. As has been stressed in this work, the fact that such arrangements would not be governed by restrictions which are now imposed to keep the two branches of the profession apart means that a client would still have direct contact with the advocate conducting the case. This would also apply if the advocate only accepted instructions from other solicitors, as there would be no restriction to prevent direct contact with the client. Convenience rather than sectional interest would rule the situation.

None of the Commission's objections to fusion question its feasibility. They are based upon what are thought to be the probable effects of amalgamation. There is little tangible evidence to support assumptions which have been made. Facts, for instance, were not elicited in respect of comparative costings, the position of very small firms or returned briefs. It is, however, clear that no fundamental principle is seen to be at stake which would render reform unacceptable e.g. the preservation of the integrity of the judiciary or the avoidance of corruption. For these reasons a continuing discussion of the problem can be expected.

PART 3—AFTER BENSON

1. Dissension within the Profession

There is evidence of public disquiet over the effects of the divided profession. Delays, procrastination, double manning and the high cost of litigation are frequently alleged. A *Sunday Times* article[1] recently described how that newspaper paid about £500 in legal costs for a simple application to a judge in the High Court. Queen's Counsel and a junior were engaged. The solicitor in the action could, if permitted, have undertaken the task, and his charges would have been one fifth of that figure. The article indicates an awareness of the consequences of the dual system which, in the past, have not attracted public interest. Within the profession, open and direct criticism of the division is now common. Barristers are unhappy with some aspects of their relations with solicitors. The delayed payment of fees for completed work has been a subject of acrimonious comment and correspondence[2] in the legal press. Late delivery of briefs and inadequate preparation of cases is another complaint. Solicitors on the other hand are moving towards the belief that the restrictive practices associated with division are not appropriate to modern requirements, both in terms of their own status and the service which they can give to the public.

As shown in the first chapter, the division arose from competing class and professional interests. To this day an element of resentment over the separation persists. This may be due to the subordinate position which solicitors occupy in the legal hierarchy. By itself, this could not justify any radical change. There is, however, a more important element. This is the conviction held by many that the present structure hinders the natural development and improvement of legal services. The substantial differences in opportunity which exist between the two branches are often overlooked and sometimes deliberately ignored. The Declaration of Bath, mentioned earlier, for instance, described solicitors and barristers as being of equal status but with different and complementary functions. Older generations of solicitors in more settled times may have thought this to be so. They were conditioned to observe a respectful and deferential attitude towards their colleagues at the Bar. In return they were treated in a polite and patronising manner.

The calm has been disturbed. Unexpectedly, the Law Society has begun to display a radical change in attitude. This became evident when the

---

1. K. Fletcher and J. Picardie, 'Why M'learned Friends are Becoming M'learned Enemies', *Sunday Times* 14 April 1985.
2. M. Wright 'Payment of Barristers' Fees.' 81 *Gazette* 1812 (1984).
    R. de Wilde 'Payment of Barristers' Fees' 81 *Gazette* 1485–6 (1984).
    M. Simmonds, 'Full Ahead for Fusion', 81 *Gazette* 1836 (1984).

Government decided to accept and legislate on the conveyancing proposals in Austin Mitchell's Private Member's Bill. A campaign to secure an extension of solicitors' rights of audience was announced and, in briefing and press material, forthright comments about the Bar were made. In criticising the operation of the 'cab-rank' principle which is designed to prevent the arbitrary rejection of instructions by a barrister on the grounds that a cause is unpopular or embarrassing it was stated:[3]

> "The rule is more honoured in the breach than in the observance in that in many areas of work the barrister whom the client and/or solicitor wish to instruct is rarely available. For example, in the Crown Court, briefs are frequently returned or passed on to a different barrister . . ."

In referring to the possibility of clients having direct access to barristers, should an extension of rights of audience be granted, it was observed:[4]

> "This would create more problems for the Bar than advantages in that it would immediately lead to the question of a contractual relationship between barrister and client and the need to provide adequate support facilities for interviewing and corresponding with clients, and for producing documentation, clients' accounts and collecting fees. In fact, direct access to the Bar would totally change the complexion of the Bar so that fusion would become almost inevitable."

The likelihood of it being said that solicitors would not be competent to practice advocacy in the superior courts and address a jury was countered. It was pointed out that already solicitor judges were presiding successfully in the Crown Court where they were required to sum up to a jury. The Law Society also pointed out that similar arguments:[5]

> "were used by those who opposed the provisions of the Courts Act 1971 permitting the appointment of solicitors as recorders and recorders as Circuit judges. Experience has shown that these objections were ill founded and that solicitor judges in the Crown Court have been successful and have had no difficulty in summing up to a jury. There is no reason to believe that solicitors should not be successful as advocates in the superior courts."

In a slightly jocular vein, a solicitor writing in *The Law Society's Gazette* indicated approval of this stand:[6]

> "This must be the first time in history that The Law Society has stopped cringing under the patronising condescension of the senior branch of the profession."

The present policy of the Bar upon the rights of audience issue is in line with the attitude in 1982 when The Law Society pressed for Circuit judges who had previously practised as solicitors to be made eligible for

---

3. The Law Society, 'Solicitors Rights of Audience Briefing Document', Mar. 1984, p. 3.
4. *Ibid*. p. 4.
5. *Ibid*. p. 4.
6. C. Railton, letter, 81 *Gazette* 1484 (1984).

appointment to the High Court bench. A letter in *The Times* from Sir David Napley supported the proposal but there was no response in the correspondence columns of that newspaper from the Bar, either officially or unofficially. According to a report of the Annual General Meeting of the Senate, the President said that the silence was intentional. Upon being asked how to respond the Solicitor-General had, at the time, advised that it would be better not to reply to Sir David Napley's letter because it had been intended to set a platform.[7]

In response to a question in the House of Commons, the Prime Minister was asked by John Townend, Conservative Member of Parliament for Bridlington, whether she would "reconsider the barristers' monopoly right of audience in the higher courts". The reply was discouraging in the short term but does not rule out the possibility of an eventual change. She said:[8]

> "the question was considered by the Royal Commission on Legal Services under Lord Benson, which reported that it would be against the interests of the client to extend the solicitors' right of audience from the lower to the higher courts. The Government accepted that advice in 1983 and it is too early to reconsider it."

A Council Member of the Law Society, giving his personal view, pointed out that the Government had tackled the solicitors' monopoly of conveyancing but had left the barristers' monopoly of rights of audience in the higher courts untouched:[9]

> "The disinterested observer might well believe that however objectively the Government may have acted it would be better if the decision involving such uneven handed treatment of the two branches of the profession had been made otherwise than by a body of whom the Prime Minister, the Home Secretary and several other members of her Cabinet were, by training, barristers."

The writer's words typify the more positive and less deferential approach to the problems of the profession which is now widespread. He asks whether, now that the wind of change is blowing and becoming stiffer:[10]

> "the profession will stand together and seek to promote change, which will ensure the public good and provide a legal profession to take us well into the next century, or whether the two branches will dissipate their considerable energies and skills in fighting each other."

As it becomes more difficult to justify and maintain the separation between the two branches of the profession, a progressive approach to the future may achieve Mr. Gaskell's objective. Clearly the Bar has

7.   R. Gaskell, 'The Wind of Change in Legal Practice.' 81 *Gazette* 2599 (1984).
8.   *Parliamentary Debates (Hansard) House of Commons*, 6th series, Vol. 59. Col. 537.
9.   R. Gaskell. *op. cit.* p. 2600.
10. *Ibid*, p. 2600.

been forced to adopt a defensive position which is bound to reduce its effectiveness. When there was complete unanimity, at least at official level, in support of the existing structure, dissent was muted and regarded with tolerance. Although the process has been exceedingly slow, a stage has now been reached where a lack of response to the call for change may cause a serious deterioration in the relations between the two branches of the profession. If this should harm the service given to the public, confidence in the legal system may be weakened.

An indication of the way in which inter-professional rivalry is likely to be accentuated is to be found in the rights of audience issue. Marcel Berlins, then *The Times'* legal correspondent, wrote at length about this topic. He expressed the view that the Benson Commission's decision not to recommend an extension of solicitors' rights of audience:[11]

> "was based on an unconvincing premise and illogical reasoning. Compared to the rest of the report, the chapter dealing with right of audience pays least service to the interests of the public and most to protecting the narrow financial interests of the legal profession or rather one part of it."

He points out that there is nothing in the report to show that investigations have been made to find out whether barristers are truly specialists and that they perform their work satisfactorily. In the absence of a qualitative judgement, the wrong questions have been asked and answered.

During a period when *The Times* was not published, Mr. Berlins had the opportunity to visit a number of courts and assess the standards of advocacy being practised in criminal cases. As an independent observer with a knowledge of the practice of the law he was in a position to give an unbiased account without being concerned over the reaction of either branch of the profession. His findings cast doubt upon the view, implicit in the Commission's report, that the services rendered by all barristers are satisfactory and of a high standard. The whole basis of support for the dual system is the assumed excellence of the Bar's service, a service which, it is maintained, would not be forthcoming if solicitors were allowed to have a right to take cases in the Crown Court. In questioning this view he gives examples of his observations:[12]

> "I was appalled. It was not just that so many young barristers seemed incapable of forming a grammatically correct English sentence (and I am not talking about 'immigrant lawyers'). Much more distressing was the poor, sometimes inexcusable, standard of presentation of the lay client's case. I was present on two occasions when counsel managed to forget the crime with which his client had been charged. I saw more than one example of counsel clearly being unaware of the leading relevant case or the relevant

11.   M. Berlins, 'Rights of Audience', 129 *New Law Journal* 1116.
12.   *Ibid.* p. 1117.

piece of legislation. Mistakes about the detail and circumstances of the crime and, in pleas of mitigation, about the defendant's age, occupation and personal circumstances were commonplace. I did not try to ascertain the reasons for the incompetence but it could not all have been a result of late briefs."

Under the dual system it is often assumed that the Bar is a body of specialists comparable to the consultants of the medical world. Traditionally counsel's opinion has been accepted as an authoritative statement given by someone with special knowledge and experience upon which a client can rely. The term 'solicitor's opinion' is rarely used and would carry little weight with the public if it were. A correspondent in *The Law Society's Gazette* illustrated this anomaly in referring to the advice of leading counsel taken by The Law Society upon the question of a judicial review of the Master of the Rolls' refusal to approve new indemnity insurance rules. He wrote:[13]

"With the greatest respect to the Bar, why leading Counsel? Are we to believe that among the entire body of members of The Law Society, among the experienced and highly talented members of the Council and/or their professional colleagues, there was not to be found a solicitor capable of advising in depth on this point?"

The question is rhetorical as, in fact, an abundance of solicitor experts practice in all branches of law. The prestige attached to 'counsel's opinion' is probably a survival from the days when solicitors were merely clerks and law agents.

General criticism of the legal profession is not new. It is, however, possible to identify specific areas where there may be justification for complaint. Now that conveyancing has been removed from the arena, litigation and representation in court are bound to attract more attention. For most of this century the lucrative monopoly in conveyancing has been accepted as a reward for being excluded from the higher reaches of the law. This balance has been upset and the younger members of the profession, who now predominate, are unlikely to remain passive if reforms which would improve their opportunities are blocked. Lord Benson recognised how contentious the rights of audience question has become when he commented:[14]

"The lay public is disturbed by the apparent differences of opinion within the profession which often appears to be divided against itself. The demarcation dispute with the Bar on the rights of audience is one example but, as you know, there are many other factions. It would be helpful if the public could be assured that these internal differences will soon be resolved and that the profession will be able to move forward as a united body in its responsibility to serve the public."

13. M. D. Varcoe-Cooks, letter, 81 *Gazette* 2423 (1984).
14. Lord Benson 81 *Gazette* 1251 (1984).

Lack of harmony is becoming evident in the working relationships within the profession. Since solicitors have been given the limited rights which they now enjoy in the Crown Court comments have been made about the treatment which they receive from judges. At one time this happened only occasionally and was regarded with good natured tolerance. Now a note of resentment is detectable in published accounts of the discourtesy and sometimes rudeness which a few judges in the Crown Court have shown towards solicitors appearing before them. Unfortunately, the experiences of some solicitor advocates indicate that antagonism of the kind described may result in injustice to the client. A well-known columnist writing in *The Law Society's Gazette* under the pseudonym Sebastian Cullwick, tells of his personal experience when first appearing in the Crown Court to conduct an appeal against a Magistrates' Court decision. He was first ordered to leave the barristers' robing room, being informed that it was not a room for solicitors. At the beginning of the case the judge said "What are you doing here?" Explaining that he was representing an appellant, the judge replied, "Let's get on with it". The solicitor relates:[15]

> "from that moment I had lost my case. There was total antagonism and lack of co-operation throughout the proceedings; the barrister appearing for the respondent was anything but civil, the judge was positively rude. My client thankfully realised why he had lost his appeal. Others sadly have had similar experiences . . ."

Another instance of this kind of treatment is related by a London solicitor.[16] Appearing before a judge in chambers at the Central Criminal Court to make a bail application he was, correctly, not robed. The judge seeing only the prosecuting barrister there, in wig and gown, spoke to the clerk of the court. The clerk turned and pointed to the solicitor whereupon the judge said "What's he doing here? He's not allowed to appear in this court." The clerk apparently, out of earshot, corrected the judge. The solicitor goes on to say how his address to the court was punctuated by the judge's cavernous yawns and that he left the court without having once been addressed by name.

The extent of the problem and the variety of its manifestations is illustrated by yet another example. A solicitor was acting for a client who was committed by a Magistrates' Court to the Crown Court for sentence. The case was called on at 10.55 a.m. The judge, noticing immediately that a solicitor was taking the case, brusquely announced that the Bench was minded to amend the legal aid order to include representation by counsel and gave until noon for a barrister to be instructed. The client stated that he was satisfied with the solicitor and would prefer the hearing to

---

15. 81 *Gazette* 1414 (1984).
16. J. Mackenzie, 'Rights of Audience—Ill Judged' 81 *Gazette* 2735 (1984).

proceed. On being advised that it might not be in his best interest to spurn the offer, the client reluctantly agreed to an adjournment. A barrister was found and given the papers and notes of a plea in mitigation already prepared by the solicitor. At 11.30 a.m. the case was called. The barrister appeared and made the plea almost word for word as it had been written. The solicitor described the experience as humiliating, particularly as it took place in full view of other barristers and the public.[17] The serious aspect of this incident is that the client's right to select an advocate was interfered with by the court.

The tensions which Lord Benson referred to are not only concerned with right of audience. The denial of opportunity to skilled and experienced practitioners to serve in certain judicial posts is another cause of discontent. A correspondent in *The Law Society's Gazette* has drawn attention to an advertisement for applications by members of the Bar or of the Faculty of Advocates for appointment as Deputy Judge Advocate. He points out that all members of the profession have a right of audience before courts martial. Yet, despite the fact that many solicitors have considerable experience in these courts they are excluded from presiding over them. "Is not this" he asks "another example of wholly unjustifiable prejudice against solicitors and in favour of the Bar?"[18]

For as long as the dual system exists, customs and rituals, unimportant as they are, will continue to emphasise the division. Those who observe them may be oblivious of their effect. For instance, the term 'my learned friend' which barristers use when addressing each other becomes 'my friend' when referring to a solicitor. The implications in the distant past may have been obvious. Today it can be used slightingly and without reason. A practitioner describes how a member of the Bar who, when opening, referred to him as:[19]

> " 'My learned friend' went on to say 'I mean my friend' . . . I can picture to this day the polished raising of the registrar's eyebrows at this juncture. One could almost say that he winced at the almost calculated insult implied in these words."

This new and firm stand is a break with the past. Instead of accepting rebuffs and discourtesy in silence, criticism is more openly expressed. The extent of the discontent is revealed by the solicitor who has suggested that a practitioner, believing that he had been treated with discourtesy, should write personally to the judge:[20]

> "expressing politely his disappointment at the judge's rudeness and

17. K. Hall, 'Solicitor Advocates', 81 *Gazette* 3141 (1984).
18. D. M. Philips, 'Discrimination' 81 *Gazette* 1254, 6 (1984).
19. A. C. Cunnew 82 *Gazette* 5 64 (1985).
20. P. J. Martin, 'Solicitor Advocates and the Judiciary' 81 *Gazette* 3385 (1984).

partiality (perhaps not in those words) and hoping for a reply. If not
satisfied [he] should write to the Lord Chancellor. We have to act
individually as well as collectively if we are to get anywhere as a profession
(e.g. with rights of audience)."

2. Conveyancing

The Royal Commission on Legal Services was appointed in July 1976,
cost £1.25 million and reported in October 1979. Its terms of
reference were limited to an examination of the organisation and
methods of the legal profession and court procedures under the existing
legal system. The recommendations made did not represent a radical
departure from established practices. Apart from a number of relatively
minor aspects, the existing structure was thought to be satisfactory.
Proposals were made in evidence to change a number of practices upon
which strong views had been held by reformers for many years. These, if
adopted, would have affected fundamental aspects of the services
available to the public and related to conveyancing, the structure of the
profession and the rights of audience of solicitors. The proponents
believed that they would improve legal services.

Since the Benson Report, the legal aspects of conveyancing have
continued to attract comment and criticism. Conveyancing charges have
been a constant source of complaint for several decades. For many,
contact with a solicitor has been limited to a single property transaction.
The eventual bill, which probably included stamp duty and fees paid to
the Land Registry, has been seen as the solicitor's charge and often
caused resentment. With this background, the Commission investigated
the system of conveyancing and the restriction which prevented
unqualified persons, not employed by solicitors, preparing documents of
title for a fee. Extremely detailed information upon conveyancing
practices in this and other countries was obtained.

The restriction imposed effectively kept this lucrative work in the
profession and, at the same time, protected the public against unethical
practices, incompetence and fraud. As a consequence, and over a long
period of time, the majority of solicitors' practices had become heavily
dependent upon conveyancing fees which formed a major part of their
income. To a degree this income has allowed some to undertake
unprofitable work. Many injustices have been righted and anxiety
relieved through the subsidy which conveyancing income has provided.

The legal aid scheme alone rarely provides adequate income to make a
practice viable without revenue from other work. To some extent a
proportion of cases which involve the use of barrister advocates show

little net profit. The cost of providing supporting services and conducting cases in the courts make litigation practices which rely entirely upon this type of work the exception rather than the rule. Practices and the services which they offer to the public are therefore affected to a great degree by the income arising from conveyancing. At the time of the Benson Commission report no radical change in the work available to the profession was envisaged. It was estimated that about one third of income of solicitors came from conveyancing.

Against this background, relief was expressed by the profession when the Benson Commission recommended that the restrictions upon conveyancing should not be modified. Strangely, and despite the climate of opinion evidenced by sustained press campaigns and public disquiet over the cost of conveyancing, the Commission suggested that the monopoly should be extended and strengthened. It was proposed that only a solicitor should be permitted to prepare a contract for the sale of land. This, it was thought, would give greater protection to the public by ensuring that full control could be exercised over conveyancing, so preventing incompetence, fraud and defalcations.

3. Rights of Audience Campaign

Subsequent events proved this to be a complete misjudgement of the situation. The Government, by promising to enact the proposals in Austin Mitchell's House Buyers' Bill 1984, rejected the Commission's conclusions upon this major issue. Legislation which has followed represents a consensus of the views of all political parties. Despite objections from the profession, it became clear that none would prevail over the force of public opinion. It is not surprising that The Law Society reacted quickly by taking a fresh look at the role of solicitors and possible new areas of work open to them. In early 1984 the campaign to secure universal rights of audience was announced. The likelihood that, if granted, this would lead to fusion was accepted. This possibility was not thought to be against the public interest.

An inconsistency has now arisen which does not appear to have been perceived by the Government. Competition for work in the superior courts is thought to be undesirable. An inevitable weakening of the Bar would, it is maintained, be a consequence. Yet the introduction of licensed conveyancers is acceptable even if it would weaken the solicitors' profession. Both reforms are likely to result in the transfer of income to competitors on a substantial scale. Why this is thought to be against the public interest in one instance and not in the other has not been explained.

This piece-meal approach has directed attention to the sectional interests within the profession. The leaders of the Bar, including the Attorney General, delivered a riposte to The Law Society's rights of audience campaign by asserting that:[21]

> "There can be no sensible suggestion that the loss by the solicitors' profession of the conveyancing monopoly alters this well-settled public interest in any way."

The stand taken indicated that the issue was thought to have been finally settled by the Benson Commission. The Chairman of the Bar at the time, Michael Wright, Q.C., agreed with this view when he commented that the campaign "Rises no higher than the level of parochial self-interest".[22]

Seen in a wider context, the structure of the profession and rights of its members are subjects of increasing interest to everyone. It is clear that they have a direct and profound effect upon the nature and quality of legal services. Evidence on these subjects submitted to the Benson Commission was prepared almost a decade ago in a different political and social climate. Since then, dramatic and radical political change has been initiated, which pays scant respect to traditionalism and vested interests. "The professions should not be unnecessarily sheltered from the stiff breezes of competition . . . " are the words of a Home Secretary. The Prime Minister has shown her determination to pursue this aim to be undiminished in saying: "I would like the Governments I led to be seen . . . as Governments which tackled the vested interests which had been immune for years—the trade unions, the nationalised industries, local government, the monopolies in the professions." This aim is difficult to reconcile with the selective use made of the Benson Commission's recommendations.

The Law Society, as a first step in securing an extension of solicitors' rights of audience, suggested an amendment to the Matrimonial and Family Proceedings Bill which came before Parliament in early 1984. The Bill included in Part V proposals governing the allocation of family proceedings in the High Court. Demarcation rules prevented solicitor advocates conducting defended divorce suits commenced in the Principal Registry of the High Court, or proceedings where there has been a breach of an order of the court in the form of a matrimonial injunction, or an appeal from a decision of a Magistrates' Court in a family matter to the Divisional Court of the Family Division of the High Court. Part V of the Bill made it likely that defended divorces would usually be heard in the County Court where solicitors may appear as advocates. Principal Registry proceedings would be deemed to be dealt with in the County Court so enabling solicitors to deal with them as advocates. The Law

---

21. F. Gibb, 'Bar Leaders' Riposte to the Law Society' *The Times* 3.4.1984.
22. M. Wright, 'Rights of Audience' 81 *Gazette* 1856 (1984).

Society sought the removal of restrictions upon solicitors acting as advocates in family proceedings in the Family Division of the High Court and Divisional Court, the most significant category of cases being appeals from magistrates' decisions—there were 344 in 1982. The amendment was lost.[23]

If considered merely as a means of providing more work for solicitors, the proposal would have little merit. Reasons in support given by The Law Society, however, are concerned with the public interest. When a solicitor acts there is direct contact between the client and lawyer. This helps to reduce the stress of what is often a disturbing experience. In addition, more frequent interviews and an adequate pre-hearing conference are possible. The advocate has a greater opportunity to become familiar with the facts and background of the case. This contrasts with the position of a barrister who is often expected to assimilate and present a case in a short space of time. With the resulting inadequate preparation a client's case may suffer. Personal relationships extending over years and the welfare of children are generally the subjects for adjudication. To be forced to bring a second lawyer into the proceedings, often a stranger to the case and client, is hardly an arrangement that can be said to benefit the client. The Law Society also points out that if solicitors could handle a case throughout, public money would be saved through the reduction in fees.

Since the beginning of the Law Society's campaign, the rights of audience issue has been brought before Parliament. Austin Mitchell introduced a Bill, under the ten minute rule, to promote the reform and unity of the legal profession by granting solicitors universal rights of audience in all courts and relaxing the restrictions upon the manner in which barristers practise. The latter included provisions to:[24]

"regulate and provide for advertising of pupillages and tenancies in barristers' practices and to enable barristers to establish practices anywhere in England and Wales with direct access to those seeking legal advice and when appropriate, representation, there being no mandatory intervention of any solicitor's or barrister's clerk or any other person whatsoever; to enable barristers and solicitors to practise together in any mutually acceptable form; to enable barristers to litigate for professional fees; to enable barristers to advertise; and to abolish the rank and title of Queen's (or King's) Counsel and the two Counsel rule."

Althouth the motion was lost by 32 votes, those in favour numbered 119. The Law Officers may have been alarmed by the possibility of Mr. Mitchell's earlier success in the field of conveyancing being repeated. This would account for the Prime Minister and members of the Cabinet

23. The Law Society 'Solicitors' Rights of Audience Briefing Document' Mar. 1984. p. 3.
24. Hansard. H. C. Deb., 11 June 1985, col. 759.

attending and voting against the Bill. Those who gave it their support included Michael Foot, David Owen and David Steele. Conservative supporters included John Townsend, Reg Prentice, Teddy Taylor and Anthony Beaumont Dark.

4. Prosecution Service

The conduct of criminal prosecutions in the Crown Court has always been carried out by barristers in private practice and instructed by county prosecution departments. The Law Society at the time of the Benson Commission accepted the desirability of this arrangement and indicated that the right of audience in the Crown Court should not be extended to solicitors so employed ". . . unless there is a statutory separation of the office of prosecuting solicitor from the police authority."

Subsequently, the Royal Commission on Criminal Procedure was appointed and reviewed the rights of audience position in the context of an independent prosecution service. The Law Society then proposed that solicitors in the service should have the right to conduct prosecutions in the Crown Court. The divided profession again created an anomaly as solicitors and barristers were to be eligible for appointment as Crown Prosecutors. The Bar opposed any extension of solicitors rights and the problem was resolved by enacting the following provisions:[25]

> **4.**—(1) Crown Prosecutors shall have, in any court, the rights of audience enjoyed by solicitors holding practising certificates and shall have such additional rights of audience in the Crown Court as may be given by virtue of subsection (3) below.
>
> (2) The reference in subsection (1) above to rights of audience enjoyed in any court by solicitors includes a reference to rights enjoyed in the Crown Court by virtue of any direction given by the Lord Chancellor under section 83 of the Supreme Court Act 1981.
>
> (3) For the purpose of giving Crown Prosecutors additional rights of audience in the Crown Court, the Lord Chancellor may give any such direction as respects Crown Prosecutors as he could give under section 83 of the Act of 1981 in respect of solicitors.

Section 83 (3) of the Supreme Court Act 1981 gives the Lord Chancellor power to direct that solicitors shall have a right of audience before the Crown Court either generally or at specified sessions. This power, therefore, applies equally to barrister Crown Prosecutors and stipulates that the Lord Chancellor shall:

---

25. Prosecution of Offences Act 1985, s. 4 (1) (2) (3).

"In considering whether to exercise his powers under this section as respects any one or more places where the Crown Court sits, the Lord Chancellor shall have regard to any shortage of counsel in the area in question, any rights of audience formerly exercised by solicitors at any court of quarter sessions in the locality in question, and to any other circumstances affecting the public interest."

Some barristers regarded Clause 4, as it has come to be known, with "general disquiet" believing that "it would lead to fusion by the back door." Lord Hailsham indicated in the House of Lords on 17th January 1985 that it is not the Government's intention to use the section as a way of altering the existing balance of rights of audience in the profession as a whole. The Solicitor-General, however, expressed the view that no provision in the Bill, which was eventually enacted, would "stop fusion if fusion were demanded."[26]

5. Specialists

Recent developments have confirmed the Benson Commission's view that the existence of a corps of specialist advisers is of advantage to the public. The need for lawyers to specialise is emphasised:[27]

"Specialisation involves not only an adequate theoretical and practical training but also regular practice in the speciality."

Those who favour a divided profession dwell upon this as being a characteristic which would be diminished or lost with fusion. Barristers and solicitors who have acquired expertise in a particular legal subject or advocacy are known by reputation. They achieve their position by long experience and not through a set course of training and examination. Queen's Counsel, though endowed with prestige and often accepted as specialists in a particular area of the law, are chosen from those who apply for the designation without any formal test or examination.

It has been left to The Law Society to pioneer a scheme to ensure that there are practitioners in socially sensitive areas of the law who are experienced both in law and practice. A national panel of solicitors qualified to act in child care cases, called the Child Care Panel, was established in 1984. Only suitably qualified practitioners are entitled to be included. They must hold current practising certificates, already have considerable experience in the work involved and have undertaken at least five recent contested cases on behalf of either parents or children. Those without sufficient experience are required to take an approved training course, attend an interview and, if appropriate, attend a full

---

26. General Meeting of the Young Bar, 82 *Gazette* pp. 920–1 (1985).
27. Benson Commission Report, p. 366 para. 27.23.

hearing of a contested child care case. Support for the panel has been given by the Justices' Clerks' Society which assists with the arrangements, subject to the magistrates' consent, to allow solicitors to attend cases as observers. This is an advance which has come from the profession. It will ensure that solicitors instructed to protect the interests of children involved in proceedings will be experienced in that type of work. A list is published on a regional basis giving the names and addresses of solicitors upon the panel. Here may be found the germ of a truly specialist group which could be extended to other areas of the law. This would be particularly beneficial for the public, reassuring clients that practitioners chosen to assist them have been examined and their competence and experience established.

CHAPTER 5

The Need for Change

1. Is Change Necessary?

The literature upon fusion is copious and reveals a consistent pattern. When movements have arisen with the potential to sway public and professional opinion, opposition has been voiced quickly and with determination. Recently, a combination of events and emergence of opinion revealed a more widespread belief that the structure of the profession needs changing. This culminated in the Law Society's campaign for an extension of solicitors' rights of audience to the superior courts and proposals for a Family Court. The suggestion has been made that this is merely an assertion of self-interest "motivated by naked envy and greed".[1] There are, however, other factors, a number of them having already been raised in this work, which indicate that change is needed. Of the various aspects discussed, those which appear to be crucial are now examined in detail, in the light of current developments.

The provision of adequate legal services in a complex modern society is essential for the well being of the individual citizen. To maintain liberty under the law, qualified and independent lawyers must be available and free to practise without restriction. They should be entitled, both as advocates and members of the judiciary, to participate in legal processes at all levels. A divided profession, as in England and Wales, which imposes restrictive practices upon its members is not free in this sense. Rules within a profession which are intended to maintain high standards of professional conduct are necessary and acceptable. It is not possible, however, to place into this category the barrister's exclusive right of audience in the higher courts or the need for a solicitor to intervene whenever a barrister is employed. From what has already been written it will be seen that these restrictions have a profound effect upon the structure of the legal profession and the quality of service provided.

The legal system of England and Wales is unique both in its continuity, extending over six centuries, and the way in which many ancient forms and customs have survived. Tradition should not, however, be allowed to hinder or obstruct progress. A fairly recent reform, for instance, illustrates the need to abandon legal institutions which have become outdated and fail to meet the demands placed upon them. For many years

1.   R. Du Cann, *The Sunday Times*, 14 April 1985 p. 17.

after World War II it had been apparent that the Courts of Assize and Quarter Sessions were not able to cope with an ever increasing work load. Eventually a Royal Commission was appointed under the chairmanship of Lord Beeching to examine the problem.[2] The Commission, without hesitation, recommended the abolition of Assizes and Quarter Sessions and also other courts of special jurisdiction with such picturesque names as the Bristol Tolzey Court and the Liverpool Court of Passage. They were replaced by the Crown Court with sessions in places accessible to the main concentrations of population.[3] Archaic expressions and customs were discarded and the system was modernised and made comprehensible to lawyer and lay person alike. With deliberate planning and decisive action the confusion and muddle which had prevailed for decades was eliminated. This should allay the fears of those who find it difficult to accept that radical change which departs from tradition can be beneficial.

For the public the descriptions "solicitor" and "barrister" must be confusing. Having arisen, as already described, through historical accident, the terms do not take into account the overlapping functions of the two branches of the profession which did not exist when they were conceived. The Benson Commission acknowledged the difficulty in understanding the precise nature of the work carried out by each branch of the profession when it stated that it is:[4]

> "... an oversimplification to say merely that solicitors are general practitioners and barristers specialists, or that advocacy is the business of barristers but not of solicitors. Some solicitors specialise in particular branches of law, or act frequently as advocates; most barristers, however, regard advocacy as their main function and, as we say in paragraph 17.38, can fairly claim to be specialists in advocacy, many specialise also in specific and limited branches of the law. The distinction between the two branches may be regarded partly as that between general and specialist practice and partly as a matter of function, the solicitor acting in particular cases (and sometimes generally) on a continuing basis for the client, the barrister being retained only when circumstances require it, usually to provide specialist advice or advocacy."

Anyone who is not conversant with the legal system would be confused by this or any other attempt to describe the work of a solicitor in a rational way. Barristers are undoubtedly seen as occupying a senior position in the legal hierarchy, comparable with a medical specialist or consultant, and who deal only with the more difficult and complex cases. This impression is reinforced by the working arrangements, distinctive court dress, language, customs and institutions of the Bar which set its members apart from solicitors. Although, occasionally, reference may be

2. The Royal Commission on Assizes and Quarter Sessions' Report 1969 Cmnd. 4153.
3. *Ibid.* pp. 64–5 para. 174.
4. Benson Commission Report, p. 188 para. 17.6.

made to the equal status of the two branches, no convincing attempt is made to dispel the general belief in the Bar's pre-eminence. The fact that higher reaches of the profession and the judiciary are occupied solely by barristers makes it difficult to give any other plausible explanation for the separate identity of that part of the profession.

2. Professional Education and Training

The separation of solicitor and barrister imposed at the beginning of the vocational stages of their training is never relaxed. Teachers, courses, examinations and accommodation are, as a consequence, duplicated. Proposals made for joint vocational education in the Ormerod Report of 1971[5] have been ignored and there is no sign of an intention to implement them. There are annually approximately 3,500 solicitor students and 900 barrister students (of whom 765 intend to practise). The maintenance of separate teaching systems represents a wasteful and inefficient use of the resources involved. Courses provided for both sets of students are similar. Educational requirements on entry could be integrated. It cannot be said that the dual system is necessary because of differing needs. In the absence of any other explanation, the only tenable reason for its existence is the preservation of sectional interests by keeping the two branches apart. The possibility has no doubt been recognised that if all entrants worked together at this early stage they would soon demand the kind of freedom associated with fusion. Instead of being forced to decide which career to follow when their training begins, the choice could be deferred until its end.

Young people seeking a career in the law must make a crucial decision without the opportunity of finding out where their talents lie. Some may be unduly influenced by the prestige of the barrister and apparently superior professional status. A decision to study for the Bar made upon such a misconception may be a mistake. The qualities needed in an advocate are different from those of a desk lawyer. Some will have a natural and recognisable aptitude for one or the other kind of work and make the correct choice at the beginning. Others, with little or no idea of their abilities or of the nature and demands of the work involved, will need to test the ground before taking a final step.

The dual system of vocational education and training presents entrants with a confusing situation. To have a profession with two totally separate methods of entry is an unnecessary complication. No attempt has been made to justify the duality upon the grounds of principle, efficiency or economy. Then there is the need to belong to one of the Inns of Court if studying for the Bar, and to eat a prescribed number of dinners in the

---

5. Report of the Committee on Legal Education. March 1971 Cmnd. 4549 p. 67 para. 141.

Hall. A single method of entry into the profession would remove these complications.

In a fused profession a student would not be forced to decide upon the course of his or her career at a particular stage. On qualifying there would be an opportunity to spend a period working in one or more selected areas of the law. After gaining experience and deciding which subject was the most appealing, the process of specialisation could begin with confidence and enthusiasm. A late developer could make a change of direction without disrupting his or her career.

By delaying the time at which vital career decisions have to be made, young lawyers would gain a wider knowledge and understanding of the practice of the law. Closer and responsible supervision of the beginner would be possible. The newly qualified but untrained advocate would not, for instance, be expected or permitted to conduct a case without the guidance and support of an employer who was fully responsible to the client. This contrasts with the position now where a young and inexperienced advocate may be substituted for the one originally instructed. The choice of substitute may be made by a chambers' clerk with no responsibility to the lay client. In a unified profession the need to employ separate lawyers to perform different functions and for an unqualified clerk to act as an intermediary would not exist. Only one lawyer would be involved; even if the case were delegated to an employee, a division of responsibility would not be permissible. With proper supervision, a beginner who was found to be unsuited to the particular kind of work undertaken could be advised and guided into a more appropriate area. There would be greater flexibility with none of the formalities and regulations which now govern transfer between the two branches of the profession.

3. The Deployment of Lawyers

Considerable intellectual and material resources are devoted to the training of lawyers. If they are not be wasted, the expertise of those who qualify must be effectively deployed. Their skill and knowledge need to be utilised for the maximum benefit of the public. At the same time a reasonable degree of competition is required which will enable the most talented to flourish. A divided profession is an obstacle to each of these objectives. As the location and establishment of chambers is controlled by the Circuits and the Senate through the Bar Committee,[6] the number of practising barristers and their geographical situation is restricted. Solicitors, on the other hand, although free to practise wherever they wish, are not allowed to undertake advocacy in the superior courts.

---

6.   *Supra.* p. 44.

It is in this area of advocacy where there is a great waste of talent and the deliberate elimination of competition. The number of solicitor advocates has increased considerably since the expansion of the profession began in the 1960s. There are many who practice regularly in the lower courts. As time advances these practitioners will have among their numbers a group of senior advocates of considerable experience. The existing demarcation rules prevent their expertise being fully utilised. Of those who wish to continue working in the courts, some will resent the restrictions which impede their advancement and others may accept the position with resignation. Neither is a healthy state for members of a profession whose attention should be directed to the protection and enforcement of the rights of others. The symptoms of discontent within the profession have already been described[7] and are a forboding of the ill will which may result from a rigid and unchanging attitude towards fusion. A confrontation over the rights of audience issue, for instance, already seems likely. This will be heightened if, as seems probable, the Benson Commission proposal allowing solicitors to deal with formal and unopposed matters in any court is adopted.

More strident criticism can be expected. Ultimately, concessions will, as in the past, have to be made in the hope that the gradual but inexorable move towards a single profession can be stopped. This gradualist and traditional form of adjustment conceals dangers to the profession as a whole. There are indications that the prospect of becoming a solicitor is becoming more attractive to graduates than a career at the Bar. This explains the concern expressed over the quality of entrants to the Bar. A survey was instituted by the planning committee of the Senate to determine "whether the proportion of first class law graduates seeking to be called to the Bar had fallen." The first stage of the investigation revealed a significant change in the proportion of Oxford and Cambridge law graduates joining the respective branches of the profession. A table of statistics published by the Senate is set out below:[8]

Oxbridge Law Graduates

Year of Graduation	Oxford Firsts		Cambridge 2.1's	
	% practising as barristers	% practising as solicitors	% practising as barristers	% practising as solicitors
Early 1950s	38	14	29	21
Late 1950s	28	23	16	27
Early 1960s	28	22	22	38
Late 1960s	33	18	19	41
Early 1970s	32	21	17	33
1976	15	35	16	29
1977	28	45	20	42

7. *Supra.* pp. 83–90.
8. Annual Statement, 1981–2 pp. 6–7.

The proportion of more highly qualified solicitor entrants has increased markedly over the period 1950–1970. Degree class lists from other universities "show that a lower proportion of first class graduates go to the Bar compared with Oxford and Cambridge."[9] The final report of the survey analysing "the numbers of persons with varying class of degree from different universities who have been called and remain in practice" was submitted to the Senate during the year 1983–84[10] but has not been published.

Oxford University Appointments Committee, in its latest report,[11] comments upon the fact that for several years senior members of the Bar have been expressing anxiety about the quality of entrants. Figures given show that of 57 graduates who started their training for the Bar in 1984, 6 had firsts in Law and 7 in other subjects. Solicitor entrants numbered 196, of whom 14 had a first in Law and 4 in other subjects.

Cambridge University Careers Service has compiled statistics showing the first destination of law graduates, the most recent being for the year 1983. Of 266 graduates, 105 intended to become solicitors and 33 went to the Bar. The system of classifying degree passes divides degrees awarded into first, second class 1 and 2, third and others. The distribution between prospective solicitors and barristers is shown below:[12]

Class of degree	Numbers Graduating		Going to Solicitors		Going to the Bar	
	1983	1982	1983	1982	1983	1982
1	36	29	21	15	2	5
2:1	135	138	63	71	20	13
2:2	77	79	21	24	11	9
3	12	15		3		1
others	6	3		1		
Total	266	264	105	114	33	28

It will be observed that in the 1 and 2:1 group 75% were solicitor entrants. This follows a trend in previous years. It is possible, although no data is available, that the number of firsts going to the Bar may be depressed by a number of entrants undertaking higher studies before-

9. *Ibid.* 1982–3, p. 48.
10. *Ibid.* 1983–4, p. 23.
11. Oxford University Appointments Committee Report for 1983–4, pp. 7–8.
12. Cambridge University Careers Service, First Destination Statistics for Law Tripos Part II 1982–3.

hand. Nevertheless, it is apparent that those with high degree passes are, in increasing numbers, becoming solicitors.

4. The Location of Lawyers

The Benson Commission's prediction that fusion will reduce the number of small firms and cause an increase in the proportion of larger city based ones may not, as shown,[13] necessarily have a prejudicial effect upon legal services. Of prime importance is the need to supply legal services of a high standard. It is not possible for any single practitioner to advise upon all aspects of the law. Unless a practice is of a modest size employing skilled staff, work must be restricted or outside help sought. There is a temptation for some sole practitioners to undertake matters which are beyond their capacity. This is a constant dilemma and a strong reason for encouraging larger groups. If fusion brings this about, the public will benefit from an improved service and the profession from an enhanced reputation.

The accessibility of solicitors is not always matched to the needs of clients. They are often scarce in the inner city areas and remote country locations. Fusion could improve the position in the former and provide a greater degree of decentralisation in the larger connurbations. With stronger and more comprehensive advocacy services serving the public direct, lawyers would have an incentive to open offices nearer to clients. Instead of merely receiving instructions to be passed on to other lawyers, often a considerable distance away, they would be available in the areas where services were needed.

The provision of legal services in remote country areas is a problem different in kind. Where legal assistance is needed by those who are unable to travel, the voluntary agencies can always help with transport. Even urgently needed medical services are often situated at a distance from prospective patients. This is not thought to be a hardship. No legal problem is a matter of life or death, and availability of a comprehensive and skilled service is the primary concern, not geographical accessibility. Should the demand for a solicitor not be sufficient to support a single practitioner, fusion is unlikely to affect the likelihood of one setting up a practice. The kind of work which makes a new practice viable does not depend upon the availability of barristers, as they are rarely needed. If, in a unified profession, it were necessary to consult a specialist in another firm or one practising as a consultant, this would not affect the growth of the practice in any way. The wholesale loss of clients is unlikely, for the occasions upon which aid of this kind is called for would be few.

13. Benson Commission Report, p. 201, para. 17.45.

The client seeking advice quickly and at the minimum cost is better served by a firm with the capacity to give a comprehensive service from its own resources. A branch office of a larger firm will have a fund of experience and support at its command. An example is to be found in the conduct of claims arising from road accidents and those from injury received at work. Invariably the very small firm, which does not specialise in litigation, will rely almost entirely upon solicitor agents to conduct an action of any magnitude or complexity. Its function is limited to administrative acts and taking statements or proofs of evidence. Because of the pressure and diversity of work involved in running a small practice often even these limited tasks do not receive adequate attention. This can lead to the premature settlement of an action to the disadvantage of the client. There is also a danger that the division of function under these circumstances may result in inadequate preparation for trial and weaken a case.

The medium sized partnerhip is better equipped in every way to handle the type of claim described in the previous paragraph. Its staff will be completely familiar with the preparation of cases and the assembly of evidence. Medical and other specialists will be known who are conversant with trial procedures and accustomed to preparing reports. Adequate and professionally drawn plans and photographs of high standard can be prepared well in advance. No advantage is likely to be lost through the lack of a full and detailed knowledge of pre-trial procedures. In a fused profession, medium sized firms with full time advocates would be a distinct advantage to the client in the majority of cases which come before the courts. The likelihood of small firms undertaking work beyond their capacity would also be reduced.

5. The Returned Brief

The returned brief phenomenon described earlier is a problem which, to the author's knowledge, has existed for at least thirty years. From enquiries made, the practice has actually increased over the past ten years and shows no signs of diminishing. Three members of the Benson Commission examined and criticised the practice. They expressed their views in a dissenting note saying that:[14]

> "...inadequate instructions and last minute meetings with defendants, constitute a risk inherent in the two-tier system."

Fusion offers a way of tackling what must now be regarded as an incurable defect of the divided system. When cases are handled from

14. *Ibid.* p. 817 para. N 5.18.

beginning to end within a firm of solicitors it is less likely for an inexperienced advocate to be substituted twenty-four hours or so before a hearing. Close contact and consultation which must prevail among the members of a practice ensure that contingency plans to cover any clash of engagements are well established. The discipline needed to run a practice prevents briefs being exchanged between advocates at short notice merely to ensure an even distribution of work. A more settled and organised regime prevails. This would be the position in a unified profession. Should it be decided to employ an advocate from another firm or one who practises as a barrister does today, there would be further advantages over the present system. Arrangements would not be made through an intermediary acting in the capacity of an agent. The advocate employed would be personally responsible and act upon a contractual basis. Under a normal and reasonable code of professional conduct the return of a brief without adequate notice and substitution of an advocate with no previous knowledge of the case could become a matter for disciplinary proceedings.

There is a need for the profession to adapt to the needs of the client. At present, the opposite is the case and the client is obliged to accept the rules and conventions required to preserve a divided profession. It is possible to make a complaint to the Senate of the Inns of Court and the Bar if it is thought that a brief has been returned without adequate notice or reasonable excuse. A lay client is, however, unlikely to use this procedure for several reasons. In many instances the change of barrister, sometimes less than twenty-four hours before a hearing, is only known to the solicitor and chamber's clerk. The client will be informed of the situation on arriving at the court. His or her consent is taken for granted and the solicitor accepts the position because it happens so frequently. Once the case has been heard the barrister disappears from the scene. If the client's interests have been affected by poor representation the possibility of making an appeal against the judgement will be the first consideration. This and the nervous strain involved usually override any thought of becoming involved in another dispute i.e. disciplinary proceedings against the barrister. The solicitor is unlikely to encourage a complaint. It would usually be an unprofitable distraction to do so. Rarely, if ever, is reference to an advocate's incompetence made at a hearing or in a judgement. The difficulty of proving a complaint is therefore insurmountable.

6. Specialist Lawyers

The ever increasing demand for specialist practitioners is generally acknowledged. It has been shown that many solicitors as well as barristers now concentrate upon limited aspects of the law to the extent that they are true specialists.[15] Traditionally, the Bar has been considered to be the specialist branch of the profession, but this is no longer so. An exclusive right of audience in the superior courts cannot be classed as a specialist function. Advocacy per se when compared, for instance, with conveyancing, is a specialist activity. Practitioners who achieve a high degree of competence in either are specialists in the true sense of the word. If skilled advocates are excluded from particular courts, this does not make them non-specialists. It merely imposes an artificial restriction upon their activity. Venue makes no difference to the competence and expertise required to conduct a case. Frequently, cases are heard at County Court or Magistrates' Court level which involve issues of greater social and legal importance than many dealt with in the High Court. A logical and efficient system would endeavour to match the skill and proficiency of the advocate with the complexity and importance of the case. With specialists in advocacy and law in both branches of the profession, the existing arrangements do not appear to be either the most efficient or cost effective way of supplying their services to the public.

The trend towards increased specialism among solicitors is now actively encouraged, following the Benson Commission's Report. Current developments indicate that solicitor specialists are emerging with experience in particular areas of the law which meets a specified standard or who have attended a course of training and have been examined. This contrasts with the barrister specialist whose status is not gained by formal post-qualification training or examination. A scheme has been introduced by The Law Society for the establishment of a panel of solicitors competent to deal with child care cases.[16] It has long been recognised that specialised knowledge of the law and practice in this field is necessary to ensure that the rights of parents and children are protected. Ignorance of the special nature of child care proceedings can lead to confusion and injustice. An advocate who is unaccustomed to the procedure and aims of cases of this kind is at a disadvantage. Hearings do not follow the pattern of criminal proceedings in the Magistrates' Court and the objectives are different. The Child Care Panel was introduced to provide a list of solicitors suitably qualified and experienced in his type of work to be available in the court office for the guidance of potential clients. For the same reason, a panel of solicitors with special knowledge of the law and procedure governing Mental Health Review Tribunal proceedings has been established.[17] For the

15. *Supra.* pp. 55–6.
16. Approved by Council of the Law Society at its meeting on 19th July 1984: 81 *Gazette* 2894 (1984) *supra* p. 95.
17. 80 *Gazette* 468 (1983).
     80 *Gazette* 2377 (1983).

Magistrates' Court the duty solicitor scheme has been introduced.[18]

Society is increasingly being regulated by statutory law and delegated legislation. As industrial processes become more capital intensive and service industries expand, the need to legislate for the health, safety and rights of employees, the conduct of trade and the promotion of harmonious industrial relations grows. Social needs in the form of welfare benefits, the resolution of problems accompanying matrimonial breakdown and the care of children are subject to continual review and amendment. The process is accelerating, and with new technology there is no limit to the amount of legislation that can be enacted, stored and instantly retrieved. A great deal of this material is complex and some is of a technical nature. A knowledge of the subject matter is often needed to enable a lawyer to understand its meaning and effect. It is here that the services of a specialist are required if sound advice and effective representation is to be obtained. A fused profession would be in a better position to respond to this demand. Post-qualification training would be available for all lawyers. This could be planned with the whole profession in mind. There would be no need to provide separate courses for two branches of the profession, or duplicate the conditions of qualification. Above all the system could be rationalised and made comprehensible to the public.

7. Development of the Lawyer's Potential

It is in the public interest that all lawyers, whether barristers or solicitors, should have the opportunity to realise their full potential. Those who are inefficient, because they find their allotted tasts difficult or tedious, should be able to change the course of their professional career quickly and easily. The barrister who, after years in practice travelling from court to court, find the demands of advocacy wearisome may welcome the opportunity to settle down as a desk lawyer. The solicitor who is highly specialised in a particular area of the law may have a great deal to contribute if allowed to appear before the High Court in cases involving his or her speciality. Distinguished practitioners of long and varied experience who have acquired the habit of calm and reflective judgement are eminently suitable for appointment to high judicial office. The present division does not make a change of activity of this kind easy. The problem is particularly difficult for the solicitor who must sever his or her established professional connections and source of income upon transferring to the bar. For a barrister the difficulty is less. It is possible, on leaving the Bar, to take up an appointment with a firm of solicitors in

18. 82 *Gazette* 3313 (1985).

an unqualified capacity before fulfilling the conditions stipulated for admission. In a fused profession none of these problems would arise. A lawyer would be able to settle into the type of work which suited his or her talent, inclination and ability.

The developing post-qualification programme for solicitors already described is creating considerable resources in the form of highly trained and competent practitioners. The divided profession restricts the use made of this fund of experience and knowledge. Solicitor specialists are denied the opportunity of influencing the superior courts, and cannot make a direct contribution to the growth of case law. Developments may be delayed which their practical experience would have brought to light much sooner.

Fusion would amalgamate the intellectual and material resources of the two branches of the profession and place them under the control of a single governing body. With a planned scheme of post qualification education, specialist or higher qualifications would be available for all lawyers. Ability and competence would then be the criteria for progress, unhampered by the artificial restrictions and antagonisms which accompany a divided profession. Competition would provide an incentive to efficiency in all aspects of legal practice, so improving the service provided for the public.

8.   The Cost and Quality of Legal Services

The cost of legal services is a subject of perennial interest to journalists and a constant source of complaint from the public. For decades, conveyancing was singled out for particularly harsh criticism. This has subsided with the introduction of outside competition from non-lawyers. Attention is now directed to the cost of litigation and representation before the courts. The civil procedure review which the Lord Chancellor has instituted reflects the disquiet felt over the failings of the present system. Where these affect the fees paid by litigants the question of fusion arises. This is a reform which would lower the cost of employing an advocate in a considerable number of cases.

There are instances where the joint effort of two or more lawyers may be justified because of the nature or complexity of the issues involved. There are many more, probably the overwhelming majority, which a single lawyer, employing supporting staff, can handle satisfactorily. Inefficiency arises from the insistence that a solicitor and barrister must be engaged and paid for when a case comes before a particular class of court. Where this amounts to unnecessary double manning it is not in the interests of the client and does not contribute to the effective administration of justice. A lawyer engaged to further a client's interests should have complete freedom to decide how representation is to be arranged. As it is, this is not possible because of the restrictions imposed.

The Crown Court provides illustrations of the inhibiting effect of the divided profession upon attempts to improve the service given and reduce its cost. Sessions of this court are held throughout the country. The volume of work they undertake has shown a continuous increase. Most solicitors' firms of any size practise in them. This is one of the areas in which substantial savings could be made if there were a fused profession. The present system prevents one lawyer dealing with a case from beginning to end (except in a limited number of instances). A solicitor, in drawing a brief, will have performed a major part of the advocate's task. This work, for which the client pays, is wasted should the brief be returned shortly before a hearing and then accepted by a substitute. Without adequate time to assimilate its contents and advise upon any further preparatory work which may be necessary, presentation of the case may suffer. By dividing the work and responsibility between two lawyers in this way there is no safeguard or guarantee that it will be properly carried out. It is rare that one will criticise the other for to do so often would destroy confidence in the system. In a fused profession, another lawyer could be brought into a case but this would be entirely at the discretion of the one first instructed, who would need to convince the client of the need for extra help. The type of court involved would not be an influencing factor. Taxation or a right to challenge charges made would, in any event, protect the client against the unnecessary use of outside advocates or advisers.

The Benson Commission did not agree that a significant overall saving in costs would accompany either an extension of the right of audience of solicitors to the Crown Court or outright fusion. The Law Society, however, has indicated that in a situation comparable with fusion, i.e. where there was parity between solicitors and barristers as advocates in the Crown Court, substantial savings in costs would be achieved. This would be the case if:[19]

> ". . .lawyers employed by the new prosecution service were free to prosecute in the Crown Court. Costings prepared by The Law Society show that in 67% of all cases in the Crown Court it would be cheaper for the service to deploy its own employees in the Crown Court, than to instruct a barrister practising from chambers."

The situation can be likened to that of a firm of modest size having advocate partners in a fused profession. Savings would be inevitable

---

19. A. Hoole, 'The Independent Prosecution Service: The Law Society's View.' *The Lawyer*, Nov. 1984 p. 4.

when comparing their charges with the cost of employing barristers under the present system. The point was inadvertently conceded by the Benson Commission when it stated:[20]

> "It appears to be correct that an extension of solicitors' work in the Crown Court would have a serious and disproportionate impact on the income and capacity of barristers to continue in practice . . ."

The lost income would, in part, be diverted to solicitors. The Law Society's costings indicate the extent to which this would happen with prosecutions. Similar conditions would prevail with the representation of defendants. If lawyers in a fused profession did not need to call in outside assistance their charges would be lower. A great deal of the saving would benefit the Legal Aid Fund and ultimately reduce public expenditure.

It must be considered whether a reduction in cost brought about by fusion would affect the quality of the service provided. Any possible decline in standards would be an important factor to consider before making irreversible changes to the system. The main contention of the Benson Commission is that the quality of advocacy would fall in a fused profession or if solicitors were granted increased rights of audience in the Crown Court. There are, however, indications of definite advantages which would accompany fusion, additional to the lower cost of representation. At present, a solicitor acts as a means of communication between the client and barrister, often performing tasks which are well within the province of an unqualified clerk. There are cases which justify the attention of two lawyers but, even then, it is not essential to have a divided profession for them to be provided. The insistence that a solicitor must intervene when a barrister is employed is in many instances otiose. Fusion would eliminate this rule. A client would then have a single lawyer totally responsible for the conduct of his or her case.

9.   Choice of Advocate

Another indirect consequence of the divided profession is its effect upon the client's freedom of choice when engaging an advocate. The Bar's monopoly in the superior courts is deliberately imposed as a matter of policy. There is also a hidden factor which interferes with a client's choice. It is the substitution of a barrister at short notice who is often unknown to the solicitor or client. The frequency of this practice makes the 'cab-rank' concept entirely theoretical. There is no free choice when an unknown barrister substitute, selected by a chambers' clerk, is seen for the first time on the steps of the court. All conscientious members of the

---

20. Benson Commission Report, p. 216 para. 18.52.

legal profession should regard this as a serious breach of professional ethics, yet it persists. In a single profession the choice of advocate would rest entirely with the client.

10.　Client's Convenience

In the mass of articles and letters which have been published in the legal press over the years upon the topic of fusion the wishes and feelings of the client are rarely mentioned or discussed. Although many rules of etiquette and unwritten conventions are observed, the client is rarely, if ever, informed of them or their purpose. To a great extent, the public is ill-informed of the manner in which the legal profession is organised and the effect this has upon the service provided. It is accepted as normal that a barrister will not interview a witness or see a client alone. Rarely, if ever, is any explanation given of the absence of a pre-trial conference in the solicitor's office. The client is never prompted to ask why a senior and experienced solicitor, on occasions, adopts a subordinate and supporting role when a young and inexperienced barrister is conducting a case. It is no reflection upon the barrister to comment upon this, but the client's confidence must be weakened when observing such a strange reversal of the usual order. If lawyers discussed more openly the relevance of these practices, moves to modify or abandon them would be made. As it is, there is a general insensitivity to the barrier which exists between barrister and client. This leads, for instance, to the unquestioning way in which the return of a brief is accepted. The client has no idea that the barrister first instructed has passed the brief to someone else until an hour or so before the hearing when the substitute arrives. The client will not have been consulted and the change may even have been made without the solicitor's knowledge. It is not difficult to imagine the bewilderment of the client who, for instance, faces a possible custodial sentence or the parent whose child may be taken into care.

The difficulty of arranging a conference between barrister and client before the hearing of a case is another problem aggravated by division. Barristers need to have adequate premises located near to the clients they serve. In some provincial cities there are chambers which satisfy these requirements. This is not always so and even in the Inns of Court facilities for conferences are often not ideal. In any event, visiting chambers may involve a not inconsiderable amount of travelling. Because of the rule that a conference must not take place in the office of a solicitor, the tendency is to postpone the first meeting between barrister and client until arriving at court. With fusion, a lawyer would have the right to become established anywhere without the need to obtain permission from the profession's governing body. Demand would be catered for in the most efficient and economical way. Competition would ensure that those who provided the best facilities and service would prosper. The client's convenience and interests would be paramount.

11. Licensed Claims Specialists

There is a danger to the profession in confining the solicitor's role in the superior courts to the preparation of cases and the administrative work of an action. With larger firms these tasks are performed efficiently. Others, however, do not possess the resources necessary to conduct actions effectively. There is a parallel with conveyancing. For decades, efficient firms have been penalised by the slow and expensive mediocre ones who misused the monopoly they possessed. Eventually, when the public became aware of the drag which this placed upon progress, the current changes were forced upon the profession. As a consequence traditional attitudes have altered dramatically; almost beyond the belief of older practitioners. Advertising, contested for generations, is commonplace. Cost cutting upon an unprecedented scale has encouraged the introduction of new technology. Perhaps the most radical of all developments is the opening of conveyancing "shops" which cut across the demarcation line between estate agent and solicitor. Here is a definite improvement for the client. A reduction in cost joined with improved efficiency and convenience. Instead of dealing with estate agent and lawyer, property selling and transfer is co-ordinated by one person.

Litigation, is another clearly identifiable area of solicitors' work. It could become the next target for reform. If there is no relaxation of the Bar's monopoly, solicitors may meet competition from another source. As with conveyancing, the preparation of a case to be argued by a barrister advocate is not a task which always requires or receives the attention of a fully qualified lawyer. This is evidenced by the number of legal executives and unqualified staff who man the litigation departments of solicitors' firms. Some may argue that supervision is always provided by a solicitor. This was said to be so with conveyancing. In reality, it is well known that only nominal control is exercised in many instances. Again it can be questioned whether this is the most efficient way of providing an effective service at reasonable cost. To an impartial observer the conveyancing experience may give a lead to the kind of reform that is called for.

When a barrister is employed in an action the solicitor's role should, primarily, be investigative. The procedural aspects do not normally require the attention of a fully qualified lawyer. They are more likely to be efficiently performed by a specialist legal executive whose attention is directed solely to the management of the proceedings. If the solicitor neglects to scrutinise the legal and evidential features of a case, his or her raison d'être disappears. This, regretfully, is a not uncommon failing. It is prevalent when a non-specialist solicitor undertakes a diverse range of work and does not specialise. Larger firms with adequate resources do not have this problem. There is, however, always, the possibility that they may suffer, as with conveyancing, because of the poor reputation of smaller, inefficient ones.

Any reformer looking at the situation impartially will seek to compare the improvement in conveyancing services with other areas of legal work. By encouraging special attention to be given to the work involved in preparing and conducting an action, efficiency and productivity would increase. There does not appear to be any reason why this work should be entrusted solely to solicitors and their employees. Licensed claims specialists permitted to instruct barristers could provide highly developed and integrated services dealing with all aspects of particular types of work, e.g. common law and statutory claims for personal injuries arising out of road accidents or at work. It is even possible that a government may be persuaded that charging by way of contingency fees would be appropriate to match the commercial motive of licensed claims specialists. All of this is more likely to happen if the divided profession remains. With a single category of lawyer, however, the problems associated with division would be fewer. Firms would be free to develop highly specialised services. Advocates at all levels could adjust their working arrangements to suit the demands of the public. With competition, a better service would evolve and so remove the critics' argument for radical change.

By resisting the call for fusion this process, which began with conveyancing, may continue unabated. Solicitors, already excluded by the Bar from a sector of the work and opportunities which are the province of a lawyer, may find a further inroad being made into their work. Banks and trust corporations are not likely to rest until they have acquired the right to take out grants of representation so that they can administer estates, without a solicitor's help, from beginning to end. It is logical and may become a matter of urgency that the solicitors' branch of the profession should be strengthened and its prestige improved. Fusion, with the co-operation of the Bar, is the preferable way of achieving this end. For a strong and independent legal profession to survive its members must have equal rights, within the system, to choose the kind of work they wish to undertake. Within the profession safeguards can be introduced to ensure competence in the various areas of activity but no practitioner should be excluded from advancement in his or her chosen work. The alternative to a single profession may be the gradual dispersion of specific functions to independent groups in the manner already described. Instead of one governing body, accountable to the public and exercising strict disciplinary powers, a number of separate controlling bodies would be required. The bureaucracy to run them would be extensive and add an unnecessary complication to the legal system.

With fusion, the specialist services now provided by both branches could be integrated. Practitioners could work with firms and be available for public consultation or become consultants to the profession. Changes in an individual's manner of working would not be inhibited by rules of etiquette. The need to abandon old concepts is shown by the merger of property selling and conveyancing in the new service offered by solicitors. Traditionalists repeatedly reject such an idea as undignified and damaging to the reputation of the law as a learned profession. Now that this myth has been destroyed, the establishment of licensed claims services outside the profession may be the next development. The derogatory description of "ambulance chasers" may be applied to them. This is not necessarily an objectionable epithet. It is sometimes only at the time of an accident or immediately afterwards that evidence to justify a claim may be available. With fusion a relaxation of rules of professional etiquette would encourage the provision of legal services where they are needed.

12. Division of Function

The division of function between solicitor and barrister is clear but the allocation of responsibility is not definite. "Who", it can be asked, "is the captain of the ship?" The answer is by no means certain. Dillon L.J. in *Davy-Chiesman v. Davy-Chiesman and Another,* a case concerning the liability of a solicitor who acted throughout upon the advice of an experienced barrister, observed:[21]

> "Undoubtedly, however, and rightly, the solicitor is in very many circumstances protected from personal liability if he has acted on the advice of experienced counsel properly instructed. This is inherent in the division of the profession into two branches, a division which, in my experience is normally highly beneficial to the litigant and to the community at large. But protection to the solicitor is not automatically total. The solicitor is highly trained and expected to be experienced in his particular fields of law and he does not abdicate all responsibility whatever by instructing counsel."

In this instance, the judge in the court of first instance had concluded that the solicitor was exonerated from blame in accepting the advice of counsel, properly instructed. On appeal, the opposite view was taken.

21. [1984] 1 All ER 334–5.

This indicates the uncertainty which arises from the fact that two lawyers are involved in the conduct of a case.

A comment often made when fusion is discussed is that in a single profession there would still be a division of function. An advocate could not be expected to prepare every case and interview all witnesses. This is perhaps true but the arrangements would be made within one office and adjusted to suit the circumstances at the time. If an outside lawyer were called into the case none of the existing rules of etiquette would apply. Clients and witness could be interviewed in either lawyer's office, direct contact between the client and advocate would be permissible. Above all, the lawyer who accepts a case would remain fully and totally responsible for its conduct from beginning to end and liable to the client for any dereliction of duty. The Benson Commission did not appear to appreciate the anomalous position of the solicitor who relies upon a barrister to advise and conduct a case but is expected to retain overall control. This is revealed in the following observation:[22]

> "As to attendance in court, we consider that the profession, the judiciary and those responsible for the administration of the courts should settle what is required in various categories of case. We question whether it is invariably necessary for a barrister to be accompanied by a solicitor. Some pleas in mitigation and some County Court cases, for example, if properly prepared, may require no more than the attendance of an advocate in court. In such cases we consider a barrister should be permitted to appear without a solicitor."

This would be a difficult procedure to devise. As the case cited shows, even judges disagree over the culpability of a solicitor who acts upon an experienced barrister's advice which proves to be faulty. The view of the judge in the first instance was contradicted on appeal when May L.J. said:[23]

> "I do not forget the evidence of the forcefulness of counsel's personality, nor his experience, which the judge accepted. But making all allowances for that, I cannot avoid the conclusion, differing respectfully from the judge, that this solicitor did abdicate responsibility for his proper part and role in the relevant litigation. I think he relied blindly and with no mind of his own on counsel's views on which, it must or ought to have been apparent to him, some question should have been raised."

The problem for a client wishing to prove neglect of duty can be imagined if, under a pre-arranged procedure, it had been decided that a solicitor need not accompany the barrister in court. Should a course of action then be taken against the client's interests it would be exceedingly difficult to say who was responsible. Attempts to simplify and rationalise

---

22. Benson Commission Report, p. 299 para. 22.44.
23. [1984] 1 All ER 333.

the solicitor/barrister relationship will always be thwarted because it is not a contractual one. Fusion would eliminate the need for deciding questions of responsibility in this context by placing an absolute duty upon one lawyer to handle a client's case competently.

13. The Judiciary

To preserve the divided profession it has become necessary to create two tiers of judges. Solicitors still cannot progress beyond Circuit judge level despite attempts to allow them to serve upon the High Court bench. This amounts to discrimination against one class of lawyer and is inconsistent with the principles of an open and democratic society. As with rights of audience, if the position is not rationalised, relationships between the two branches of the profession will deteriorate. The creation of a single legal profession would resolve the problem. Judges would then be selected from the one category of lawyer and no anomalies would arise.

It is a statistical certainty that more practitioners with the qualities needed in a judge will be found among a larger group of lawyers than in a smaller one. The terminology used to describe each group is immaterial but the opportunity for their members to develop the talents they possess is of importance. Until there is parity between them it will always be possible to bar progress by asserting that barristers are more suitable to preside over the courts in which they alone can practise.

The truth of this assertion cannot be assessed unless an objective comparison is made. This is possible at Crown Court level. Although no published study exists, it is certain that the Lord Chancellor's department will have observed solicitor Circuit judges and Recorders at work. No criticism of their effectiveness has been recorded and appointments continue to be made. Apart from the question of competence, which is no longer at issue, the judiciary in a pluralistic society should, in its composition, be representative of society as a whole. This cannot be said to be the case at present. Although a gradual change is taking place it has not matched social trends generally. The Benson Commission showed an interest in the social background of student lawyers but this was not followed through with detailed research. Statistics produced for the years 1976 to 1977 lead to the conclusion that:[24]

> "graduates studying subjects leading to a professional career are likely to come from a professional or managerial background but that the law does not differ markedly in this respect from other professions."

Perhaps of more significance than this observation is the information given by the Middle Temple which shows that in 1977 and 1978 only 14%

---

24. Benson Commission Report, Vol. 2 Surveys and Studies, pp. 57–61.

of those admitted to the Bar had fathers in manual occupations. The figure given for Gray's Inn is 8%. These figures are stated to be based upon 70% of all admissions. The educational background of students, lawyers and judges was not investigated. Studies in the past have shown that among the higher judiciary a majority were educated at fee-paying schools.[25]

There is a need for the diversity of society to be reflected in the judiciary. Decisions of the courts are frequently criticised on the grounds that they are politically and class biased. The use of legal procedures to resolve trade union and industrial disputes has increased dramatically. Injunctions to restrain workers and union officials are commonplace. Unions as entities are fined and their assets sequestered. It is here that the role of the lawyer in advising and initiating action is fundamental to the preservation of democratic rights and the freedom of association. Any suspicion, however unjustified, that the immense power of the judiciary is not wielded impartially lessens respect for the rule of law and hinders the lawyer's task. In a fused profession there would be a much larger body of practitioners from which to select the higher judiciary. All lawyers practising as advocates, and others with the necessary qualities, would be eligible for appointment. With the wider range of experience, and diverse social and educational background of a combined legal profession a more representative judiciary could be selected.

In a single legal profession a more open way of appointing judges at all levels could be devised. It has always been considered that, as a general rule, long and continuous practice as an advocate develops the skills necessary for judicial office. The method of choice now used is based upon the existence of a relatively small Bar and personal contact. With a larger, uniformly structured profession, a formal scheme of selection and training would be more appropriate. This would be possible without the danger of creating a professional judiciary. Training could begin by appointing suitable candidates to serve in minor judicial posts on a part-time basis early on in their careers. With training schemes organised by the profession and the Lord Chancellor's department, performance could be monitored over a period of years and promotion awarded upon the basis of achievement. The mystique and secrecy which now surround the appointment of the higher judiciary would be eliminated and a more democratic process instituted.

14. Specialised Courts

Statutory tribunals, which adjudicate upon questions arising in relation

---

25. C. Neal Tate, 'Paths to the Bench in Britain', *Western Political Quarterly*, U.S.A. Vol. 28, No. 1, p. 108.
J. A. G. Griffith, *The Politics of the Judiciary* 3rd Ed. 1985, p. 26–7.

to particular areas of legislation, have proliferated since World War II. Employment, social services, mental health and immigration are a few examples. There is an advantage for the parties concerned in having the law interpreted and applied by specialists in the subject matter. Familiarity with the problems involved is more likely to lead to consistent decisions. Family law is an area which suffers through a lack of coherence in the Courts which deal with its various aspects. There is overlapping of jurisdiction between the County Court and Magistrates' Domestic Courts which results in differing approaches to the same problems. There has been authoritative and convincing support for a single unified Court to deal with all family matters, including care proceedings. The Law Society,[26] in a consultation paper, has outlined proposals for a Family Court and a Families Appeal Court to deal with all first instance decision-making. The Court would incorporate the High Court Family Division, County Court family jurisdiction, Magistrates' Court domestic jurisdiction, Juvenile Court care proceedings and Crown Court appeals against Magistrates' Courts decisions in family matters. Solicitors and barristers would, it is envisaged, have equal rights of audience in all cases before the Family Court and Family Appeal Court.

The Bar is unable to accept the rights of audience provision. This is a striking example of the effect of a divided profession. Clearly, the proposed new courts, by amalgamating courts in which differing rights of audience exist, could not function if any attempt were made to retain those differences. It would be impossible to devise a scheme in which advocates were discriminated against in the same court. As a consequence a reform may be blocked, not on its merits but because of the way in which the legal profession is organised.

Similar proposals have been put forward to establish a specialist Housing Court.[27] This also may not prove acceptable if the rights of audience issue is raised. It should be added, however, that the arguments in favour of this type of specialist court are not yet very far advanced. The point is mentioned to show that the profession as a whole is prevented from working together upon questions affecting the public interest. In a unified profession sectional interests would no longer interfere with reform.

15. Legal Aid

A disturbing trend in legal aid work has been revealed by Robert Johnson, Q.C., Chairman of the Bar Fees and Legal Aid Committee, and

---

26. 'A Family Court'. Consultation paper issued by The Law Society Family Law Committee 82 *Gazette* 1137 (1985).
27. M. Jackson, 'Housing Courts' 82 *Gazette* 1002 (1985).

Michael Hill, Q.C., Chairman of the Criminal Bar Association. In an interview they both agreed that serious shortcomings are evident in the quality of work which is legally aided. Mr. Johnson went as far as to say:[28]

> "The legally aided fees in civil work are a long way behind the privately paid fees. The consequence, of course, is that a young man starting at the Bar starts on legal aid and as soon as he has developed the sort of practice where he is getting private work then he or his clerk tends to phase out the legal aid work. So nowadays the best people at the civil Bar tend to do very little legal aid. In that sense the legally aided client does not get the same quality of counsel; obviously there are lots of very distinguished exceptions, but I think that's a trend which distinguishes the present situation from 25 years ago."

The position with criminal legal aid is different but just as serious. Mr. Hill relates how inadequate fees paid to barristers in legal aid cases are and that as a consequence he believes:[29]

> "that criminal trials take too long and the cost to the public is enormous. The only sensible way of attacking this is to make the trials more efficient which means accelerating preparation and also accelerating the time at which cases come on for trial. The Lord Chancellor may say that that will increase the cost of criminal legal aid work. I suspect that will probably be true initially, but it may be a price that we have got to pay."

Higher fees, he considers, should be paid for preparation. This would make it more worthwhile for the barrister to commit himself to preparation, resulting in shorter trials. At present, because of the listing system, a barrister may not be available to appear in a case in which instructions have been received months before the actual trial. In such instances preparatory work is unpaid and of no use to the barrister who eventually accepts the brief. The pressure to cut back legal aid remuneration has, according to Mr. Hill, reduced the amount of Magistrates' Court work available to the Bar. Solicitors are taking cases themselves because the amount allowed under 'solicitor only' legal aid certificates is not sufficient to pay for counsel to be instructed. Magistrates' Court cases in the past provided training for young barristers before they took cases in the higher courts. Now, according to Mr. Hill, with less experience in the lower court this:[30]

> ". . . may explain why there is criticism about the level of competence of people who appear in indictment cases. They are cutting their teeth on work that is larger and more difficult than the work my generation cut their teeth on."

---

28. R. Johnson and M. Hill, 'Legal Aid Comment', 82 *Gazette* 580 (1985).
29. *Ibid.*, p. 581.
30. *Ibid.*, p. 581.

These three criticisms alone indicate that the divided profession is not functioning well. To learn that the best people at the Bar do very little civil legal aid work, that criminal trials take too long and that there is a low level of competence among those who appear in indictment cases is disturbing. These symptoms can be taken as a sign that a radical change in organisation is necessary. Bearing in mind the continued restraints upon public expenditure, any increase in fees will only act as a palliative.

Fusion would enable the problems to be dealt with by eliminating double manning where not essential and allowing different working arrangements to be developed. With the support of partnerships and simplified costing, substantial economies could be made. Above all, the strain now being imposed upon the criminal Bar could be reduced for the benefit of the practitioner and the client.

Mr. Hill places the blame for the deteriorating position of the criminal Bar upon those who are responsible for fixing levels of remuneration. The problems he describes, however, appear to be an indictment of the whole system. Separation militates against their discussion and solution by the whole profession.

CHAPTER 6

How Change Can Be Achieved

1. Objective

The task which lies ahead is to bring the vast corpus of knowledge and experience of all qualified lawyers into the mainstream of the legal system. Painful adjustments to modern circumstances have been accepted in industry, commerce and the academic world, even to the extent of the loss of employment. With an ever growing need for legal services it seems unlikely that fusion would cause real hardship. There may be alterations in working arrangements and the removal of some privileges previously enjoyed by the Bar. The changes can, however, only affect a relatively small group and amount to a surrender of exclusive rights in the higher Courts. Customs of a ritualistic and social nature, pleasant as they may be for the participants, may wither away and ceremonial dress be discarded. In return, a single and undivided legal profession will arise unhampered by restrictive practices and internal dissension. The energies and talents of all lawyers can then be concentrated upon the provision of an effective legal service.

2. Governing Body

In considering how a unified profession would be governed, the nature of the existing professional bodies must be taken into account. These have been described in detail in Chapter 3. Summarised they show that with solicitors the organisation is formal, uncomplicated and in accord with modern institutions. The Law Society is the single controlling body, having a written constitution which provides for a governing council elected from its members. The council's responsibilities include the provision of legal education, requirements upon admission and the exercise of professional discipline. An annual report is published upon its various activities together with detailed accounts and a financial statement. Income is derived from the subscriptions of members and the Society does not rely upon income from assets or freehold properties of the magnitude of those owned by the Inns of Court.

A permanent staff of officials headed by the Secretary General carries out the policies laid down by the Council. The Society organises post qualification education and contributes to law reform. Being relatively recent in origin, its members do not observe the customs or ceremonies of earlier times. A Lay Observer, appointed by statute, reports annually upon its activities and those of its members, and a compensation fund, together with a system of compulsory insurance protects the public against financial loss due to the negligence or dishonesty of practising solicitors.

As described in Chapter 3, the organisation and finances of the Bar are complex. Every barrister, both as a student and when practising, must belong to one of the Inns of Court. The Inns are represented on the Senate of the Inns of Court and the Bar, which is the profession's controlling body exercising disciplinary powers and responsible for legal education. The Council of Legal Education, under the Senate's direction, provides educational facilities. The Bar Council, also represented upon the Senate, is concerned with the affairs of the Bar but is constituted under the Senate regulations. Barristers, with some exceptions, are expected to belong to a Circuit, an autonomous organisation based upon the court Circuits. The main source of income is from lettings of real property, and involved financial arrangements provide for the support of these bodies. These are described in the report commissioned by the Benson Commission.[1]

Separation within the profession ensures that these marked differences of organisation persist. Traditional observances and the social nature of the Inns of Court foster intense group loyalty. Coupled with a close relationship with the higher judiciary, there is every incentive for this group to keep its identity and privileges intact. This may explain why no attempt has been made in recent times to bring the two branches of the profession closer together, either for educational or professional purposes.

If fusion is to be achieved then eventually the two professional bodies will need to consider how they are to join forces. Sir John Donaldson, Master of the Rolls, when addressing a Law Society conference, indicated the kind of problem which arises when established patterns of the profession need altering. He said:[2]

> "Today, more than for many years past, we are being pressed to make changes in the profession. And make no mistake about it, we should do so and we want to do so. We should remove the mystique which is one of the reasons why the public hesitates to consult us. We should supply a better and wider service using all the aids now becoming available to us through modern technology."

1. *Supra.* pp. 35–7.
2. Sir John Donaldson, 'Change and Reform', 81 *Gazette* 2985 (1984).

This is a call to modernisation which will be echoed by the younger members of the whole profession. It is one which may not be heard by those who do not appreciate the speed of technological and social transformation. The status quo was, until only recently, unreservedly accepted by both branches of the profession. Now a change of attitude is discernible. The Law Society acknowledges that its rights of audience policy could lead to fusion. It is, therefore, prudent to consider how the eventual amalgamation should take place. To foresee a change without planning for its introduction can lead to unsatisfactory and involved adjustments taking place over a long period of time. These may be more concerned with the preservation of sectional interests than the public interest.

A single unified legal profession would need to be governed by one body. Its structure could, with only minor changes, be based upon that of The Law Society. It would be neither practicable nor in keeping with democratic principles to retain institutions resembling the Inns of Court. Their self-appointed Benches which exclude the general membership from control are not compatible with a larger organisation having an elected leadership. The Inns, venerable and interesting as they are, contribute a great deal to the mystique of the law mentioned by Sir John Donaldson. With the English attachment to ancient survivals and traditional forms no doubt a place would be found for them comparable to the livery companies of the City of London. Without power, but serving as reminders of past glories, their continued existence would not affect the restructuring of the profession which unification would bring.

This suggestion can be expected to arouse considerable opposition and dismay. It must, however, be asked whether the Inns are indispensable to the effective administration of justice in a modern society. Generalised comments about the desirability of maintaining a collegiate atmosphere are not specific or compelling enough to provide a basis for determining their value. An assessment of the functions they perform is more appropriate. Educational activities in the form of moots and lectures, as provided by the Inns, are not unique in any way and could easily be provided by the governing body of a single profession. The contact which exists between the judges and Inn members, whether social or professional, could take place equally well in a single profession for the benefit of all practitioners. Social activities and dining facilities may not be possible upon the scale now enjoyed by members of the Inns. Local Law Societies, however, could provide adequate opportunities for lawyers to associate socially and for educational purposes. The development of these societies would be a means of providing regional organisations for the whole profession. The Benson Report recommended the establishment of such local groups to promote and carry out the policies of The Law Society.[3] This would encourage participation in matters affecting the profession and prevent the over-centralisation of its control. For the public there would be easier access to the complaints procedure and the possibility of grievances being redressed at local level.

An opportunity would arise to channel the resources of the Inns into the provision of educational facilities for the benefit of the whole profession. In particular, post-qualification specialist training is an area where, with adequate financial support, there could be rapid expansion. With the emergence of highly trained specialists the image of the lawyer generally would improve. Competition from unqualified practitioners would be met by the provision of efficient and competent services in all fields of the law. This, to some extent, may alleviate a loss of revenue to licensed conveyancers.

3. Enabling Act

If it is decided that fusion is to be introduced and the profession governed by a single body, similar in character and form to The Law Society, timing becomes the next important consideration. A planned transition to the new structure is preferable to sudden change. However there is no reason why this should take an unreasonable length of time. Once fusion has become a settled objective undue delay could cause as much disruption as abrupt change. This would apply particularly to new entrants to the profession who, if the change-over were prolonged, would be faced with the dilemma of deciding which branch to enter.

Legislation to amalgamate the two branches need not be complex. A short enabling Act providing for the constitution of a Legal Practitioners' Commission charged with the task of unifying the two branches by a specified date and granted appropriate powers would be adequate. Five years would seem to be a reasonable time in which to complete the task. Transitional orders or directives could deal with the introduction of joint legal education, qualification requirements, the transfer of barristers to solicitors' firms, rights of audience and the progressive opening of judicial posts to solicitors and barristers on equal terms.

4. Professional Description

It would be appropriate when drafting an enabling Bill to decide upon the designation of practitioners in the single profession. Although "solicitor" and "barrister" could be preserved, the public would undoubtedly find the situation confusing as the distinction would be

3.   Benson Commission Report, p. 392 paras. 29.43–7.

without meaning. There would also be the danger of unofficial groups endeavouring to restore the division which had been abolished. With a single qualification it would be ambiguous to give practitioners two descriptions. One title which conveys to the public the true function of its holder is a more logical and sensible arrangement. There seem to be four alternatives; advocate, counsellor-at-law, attorney-at-law, or plain attorney. Attorney has the advantage of being understood by most people if only through the influence of television programmes from the United States. The word has, of course a much earlier origin in this country and the fact that there already exists an Attorney General makes its choice a natural one. Arguments against the use of this description have always referred to the past history of the attorney. This can be dismissed, for apart from its distance in time many of the alleged unpleasant characteristics of the earlier bearers of the description are inaccurate and misleading.[4] If objections to the title had any merit its use to describe a senior law officer would have been abandoned long ago.

5. Transitional Provisions

A carefully planned scheme of transition to be implemented by the Law Practitioners' Commission would, in effect, accelerate existing trends towards extended rights of audience and introduce other appropriate reforms. However, instead of the uncertainty and ill will generated by the present situation, co-operation to achieve a common aim would be substituted. There would be no possibility of avoiding or obstructing transitional measures as they would have the force of law. Minor objections and procedural arrangements would be the concern of standing committees. There would be an incentive to implement all possible transitional measures by stipulating, in the enabling Act, that fusion will in any event take place on the appointed day.

Even in a divided profession a common legal educational system has been recognised as desirable. In a single profession it would be essential. This would be the first obvious subject of reform during the transitional stage. A joint standing committee, appointed by the Law Practitioners' Commission from The Law Society and Bar nominees would oversee the change. By combining the resources now devoted to the vocational teaching of law into a common system, the requirements of a single profession could be taken into account in preparation for fusion. With full consultation among those concerned with the teaching of law at all levels a clear and straightforward scheme to be followed by all entrants could be devised. Similarly, any adjustments needed at the academic

---

4.   E. B. V. Christian, *op. cit.*, pp. 55, 144 and 232.

stage would require the advice and assistance of those who now provide legal education at the universities and polytechnics.

Trends, as noted, are apparent which, if continued, will eventually lead to fusion in fact if not in name. Solicitors have been granted limited rights in the Crown Court and are eligible to serve as Recorders and Circuit judges. These concessions indicate the kind of transitional arrangements which are feasible. Present experience shows how gradual change can be effected without disrupting the system. As a beginning, a further limited extension of rights of audience in the Crown Court is conceivable. The Benson Commission opposed this move on the grounds that it would weaken the Bar. Seen as a transitional provision though, the objection is not valid because a separate Bar as now constituted would not exist in a single profession.

The position could be reached where both branches, with equal rights of audience, are working together as at present in the Magistrates' and County Court. By relaxing rules of etiquette, practising arrangements could be modified to suit the convenience of clients and improve efficiency. If all advocates were, at their discretion, allowed to take proofs of evidence, interview witnesses, attend conferences at any venue, and take instructions direct from a lay client, the public would benefit. The late return of briefs would be less likely in many instances as more solicitors would be instructed. Their practising methods make it exceedingly rare for a brief to be passed to another practitioner at short notice. Competition would reduce double manning and costs. The impact of these changes upon the Bar could not, at this stage, be ignored. To prevent the sudden interruption in their work flow which may result, the existing rule which prevents solicitors acting as agents for other firms in Crown Court cases could be retained for a period.

Some barristers may wish to anticipate fusion and work with solicitors before the appointed day. To make this possible without undue difficulty simplified transfer rules are needed. Barristers could then join solicitors' firms and undertake the kind of work to which they were accustomed. If the handling of clients' money were thought to be a problem, the passing of an examination in solicitors' accounts need be the only formal qualification required for transfer. Exemption from this examination could be granted for so long as no clients' money is handled by or under the transferee's control. When a joint qualifying examination has been introduced, new entrants to the profession would be entitled to work in either branch pending actual fusion. The problem would, therefore, only affect those called to the Bar before the new educational and qualifying regimen was introduced.

As already noted, the appointment of solicitor Recorders and Circuit judges has been a radical innovation. This reform untapped a reservoir of judicial talent. It can be expected that more appointments will be made. With a date fixed for fusion there would no longer be any reason for stopping at the Crown Court. The installation of Solicitor judges in the High Court would pave the way for the opening of all judicial offices to the whole profession.

6. Specialists

It has been constantly reiterated that specialist lawyers will increasingly be in demand. The response from solicitors has been positive and the day of the true specialist, trained, experienced and formally qualified, is approaching. During the transitional stage the courses of post quali-fication training now provided by The Law Society for solicitors could be made available for the Bar. Barristers, by undergoing the necessary training and gaining the stipulated experience, could then be placed upon specialist panels of the type already described. By bringing younger members of the two branches closer together during this period of instruction, co-operation and voluntary moves towards fusion would be encouraged.

As the number of specialists increases in both branches it does not serve the public interest to restrict access to them. Until actual fusion, it would be of immense benefit to clients if they had the option of taking an opinion direct from a specialist. Company directors, accountants, businessmen etc. would be able to obtain advice quickly from those qualified to give it. By permitting this during the transitional stage a larger pool of experience and talent would become more easily available. Where a solicitor did not intervene, costs would also be reduced. This relaxation of present rules of etiquette would allow adjustments to be made in working arrangements if shown to be necessary. This advance notice of the kind of problems which may arise in a single profession would allow them to be resolved sooner.

7. Hardship

As the transitional arrangements leading to fusion progress, barristers would be able to plan for the future by adjusting their working arrangements. They could decide whether to join existing solicitors' practices, form partnerships or practise as they do at present. Initially, though, there may be difficulty in matching their services to demand. As with any departure from long established routines, change may bring temporary disruption.

It is possible that younger barristers, endeavouring to build up their practices, may be apprehensive about the future. Competition for less exacting work is bound to increase when solicitors' rights of audience are extended. This will be an incentive for barristers to join existing practices. The benefits of doing so may well outweigh the insecurity and struggle which those who lack private means, privileged educational backgrounds or social connections endure at the beginning of their careers. Even the smallest partnership allows its members the opportunity to concentrate more intensively upon their chosen work without the distraction of these factors or the vagaries of the chambers system. The back-up of unqualified staff and articled clerks gives the most junior practitioner support which is not forthcoming at the Bar.

Senior barristers, who have not been fortunate enough to secure a judicial post or become established as specialists, may be justifiably worried over the consequences of fusion. A lurking fear of financial insecurity and diminishing prospects of advancement which may already exist could become more acute. For them the prospect of finding a suitable opening in a lawyers' firm of modest size could be a blessing in disguise. It would offer a respite from the pressures which increase as the years advance.

Should it prove difficult for some to find alternative openings and if their practices decline, possibly the most serious problem will be that of retirement. Pension arrangements made at the time of high income and before inflation eroded their value, may prove impossible to maintain. The profession as a whole could reduce the impact of this situation, if it arose, by creating a fund to ensure that pension contracts are maintained at a reasonable level in cases of extreme hardship. Admittedly, great tact would be needed in devising a scheme but in principle it would be little different from redundancy payments which those in employment are entitled to receive.

CHAPTER 7

The Future—A Prediction

For almost one hundred years trends in the legal profession were not difficult to foresee. After the pro-fusion agitation was contained and eventually subdued at the beginning of this century little altered. It is only recently that factors which portend a profound change in the established order have arisen. First, the expansion which has taken place in both branches has reduced the size and influence of the older age group of practitioners. Secondly and probably more far reaching, the transfer of a considerable proportion of conveyancing work to licensed convey-ancers is likely to affect the viability of smaller practices with a restricted work range. Thirdly, the information and communication revolution is gathering such momentum that even radical changes are overtaken by new developments in a short space of time. An attempt has been made in the following paragraphs to predict the state of the profession when the 21st century begins.

We are now at the beginning of the 21st Century. Despite opposition, solicitors' rights of audience were gradually extended. Quite soon the differences in working arrangements between the two branches were modified. Restrictions became more difficult to maintain and this encouraged a spirit of co-operation which replaced the antagonisms of earlier years. Fusion was effected by mutual consent as demarcation lines became blurred. Once accomplished, an obstacle to the impartial and united review of problems facing the profession and the service it provided was removed. All lawyers, directing their energies to the improvement of the law and its institutions, can now make decisions without considering sectional interests or sentimental attachments to the past. As a consequence, the courts and legal procedures are being adapted to meet the needs and convenience of the people they serve.

The concept of a judicial system centralised in London has given way to courts in the regions with full jurisdiction. The distinction between the High Court and County Court has gone. Cases are allotted to judges of varying seniority according to their importance and complexity. In the centres of population lawyers practice both as consultant specialists and in partnership. The average firm has about six partners and branch offices serve outlying districts. District Law Societies now exist with permanent offices and officials to administer the policies of the Law

Society and to help the profession and public alike.[1] Data terminals accessing all known legal information[2] including precedents, commentaries and forms are available for hire by practitioners who do not have their own facilities.

The most significant advance has been the creation of specialist courts. These were not introduced in the days when the profession was divided because of demarcation disputes. To be successful it was necessary for all lawyers to have access to them. Now that fusion has made this possible these courts are flourishing and of great benefit to the public. In particular, the Family Court[3] and Housing Court[4] bring together all available remedies and processes in these respective areas under a single jurisdiction. This extends to first appeal level and cases are dealt with in the region in which they arise. The days when, for instance, a single parent with housing problems could have become involved with the Department of Health and Social Security, a Rent Officer, the County Court and the High Court over a housing problem have gone for ever.

The Family Court, originally conceived when the profession was divided, proved its worth. The initiative for this innovation came from The Law Society. A considerable body of opinion supported the need for reform of the court system when dealing with family matters. Overlapping of jurisdiction between the Magistrates' Domestic Court and County Court had resulted in a lack of uniformity in applying the law. For lawyer and client alike, the complexity of the system sometimes overshadowed the problems it was designed to solve. Now one category of court, served by specialist judges supported by staff and advocates trained in family law and problems, deals with cases from beginning to end. Organised upon a regional basis, the courts are completely separate from the rest of the court system and ensure that children do not come into contact with criminal procedures. Above all, private lawyers have co-operated to make them a success. The demarcation disputes between solicitors and barristers of the past no longer hinder progress or baffle the client. Advocates in these courts have discarded archaic dress and judges wear only a simple robe to denote their office.

Soon after fusion a complete overhaul of the costing system became possible. It is no longer necessary to distinguish between solicitors and barristers when taxing bills and making payments. The lawyer dealing with a case is totally responsible for the employment and payment of outside assistance in the form of specialist lawyers. A legal electronic

1.   Benson Commission Report, p. 395 para. R 29.6.
2.   Anon. Feature giving details of Lexis and Eurolex merger. *The Bookseller* 8 June 1985 p. 2304.
3.   The Law Society's Family Law Committee *op. cit.* p. 1137-9.
4.   *Supra.* p. 118.

communications network is now fully operative and this has simplified the taxation of costs. Details of cases are transmitted to the court registry for processing by a central computer with access to a data store of costing details. Variable, disputed or unusual items are automatically sifted and compared with previous bills and limits already established. The whole procedure has been programmed to ensure that a fair amount is eventually allowed. An incredible saving in time and labour has enabled resources to be channelled into more productive legal work.

The size of the profession, now about 75,000, has resulted in the de-centralisation of The Law Society. The district offices which have been established match the pattern of court locations. There is close co-operation with the courts and access to the registries through computer terminals in law firms' offices. For those who are unable to bear the capital cost of hardware, the Law Society has terminals available on hire giving access to law library data banks. Facilities and accommodation are provided in the district offices for specialist lawyers and advocates with higher qualifications who contract their services to the profession generally.

In retrospect, the conveyancing revolution of the 80's had a profound effect. It provided the motivation for fusion among younger lawyers. Since that time the profession has been unified. Problems and demarcation disputes which arose when it was divided have been resolved. Payments to consultants is prompt as their engagement is on a contractual basis and computerisation has eliminated the lengthy taxation process. Clients have easy access to their advisers and briefs are rarely returned. A greater concentration of specialised lawyers is now to be found in centres of population throughout the country. Conveyancing is no longer the main source of income and the procedure has become almost completely computerised. As a result, more work of truly legal nature is undertaken by firms. Advocacy in particular is conducted at all levels by lawyers who are locally based. Courts in the districts, or Circuits as they were called, now have full jurisdiction to the level of the Court of Appeal. This has produced a great deal of work for local firms and even those of a modest size employ full time advocates. Now that the structure of the profession has been simplified and rationalised a corresponding reduction in the complexity of organisation, court procedures and working arrangements has followed.

The working methods and quality of service of the profession are now closely related to new technology. A continuing and relentless advance in the capability of computers is having an incredible effect upon the viability of lawyers' firms. Only those who are able to afford the capital expenditure or leasing costs of new hardware are likely to survive.

Electronic mailing will soon be universal.[5] All forms and precedents are available from data banks and up-dated continuously. With laser printers, hard copy reproductions are available instantly. The days of keeping stocks and making sure that obsolete material has been discarded are a memory.

In civil litigation the reforms which emerged from the Lord Chancellor's Department Review of Procedure, which reported in 1987, have been fully implemented. With new technology and the accessibility of advocates in the fused system the time spent upon oral hearings has decreased. Litigants know the full facts of a case before trial. Inquisitorial procedures ensure that all matters that can be agreed before a hearing are disposed of. Settlements are more frequent and opening addresses by lawyers if there is a trial are short. As a consequence, oral argument is confined to the real issues. Judgements are much briefer and delivered in writing through the electronic communications network.

Criminal proceedings, particularly for crimes involving violence, have increased in number and the regional courts are equipped to deal with cases speedily. Local lawyers provide advocacy services and specialists are available nationally for grave and complex charges. With a limitation period, as in Scotland, for the commencement of proceedings long periods in custody, without trial, have been eliminated. Clients invariably have the benefit of a conference with their chosen advocate well before a hearing date so allowing time for adequate preparation. As a consequence trials are more efficient and lengthy addresses by advocates are rare. Unnecessary drama has been eliminated from the court room. In its place a businesslike and comprehensible system prevails. Above all, allegations of political bias on the part of the higher judiciary are now rare. Since a Judicial Commission,[6] responsible for the selection of judges, was instituted, all political parties are represented and participate in the appointment process. The immense power of the Lord Chancellor as a government appointee and member of the cabinet has been transferred to this body, which is in accord with the principles of a democratic society. Other judges cannot veto appointments. No longer is information upon prospective candidates kept in secret files which Lord Hailsham described as:[7]

> ". . . files on all the barristers, awful files with all the gossip, everything in them, including their drinking habits."

The twenty-first century has begun without solicitors and barristers.

---

5. Anon. 'Legal Electronic Communications Network' 82 *Gazette* 242 (1985).
6. *Supra*. p. 50.
7. Lord Hailsham and J. Mortimer. 'The Wig Confronts the Pen' (interview) *The Times*, 25 August 1985.

Attorneys, who have replaced them, are well respected and occupy positions of influence and prestige. Pledged to maintain freedom under the law they are no longer slaves of the past. An undivided, strong and independent profession now exists. It is better equipped to counter the destructive elements in society and combat lawlessness through an efficient and modernised legal system.

SPECIMEN DEED OF ARTICLES

It will assist The Law Society if this form is used.
In any event Articles must be similar to this specimen deed and must include clauses substantially in the form of those marked *****, which are mandatory.
Articles must be lodged with the Law Society within one month from the date of their taking effect.

. . . .

THESE ARTICLES OF CLERKSHIP dated

are made between (1)
of
("the Articled Clerk")

and (2)
of

("the Solicitor")
a partner in the firm of

Insert after the firm's name its address or, if it has more than one office, the address at which the Articled Clerk will be principally employed.

WITNESS as follows:-

*   1.   In accordance with the terms of these Articles the Articled Clerk binds himself/herself clerk to the Solicitor and the Solicitor accepts the Articled Clerk as his/her clerk for a period of   years from ("the period of Articles").

Insert the time or times of salary review. There must be at least one review during the period of Articles.

*   2.   The salary of the Articled Clerk shall be £   per annum payable   in arrear or such larger sum as the Solicitor may think appropriate upon reviewing it after   months of the period of Articles has expired.

3.   The Articled Clerk covenants with the Solicitor as follows:-

(1)   He/She will faithfully and diligently serve the Solicitor in the profession of a Solicitor of the Supreme Court of Judicature as his/her articled clerk during the period of Articles.

(2)   He/She will at all times deal properly with the money and property of the Solicitor and of his/her firm and of any of his/her or their clients or employees which shall be deposited in his/her or their hands or entrusted to his/her custody or possession.

(3)   He/She will at all times treat with the utmost confidence all information relating to the Solicitor and his/her firm and their clients and his/her or their business.

(4)   He/She will at all times during the period of Articles readily obey and execute the lawful and reasonable instructions of the Solicitor and any partner of his/her and will not absent himself/herself from the service of the Solicitor at any time during that period without the consent of the Solicitor and will at all times during that period conduct himself/herself with all due diligence, honesty and propriety.

*(5)   He/She will complete and maintain an adequate record of his/her work and experience during the period of Articles ("the Training Record") in the form provided by the Solicitor pursuant to clause 4(3) (a).

Insert any further covenants required.

4.   The Solicitor covenants with the Articled Clerk as follows:-

*(1)   He/She will take the Articled Clerk as his/her clerk and will during the period of Articles provide the Articled Clerk with the opportunity to learn the basic skills and characteristics associated with the practice and profession of a Solicitor of the Supreme Court of Judicature and in particular will:

(a)   provide the Articled Clerk with the opportunity (either in his/her own office or in the office of another practising solicitor authorised to take articled clerks) to learn the principles of professional conduct and to practise the following basic skills:

(i)   Drafting

(ii)   Communication with clients and others (including obtaining instructions and giving advice)

(iii)   Research

(iv)   Office routines, procedure and costs

(v)   Legal routines and procedures

Delete any topics not available under Articles.

(b)   give the Articled Clerk the opportunity during the period of Articles to gain reasonable experience in at least three of the following basic legal topics:

(i)   Company law and commercial law

(ii)   Family and welfare law

(iii)   Litigation (civil, criminal or before tribunals)

(iv)   Local government law

(v)   Magisterial law

(vi)   Property (including landlord and tenant)

(vii)   Taxation

(viii)   Wills, probate and trusts.

This provision will become operative in cases where secondment is necessary.

*(2)   He/She will provide the Articled Clerk with the opportunity to gain reasonable experience in at least two of the topics specified in paragraph (1)(b) within the practice of the Solicitor or his or her firm and if he/she is unable to provide the requisite opportunity to gain experience in a third specified topic he/she will use all reasonable endeavours to arrange for the Articled Clerk to be seconded for not less than six nor more than twelve months during the period of Articles to another practising Solicitor qualified to take articled clerks to enable the Articled Clerk to have the opportunity to gain reasonable experience in a third specified topic.

*(3)   (a)   He/She will provide the Training Record to be used by the Articled Clerk pursuant to clause 3(5) which shall comply with the provisions of clause 7 (a) hereof.

(b)   He/She will ensure that the Training Record is maintained by the Articled Clerk pursuant to his/her obligation contained in clause 3(5).

(c)   He/She will ensure that during each month of the period of Articles either he/she or another person delegated by him/her for the purpose will inspect the Training Record and discuss with the Articled Clerk his/her work and any general matters affecting his/her training.

· ·

(4)   He/She will allow the Articled Clerk paid study leave for the purpose of attending such course or courses as the Law Society shall specify shall be undertaken by the Articled Clerk to enable him/her to complete the second stage of training (as defined by the Qualifying Regulations 1979 – 1982) and will pay on behalf of the Articled Clerk the fees for such course or courses.

5.   In addition to any period of absence permitted by the Law Society to enable the Articled Clerk to prepare for and sit any one or more papers of the final examination the Solicitor may allow the Articled Clerk paid study leave to attend such courses as the Solicitor in his/her discretion deems appropriate.

*   6.   Any difficulty or dispute between the Articled Clerk and the Solicitor concerning the fulfilment of the provisions of these Articles or the conduct of either party in relation to these Articles may be referred by either of them to the Conciliation Officer appointed for the purpose by the local Law Society covering the area of the Solicitor's firm or at the option of either party to the Conciliation Officer appointed by a neighbouring local Law Society.

*   7.   (a)   The Training Record shall be in such form as the Solicitor shall reasonably prescribe provided that it takes the form either of a diary or of a series of check lists covering the basic legal topics specified in clause 4 (1) (b) in which the Articled Clerk is to be given the opportunity to gain reasonable experience.

(b)   During the period of Articles the Training Record shall be in the custody of and maintained by the Articled Clerk but it shall be the property of the Solicitor and available to him/her for inspection at all times.

(c)   The Training Record shall be retained by the Solicitor for at least 12 months after the expiry of the period of Articles.

(d)   At any time during the period of Articles or twelve months thereafter the Training Record shall on request be produced to the Law Society or to any Conciliation Officer acting pursuant to the provisions of clause 6.

. . . .

See Guidance Notes for
explanation and
different clauses.

8.   (a)   If the condition specified in paragraph (b) is not fulfilled either party may terminate these Articles within one month of the date on which the results of the Examination specified in paragraph (b) are published.

(b)   The condition referred to in paragraph (a) is that the Articled Clerk shall have passed not fewer than five of the papers constituting the Solicitors' Final Examination held in July   and shall have been referred in the remaining paper or papers.

9.   The Articled Clerk agrees to exclude any claim in respect of rights under Section 54 of the Employment Protection (Consolidation) Act 1978 and also to exclude any right to a redundancy payment in respect of the expiry of these Articles of Clerkship.

Insert any Additional
provisions required.

SIGNED SEALED and DELIVERED
by the Articled Clerk in the
presence of:-

SIGNED SEALED and DELIVERED
by the Solicitor in the
presence of:-

SPECIMEN DIARY

Name of Principal: ....

Name of Articled Clerk: ....

Week Beginning: ....

Date	Subject by Category	Type of Experience	Time Record (Optional)	File Title
1st March	Landlord & Tenant	Searching for Deeds Perusing & Drafting	½ hr. 1½ hrs.	Mr. G. D. Mortar & Mr. F.R. Giles – Tenancy Agreement
1st March	Conveyancing	Replying Prelim. Enquiries	½ hr.	Mrs. Brown – Sale of "The Croft"

OBSERVATIONS:

SPECIMEN CHECKLIST

LITIGATION (CRIMINAL)

(This Law Society precedent is supplied for adapting as necessary by Principals.
For list of other precedents — see back.)

NOTES: A. This checklist is suggested in case it may help at monthly or more frequent meetings of the Articled Clerk and his Principal.

B. This specimen provides examples of topics which might be selected by Principals or Firms to to cover the field of litigation (criminal) but does not purport to be comprehensive.

C. Principals and/or Firms are encouraged to prepare checklists appropriate to their own particular practices. For precedents covering other legal topics as set out overleaf please apply to the Secretary, Education and Training at The Law Society.

Name of Articled Clerk: ....

Date of Articles of Clerkship: ....

	Topics Experienced √ as appropriate	Skills Employed (e.g. Drafting, Communication, Research, Office Routines, Procedures & Costs or Legal Routines & Procedures)
1. Taking instructions from client in police custody.		
2. Taking instructions from relative of client in police custody.		
3. Attending a police station prior to charge being prepared/when client charged/ immediately after client charged.		
4. Attending Identity Parade at police station.		
5. Preparing application for bail when client in custody.		
6. Completing application forms for legal aid.		
7. Drawing up instructions to apply for bail.		
8. Advising as to appropriate mode of trial and plea.		
9. Taking written proof of statement.		
10. Taking written proof of statement of witness for defence.		
11. Preparation of plea in mitigation and attending.		
12. Preparation of case for trial in magistrates court and attending.		
13. Preparation of brief to Counsel re 11 and 12.		
14. Full consideration of prosecution depositions and advising as to appropriate form of committal.		

	Topics Experienced √ as appropriate	Skills Employed (e.g. Drafting, Communication, Research, Office Routines, Procedures & Costs or Legal Routines & Procedures)
15. Preparation for 'paper' committal.		
16. Preparation for 'oral' or 'part-oral' committal.		
17. Attending committal.		
18. Preparation of Notice of Alibi.		
19. Preparation of brief to Counsel in Crown Court.		
20. Attending Crown Court.		
21. Preparation of Advice on Appeal.		
22. Advice on merits of appeal.		
23. Preparation and completion of documents to be submitted to Court of Appeal (Criminal Division) and steps taken thereafter.		
24. Advising in motoring cases.		
25. Advice re endorsement of licence and possibility of disqualification from driving.		
26. Preparing motoring case plea in mitigation and attending.		
27. Preparing motoring trial and attending.		
28. Dealing with a 'totting up' case.		
29. Draw up Bill of Costs — magistrates courts.		
30. Draw up Bill of Costs — Crown Court.		
31. Prepare Licensing application.		
32. Attend Licensing session.		

GENERAL COMMENTS

Principal/Supervisor   Articled Clerk

(Sgd) .... (Sgd) .... Date .... 19 ....

.... 19 ....

.... 19 ....

.... 19 ....

NOTE: Further precedents of checklists for Legal Topics are available from The Law Society as follows:—

Family & Welfare Law
Local Government Law
Magisterial Law

Litigation (Civil)
Litigation (Tribunals)
Company Law & Commercial Law
Wills, Probate & Trusts

Property (including Landlord and Tenant)
Taxation

The Law Society's Qualifying (Amendment) Regulations 1982

(Regulation governing transfer of a barrister to solicitors' profession)

5. There shall be substituted for Regulation 56 of the Principal Regulations the following:—

"56 (1) A member of the English Bar who wishes to be admitted as a solicitor must first be disbarred.

(2) Unless he is able to comply with paragraph (3) he must in accordance with these Regulations have enrolled as a student with the Society and have satisfactorily completed the academic stage of training and the second stage of training.

(3) He is not required to comply with paragraph (2) beyond passing such examinations as the Society may determine if he satisfies the Society that he is a suitable person to be admitted as a solicitor and that

(a) he has, for a period of not less than three years during the five years immediately preceding his application to the Society under this Regulation, practised at the Bar in England and Wales (other than as a pupil); or

(b) his experience in the practice of English law is such that it is unnecessary for him to serve under articles of clerkship.

(4) A person other than one referred to in paragraph (3)(a) may be required by the Society satisfactorily to complete such course or courses as the Society may from time to time prescribe and/or to be employed by a solicitor in the practice of the law for a period not exceeding two years before he seeks admission."

Practice Directions

Crown Court Practice–Solicitor–Right of audience.

In exercise of the power conferred on him by s 12 of the Courts Act 1971 the Lord Chancellor hereby gives the following direction:

1. Solicitors may appear in, conduct, defend and address the court in proceedings mentioned in para 2 of this direction at any sitting of the Crown Court at Caernarvon, Barnstaple, Bodmin, Doncaster or (subject to para 3 hereof) Lincoln.

2. The proceedings in which solicitors may exercise the right of audience conferred by para 1 of this direction are: (a) appeals from magistrates' courts; (b) proceedings on committal of a person for sentence or to be dealt with; (c) proceedings in respect of offences included in class 4 in the directions given by the Lord Chief Justice with concurrence of the Lord Chancellor under ss 4 (5) and 5 (4) of the Courts Act 1971; and (d) proceedings under the original or appellate civil jurisdiction of the Crown Court.

3. The right of audience conferred by para 1 of this direction in respect of sittings of the Crown Court at Lincoln shall extend only to proceedings falling within para 2 hereof: (a) on appeal from, or on committal by, a magistrates' court in the County of the Parts of Holland, or (b) which would, but for the passing of the Courts Act 1971, have fallen to be heard by the court of quarter sessions for that county in the exercise of its original or appellate civil jurisdiction.

4. This direction shall come into force on 1st January 1972.

HAILSHAM OF ST MARYLEBONE C

7th December 1971

Crown Court Practice–Solicitor–Right of audience.

In exercise of the power conferred on him by s 12 of the Courts Act 1971 the Lord Chancellor hereby gives the following direction:

1. A solicitor may appear in, conduct, defend and address the court in—(a) criminal proceedings in the Crown Court on appeal from a magistrates' court or on committal of a person for sentence or to be dealt with, if he, or any partner of his, or any solicitor in his employment or by whom he is employed, appeared on behalf of the defendant in the magistrates' court; (b) civil proceedings in the Crown Court on appeal from a magistrates' court if he, or any partner of his, or any solicitor in his employment or by whom he is employed, appeared in the proceedings in the magistrates' court.

2. The rights of audience conferred by this direction are in addition to and not in derogation from the rights of audience conferred by the Practice Direction dated 7th December 1971.

3. This direction shall come into force on 1st March 1972.

HAILSHAM OF ST MARYLEBONE C

9th February 1972

APPENDIX F

Duties of Pupil-Masters and Pupils

The Senate has prescribed the following.

The general obligations and fupnctions of the master may be described as follows:

1. He should give specific and detailed teaching instruction in the settling of pleadings and other documents.

2. He should ensure that the pupil is well grounded in the rules of conduct and etiquette of the Bar.

3. He should require the pupil to read his papers and attempt to draft pleadings and other documents, including opinions; he should then discuss the drafts personally with the pupil.

4. He should require the pupil to accompany him to Court on frequent, but not necessarily all, occasions; he should instruct the pupil in note-taking and discuss the proceedings with him afterwards.

5. If the master has an essentially High Court practice he should arrange for the pupil from time to time to accompany more junior members of chambers to lower courts.

6. He should invite the pupil to sit in on many (but not necessarily all) conferences.

7. He should encourage a relationship between himself, his chambers colleagues and the pupil whereby the pupil is encouraged to discuss problems and receive information on matters relating to practice.

8. In the second six months the master should take a direct interest in and monitor such work as the pupil accepts on his own and in particular in his court appearances: a post mortem on the pupil's early efforts in advocacy should be part of the assistance given by the pupil-master.

9. In the second six months, the master should ensure that the pupil does not accept so large a number of briefs that his pupillage is impaired.

The obligations of the pupil are to be conscientious in receiving the instruction given and apply himself full time thereto.

Survey of Size of Solicitors' Firms

PLACE		Size of Firm—Number of Partners				
		1	2–5	6–10	11–15	16+
BRISTOL	Number of firms	7	21	5	5	–
	Total number of Branches	8	37	21	17	–
	Percentage of all branches	10%	45%	25%	20%	–
BRIGHTON AND HOVE	Number of firms	2	9	6	–	1
	Total number of branches	2	13	14	–	8
	Percentage of all branches	5%	35%	38%	–	22%
OXFORD	Number of firms	2	5	5	1	1
	Total number of branches	2	10	11	9	7
	Percentage of all branches	5%	27%	28%	23%	17%

Bibliography

BY MARTIN R. SMITH

(A) Books
(B) Periodical articles, 1950–1984

(A) BOOKS

Abel-Smith, B., and Stevens, R. *In search of justice: society and the legal system.* Allen Lane The Penguin Press: London, 1968. 384p.
Continues from *Lawyers and the courts* an analysis of the legal system as it is and how it could be improved. Ch. 9, 'The regulation of the profession' (p. 304-13), presents the arguments for fusion.

Abel-Smith, B., and Stevens, R. *Lawyers and the courts: a sociological study of the English legal system 1750–1965.* Heinemann: London, 1967. xiv, 504p.
Contains many references to fusion, particularly ch. 9, 'The barristers consolidate: trade unionism and restrictive practices' (p. 226-43).

Anon. *"Fusion" or "combination"—which? A "combination firm" sketched. By an Old Wig.* William Maxwell & Son: London, [1888]. 22p.
Commenting on the Solicitor-General, Sir E. Clarke's address (q.v.), describes the excessive costs of litigation through the existing system, and outlines how expenses might be reduced if barristers could form combinations with solicitors.

Birks, M. *Gentlemen of the law.* Stevens & Sons: London, 1960. xi, 304p.
Ch. 13, 'Solicitors in the Twentieth Century', refers to the question of fusion, but considers the bar to be rightfully 'the senior branch of the profession' (p. 294-95).

Clarke, Sir E. *The future of the legal profession: an address to the Birmingham Law Students' Society.* Stevens & Haynes: London, 1888. 11p.
Proposes that fusion would be of benefit to the public and to both branches of the profession. Reported in *The Times,* Jan. 19, 1888. For comments, see *The Times,* Jan. 21, 1888, and Jan. 25, 1888; 4 *L.Q.R.* 225; and 84 *L.T.* 247.

Committee on Legal Education, Report of the. Chairman: Mr. Justice Ormrod. Cmnd. 4595. H.M.S.O.: London, 1971. xi, 249p.
'Transfer between the branches of the profession' (para. 168). Recommends that 'Transfer between the branches of the profession should be possible without any examinations having to be taken, the only requirement being an appropriate period of pupillage or limited practice' (para. 185(37)).

Committee on Supreme Court Practice and Procedure, Final Report of the. Sir R. Evershed, Chairman. Cmd. 8878. H.M.S.O.: London, 1953. 380p.
Addendum by Sir T. Barnes, Mr. Crowther, Dr. Fletcher and Professor Marshall, recommends (para. 11) that 'the question of fusion ought to be considered forthwith by an appropriate body . . . the division of the profession into two distinct branches is one of the most obvious peculiarities of our system which invites criticism and requires to be rationally and convincingly justified'.

Commonwealth and Empire Law Conference. *Record of the Commonwealth and Empire Law Conference, London, 20th-27th July, 1955*. Solicitors' Law Stationery Society: London, 1956. 471p.

Plenary session B, 'Fusion of the two branches of the legal profession' (p. 95-124), includes papers on the systems in Australia, Canada and Scotland.

Commonwealth and Empire Law Conference. *Record of the Second Commonwealth and Empire Law Conference, Ottawa, September 14-21, 1960*. Sweet & Maxwell: London, etc. 1962. 533p.

Session on 'The legal profession of the future' (p. 419-34) includes discussion of fusion.

Forbes, J.R.S. *The divided legal profession in Australia: history, rationalisation and rationale*. Law Book Company: Sydney, 1979. xvi, 300p. [Originally published as Book supplement to *The Queensland Lawyer*, Vol. 4, 1977].

Pt. 1, 'History' includes an extensive study of the development of the divided profession in England (p. 5-27).

Hazell, R., ed. *The bar on trial*. Quartet Books: London, 1978. 221p.

Ch. 1, 'Introduction', discusses the division of the profession (p. 17-19). Ch. 8, 'Independence and fusion', argues in favour of extending solicitors' rights of audience, and of allowing barristers to take instructions directly from clients and to form partnerships with solicitors (p. 163-78).

Holdsworth, Sir W. *A history of English law. Volume XV. Edited by A. L. Goodhart and H. G. Hanbury*. Methuen/Sweet & Maxwell: London, 1965. 577p.

'IV. The legal profession' (p. 223-47) includes a section on 'The project of fusing the two branches of the profession' and 'The project of establishing a General School of Law' which would have paved the way towards fusion.

Hollander, B. *The English bar, a priesthood: the tribute of an American lawyer*. Bowes and Bowes: London, 1964. 70p.

'Fusion' (p. 65-70). He believes that the divided system is best. A solicitor will brief a barrister to appear in the County Court, rather than appear himself, because it is cheaper, and frees him to use his time more profitably. Concludes '... that the heat engendered by the client, because of proximity, is communicated to the solicitor, who becomes, quite understandably, a partisan, whereas the interposition of a barrister between the partisan and the judges helps produce that cool and calm climate in which the Court pronounces judgment'.

Johnstone, Q., and Hopson, D. *Lawyers and their work: an analysis of the legal profession in the United States and England*. Bobbs-Merrill: Indianapolis, 1967. x, 604p.

Ch. 11, 'English solicitors and barristers: implications of a split profession' (p. 357-98). Considers 'that the English legal profession and its clientele would be better off if the profession were fused'.

Justice. *The judiciary: the report of a Justice sub-committee*. Chairman: P. Webster. Stevens & Sons: London, 1972. vii, 82p.

Ch. II, 'Should the source from which appointments are to be made be enlarged?' (p. 9-31). After reviewing the arguments for and against, recommends that solicitors and chairmen of tribunals be made eligible for appointment as county court or circuit judges, and that academic lawyers be eligible for appointment to the Court of Appeal or House of Lords.

Kirk, H. *Portrait of a profession: a history of the solicitor's profession, 1100 to the present day.* Oyez Publishing: London, 1976. ix, 218p.

Ch. 9, 'Relationship with the Bar', includes a section (at 175-78) on the history of the movement for fusion, but concludes that the majority of the solicitors' profession is not interested in a system 'which may be more logical but which could certainly raise problems'.

McHugh, E. *The amalgamation of the legal professions in Ireland.* Alex. Thom: Dublin, 1915. 23p.

Citing the address by Sir E. Clarke in 1888 (q.v.) and a report of the Incorporated Law Society of Ireland in 1885, argues in favour of fusion to the benefit of the legal profession, its clients and the public at large.

New South Wales. Law Reform Commission. *The legal profession. Background paper IV.* Law Reform Commission: Sydney, 1981. 229p.

To be read in conjunction with Discussion paper No. 4. Pt. 1, 'The structure of the legal profession—a comparative survey', covers the states of Australia, England, Scotland, New Zealand, Canada, and U.S.A.

New South Wales. Law Reform Commission. *The legal profession. Discussion paper No. 4. The structure of the legal profession.* Law Reform Commission: Sydney, 1981. 2 parts. 644p.

Discusses three possible structures, *divided, flexible* and *uniform.* Considers the term 'fusion' to be ambiguous and misleading.

New South Wales. Law Reform Commission. *First report on the legal profession. General regulation and structure.* (LRC 31). Law Reform Commission: Sydney, 1982. [8], 242p.

Ch. 6, 'Legal and official distinctions between barristers and solicitors' (p. 113-139). Ch. 7, 'Restrictive practices' (p. 141-154). Ch. 8, 'The way ahead' (p. 155-156). Recommends common admission to both branches of the profession and abolition of restrictive practices. Judicial appointments should be open equally to barristers and solicitors.

Phillips, Sir F. *The evolving legal profession in the Commonwealth.* Oceana Publications: Dobbs Ferry, N.Y., 1978. xx, 318p.

Ch. 3, 'The fusion of the profession' (p. 19-26), concludes that there are no grounds for any of the new Commonwealth countries to follow the English model.

Royal commission on Assizes and Quarter Sessions 1966-69. Report. Chairman: The Lord Beeching. Cmnd. 4153. H.M.S.O.: London, 1969. 183p.

'Qualifications for circuit judges and recorders' (para. 245-48). Recommends 'that solicitors should be eligible for appointment to the Circuit bench or as recorders' (para. 485). 'Rights of audience' (para. 399-401). Although the roles of barristers and solicitors are outside the terms of reference, the Commission recommends (para. 514) that the Lord Chancellor should have power to open the Crown Court at any centre to solicitors if there is a shortage of counsel.

Royal Commission on Legal Services. Final Report. Chairman: Sir H. Benson. Cmnd. 7648, 7648-1. H.M.S.O.: London, 1979. 2 vols. 864, 765p.

Ch. 17, 'Fusion' (p. 187-202). Conclusion. R17.1: 'The legal profession should continue to be organised in two branches, barristers and solicitors.' Ch. 18, 'Rights of audience' (p. 203-21). Conclusions and recommendations. R18.4:

'Subject to the Lord Chancellor's power to extend the rights of audience in specific areas, there should be no extension of such rights in Crown Court business.' R18.5: 'There should be no general extension of the rights of audience of solicitors.' R18.6: 'A solicitor should have a right of audience to enable him to deal with formal or unopposed matters in any court.'

Royal Commission on Legal Services. [21 boxes of written evidence and 3 boxes of oral evidence submitted to the Royal Commission are available for consultation in the libraries listed in Vol. 1, para. 1.23 of the *Final Report*. A list of the individuals and organisations who gave written and/or oral evidence to the Commission is printed in Vol. 2].

Royal Commission on Legal Services, The Government's response to the Report of the. Cmnd. 9077. H.M.S.O.: London, 1983. 35p.
    The Government accepts the recommendations on fusion and rights of audience.

Royal Commission on Legal Services in Scotland. Report. Chairman: Lord Hughes. Cmnd. 7846, 7846-1. H.M.S.O.: Edinburgh, 1980. 2 Vols. xx, 444, 663p.
    Ch. 15, 'The legal profession: structure and organisation'. 'Fusion: a unified legal profession?' (para. 15.43-15.50). R15.10: 'The legal profession in Scotland should continue to consist of two branches, namely solicitors and advocates.' 'Rights of audience' (para. 15.51-15.54). R15.11: 'Rights of audience in the supreme courts should not be extended to solicitors.'

Zander, M. *Lawyers and the public interest: a study in restrictive practices.* London School of Economics and Political Science/Weidenfeld and Nicolson: London, 1968. xi, 342p.
    Ch. 12, 'The divided legal profession—advantages, real and imagined' (p. 270-99), and ch. 13, 'The case for unification of the legal profession' (p. 300-32), discuss extensively the arguments for and against fusion, leading to the conclusion that unification is in the best public interest.

Zander, M. *Lawyers and the public interest: notes to bring the book up to date.* [Typescript, submitted as evidence to the Royal Commission on Legal Services]. 1976. 93p.

Zander, M. *Legal services for the community.* Temple Smith: London, 1978. 416p.
    Ch. 6, 'Monopolies and restrictive practices', discusses the division between the two branches of the profession (p. 170-74).

(B) PERIODICAL ARTICLES, 1950–1984

1950.

Anon. 'Right of audience.' 100 *L.J.* 29.

Critical of provisions allowing unqualified persons to appear as advocates in proceedings involving legal questions before tribunals, and contending that the right of audience should be limited to qualified legal practitioners.

Anon. 'Legal education.' 100 *L.J.* 561.

The attitude of the profession to the subject of legal education is one of 'complacent apathy', and improvement cannot be achieved without a high degree of co-ordination between the two branches of the profession and between them and the universities.

Anon. 'Southampton Faculty of Law.' 100 *L.J.* 561, 570.

Describes the establishment of the new law faculty and the proposed law degree combining academic and practical training.

1951.

Anon. 'Solicitors and barristers: class distinction.' 95 *Sol. Jo.* 307.

Refers to archaic taboos on conduct of relations between barristers and solicitors, e.g. counsel not permitted to entertain solicitor friends at their inns. 'It is no longer required of the Bar that they should travel first class so as to avoid the contaminating contact of solicitors in the third!'

1952.

Howes, S. J. 'Assistant Solicitor.' [Letter]. 102 *L.J.* 96.

Letter remarking that the title of 'Assistant Solicitor' which denotes a rank in the legal civil service, may be held by solicitors or barristers.

Jones Powell, W. M. 'Solicitor-advocates in County Court.' [Letter]. 214 *L.T.* 256.

Letter complaining that solicitor-advocates are allowed to wear the same dress as barristers, i.e. gown and bands, and arguing that solicitors should wear bands only, 'marking the precedence of the barrister'.

1953.

Anon. 'Fusion.' 103 *L.J.* 565.

Disagrees with the minority recommendation in the Evershed report that there should be an inquiry into the fusion of the profession.

Anon. 'Fusion.' 216 *L.T.* 502.

Comments on the presidential address by W.C. Crocker at the annual conference of the Law Society, stating his opinion that division of work between the two branches is preferable to fusion, and deploring the growing practice of barristers doing solicitors' work, e.g. under the Courts-Martial Appeal Court Act, and in some government departments.

Anon. Current topics: 'Barristers and solicitors.' 97 *Sol. Jo.* 287.

Quotes from the address of Sir H. Shawcross to the annual general meeting of the Bar Council: '. . . the Bar should maintain a certain detachment, and not hob-nob with the other branch of the profession. The avoidance of undue familiarity between the two branches, and the maintenance of a proper demarcation . . . promoted the integrity and independence of the profession as a whole.'

Anon. Current topics: 'A case against fusion.' 97 *Sol. Jo.* 577.

In countries where centres of population are too small to support a separate bar, e.g. New Zealand, 'fusion is appropriate, but in a closely populated centre like England it would be a mistake'.

Anon. Current topics: 'Fusion or co-ordination?' 97 *Sol. Jo.* 595.

Comments on correspondence in *The Times* (August 18, 1953) from R. M. Snow, R. Cooke and R. H. Maudsley in favour of fusion, and (August 22, 1953) from B. A. Levinson who wrote that fusion in Victoria showed few advantages over the divided legal profession in New South Wales.

Anon. 'Current topics and the two branches.' 97 *Sol. Jo.* 611.

Comments on a letter in *The Times* (August 27, 1953) from Professor L.C.B. Gower who stated that, despite the advantages, fusion was unlikely in the present conditions, and proposed that either solicitors should be given a right of audience in all courts, or, alternatively, jurisdiction of county courts be radically extended.

Anon. Current topics: 'Advocacy and the division of labour.' 97 *Sol. Jo.* 643.

Quotes a further letter in *The Times* (September 10, 1953) in favour of fusion from W. D. Whitney, a member of the English Bar and American Bar.

Crocker, W. C. 'The President's address.' 50 *Law Society's Gaz.* 433.

Considers that 'the present system, expensive though it is, is perhaps to be preferred to fusion'.

1954.

Anon. 'Barristers and conveyancing work.' 218 *L.T.* 1.

Comments on the controversy about the Bar Council's ruling of 1949 that barristers in local government posts may do conveyancing.

Anon. Current Topics: 'Right of audience.' 98 *Sol, Jo.* 258.

Request by Bar Council and Law Society that barristers and solicitors should have right of audience before all tribunals.

Anon. Current topics: 'Solicitors as judges.' 98 *Sol. Jo.* 396.

Refers to City of London (Various Powers) Bill which would make solicitors of seven years' standing eligible for appointment as deputy to an assistant judge of the Mayor's and City of London Court, commenting 'qualification as a deputy judge implies fitness to act as judge'. [Bill enacted as 2 & 3 Eliz.2, ch. xxvii].

Bateson, Sir D. 'Barristers doing conveyancing work.' 51 *Law Society's Gaz.* 119. .

Statement criticising the Bar Council's ruling that barristers employed by local authorities and public corporations may do conveyancing work.

FitzGerald, R. C. 'The role of the solicitor in modern society.' 7 *Current legal Problems 1954* 33, at 51.

Considers that the continuance of the traditional system is no longer justified, and regrets that consideration of the division of the legal profession was excluded from terms of reference of the Evershed Committee.

Geach, C. D., and others. 'Fusion.' 217 *L.T.* 224, 266, 291, 304; 218 *L.T.* 26.

Letters in favour of fusion, but with dissent from the editor, from C. D. Geach (p. 224), B. Thompson (p. 266), M. J. Pearce (p. 291), A. N. (p. 304) and J. R. Bullough (218, p. 26).

Geach, C. D., and others. [Letters]. 98 *Sol. Jo.* 470, 507, 536.
In favour of fusion.

House of Commons. Questions. 98 *Sol. Jo.* 475.
'The Attorney-General said that he did not consider that there was sufficient demand for fusion . . . to justify the appointment of a committee to consider the question.' (June 28, 1954).

1955.

Anon. 'The problem in France.' 105 *L.J.* 146.
Comments on current discussion about proposals to combine the professions of avocat and avoué.

Anon. 'Fusion or status quo?' 105 *L.J.* 146.
Comments on paper by Professor FitzGerald in *Current Legal Problems 1954* (q.v.).

Anon. 'Transfer within the profession.' 105 *L.J.* 514.
Comments on the anomalies that it is easier for a barrister to become a solicitor than for a solicitor to transfer to the bar, and that a former solicitor cannot count the period as a solicitor for qualification for certain offices.

Anon. 'New rules of etiquette: French Bar.' 105 *L.J.* 802.
Minor reforms allowing a greater degree of specialisation, and permitting avocats to form partnerships of not more than three members.

Geach, C. D. [Letter]. 105 *L.J.* 237.
In favour of fusion, but proposing that specialists should first gain experience in general practice before becoming advocates in the High Court.

1956.

Anon. Here and there: 'Judge-making.' 100 *Sol. Jo.* 243.
Comparison by 'Richard Roe' of various continental systems of appointing judges.

Geach, C. D. [Letter]. 100 *Sol. Jo.* 315.
Referring to Richard Roe's comments (100 Sol. Jo. 243), asserts that because judges are appointed exclusively from the Bar, as a body they are opposed to most legal reforms and too concerned with pettifogging niceties. Solicitors possess a great fund of knowledge about where the law operates harshly, and 'it is difficult to see why members of this body should not be eligible for promotion to the Bench'.

1957.

Anon. 'Professional education.' 224 *L.T.* 177.
Refers to proposals made by I. D. Yeaman for a common period of training for entrants to both branches of the legal profession, and for easier means of transition from one branch to the other. 'The scheme adumbrated would appear to be open to certain objections. . .it might prove to be but a short step from assimilation of legal training to fusion . . .'.

Anon. 'The future of the bar, by a Queen's Counsel.' 224 *L.T.* 231.
Recommending that barristers be allowed to form partnerships, and that this would be facilitated by fusion of the legal profession.

Anon. Current topics: 'An alternative to fusion.' 101 *Sol. Jo.* 488.
Takes up Lord Evershed's suggestion (p. 490) that there should be easier interchange between the two branches. 'The bar would thus become much more truly the senior branch of the profession.'

Anon. Current topics: 'An alternative to fusion.' 101 *Sol. Jo.* 561.
Comments that Sir H. Shawcross has joined Lord Evershed in proposing easier interchange between the two branches.

Anon. Current topics: 'New Zealand law conference and fusion.' 101 *Sol. Jo.* 616.
Refers to report of the 10th Dominion Legal Conference, from which it appears that fusion in New Zealand causes some problems.

Geach. C. D. [Letter]. 101 *Sol. Jo.* 547.
Disagreeing with the editorial assumption (p. 488) that fusion is not a live issue.

Josling, J. F. 'The solicitor in the criminal court.' 101 *Sol. Jo.* 36.
Concerned with practical aspects of advocacy by solicitors in magistrates' courts.

Sim, Sir W. 'Professional ethics.' [Paper presented to the 10th Dominion Legal Conference]. 33 *New Zealand Law Journal* 107, and Discussion at 111.
Fusion of the legal profession as practised in New Zealand presents some problems.

1959.

Anon. 'The state of the legal profession..' [Signed: F. H.]. 109 *L.J.* 695.
Proposal of common basic legal education for both branches, and easier transfer from one branch to the other. Also proposes that all barristers should practise as a solicitor for several years before entering the bar at the age of thirty.

Anon. 'Solicitor's right of audience.' [Signed: M. S.]. 103 *Sol. Jo.* 589.
Refers to report in *The Times* (February 17, 1959), in which a solicitor claimed right of audience to appear in the High Court in a bankruptcy matter, under s. 152 of the Bankruptcy Act, 1914. Under s. 89 of the County Courts Act, 1959, solicitors have statutory right of audience in the county courts.

Anon. Current topics: 'Solicitors as judges?' 103 *Sol. Jo.* 1011.
Refers to a debate in the House of Lords in which Lord Chorley argued in favour of solicitors being considered for judicial appointment.

1960.

Anon. 'The state of the bar.' 110 *L.J.* 405.
Referring to 1959 Annual Statement of the General Council of the Bar, comments on declining numbers of bar students, and welcomes discussions on assimilation of professional examinations common to both branches, and consideration of partnerships at the bar.

Anon. 'Solicitors at the Central Criminal Court.' 110 *L.J.* 758.
'Barristers, fully robed and wigged, have the privilege of access to the cells through the dock entrance, but solicitors, it appears, may not use this way as of right.'

Anon. County court letter: 'The legal outlaw.' 104 *Sol. Jo.* 1046.

S. 89(c) of the County Courts Act, 1959, denies right of audience to a solicitor retained as advocate by, or acting as agent for another solicitor, but does not prevent a solicitor so retained from conducting a case; he is merely forbidden to 'address' the court.

Brown, J. F. 'Solrs. and Col.' 104 *Sol. Jo.* 838.

Comparison of American and English legal professions, but believes that the English system would not be improved by fusion.

1961.

Anon. 'Legal office: qualifications.' 111 *L.J.* 366.

The Legal Profession (Qualification for Office) Bill is welcomed, 'since by widening the circle of those who may be eligible for appointment to judicial or other legal offices, the way will be paved towards a much freer transfer between the two branches of the legal profession'.

Anon. 'Fusion for beginners?' [Letter, signed: Fuse-Box]. 105 *Sol. Jo.* 14.

Proposes that newly-called barristers should be employed for a few years by a solicitor, doing 'solicitor's work', to gain experience of the practical aspects of the law.

Anon. 'Fewer barristers.' 105 *Sol. Jo.* 536.

Argues that the best young solicitors of the right calibre should, after a few years' practice, proceed to qualify for the bar.

Anon. 'Solicitors and barristers.' [Letter, signed: Ten Year Man]. 105 *Sol. Jo.* 591.

Disagreeing with the editorial suggestion (p. 536) that the best young solicitors should be creamed off to improve the calibre of the bar.

Anon. Current topics: 'The future of Bench and Bar.' 105 *Sol. Jo.* 955.

'No doubt that practice at the bar is the best preparation for the bench.' Considers that solicitors and academic lawyers with judicial ambitions should have practice at the bar.

Anon. Current topics: 'The supply of judges.' 105 *Sol. Jo.* 995, 1012.

Referring to House of Lords debate on the Criminal Justice Administration Bill (25th November, 1961), comments that solicitors ought to be eligible for the county court bench, and that more county court judges should be promoted to the High Court.

Anon. 'Solicitors and barristers: some comments on the common education proposals.' [Signed: J.C.B.]. 58 *Law Society's Gaz.* 719.

Discusses recent official attitudes to common education and transfer, and suggests that the two branches are likely to resist change, at the cost of service to the public.

Geach, C.D. 'Apartheid.' [Letter]. 105 *Sol. Jo.* 364.

'The most brilliant and experienced solicitor can never aspire to a judicial post, must accord precedence to the most junior and backward counsel, and must avoid any danger of contamination by appearing over-friendly with a barrister.'

Hicks, D. T. President's address: 'Professional development for the future.' 58 *Law Society's Gaz.* 419, at 422.

Argues for reform of legal education, but against fusion.

Jacobs, S. J. 'Solicitors and barristers.' [Letter]. 105 *Sol. Jo.* 606.
  Also disagreeing with the suggestion (p. 536) to cream off the best solicitors as recruits to the bar.

1962.

Fielding, H. 'Fusion of the profession.' [Letter]. 59 *Law Society's Gaz.* 401.
  Fusion advocated by a Canadian solicitor/barrister who has also practised as a solicitor in England.

Harris, D. 'Fusion of the profession.' [Letter]. 59 *Law Society's Gaz.* 479.
  In favour of fusion: less expensive and more efficient.

Moeran, E. 'Fusion of the profession.' [Letter]. 59 *Law Society's Gaz.* 666.
  Against fusion, likely to reduce solicitors' capacity to give 'friendly, worldly, and on occasion . . . spiritual comfort which our clients often seek'.

Trenchard, J. C. 'Fusion.' [Letter]. 59 *Law Society's Gaz.* 612.
  In favour of barristers being recruited from the solicitors' profession.

1963.

Anon. Editorial: 'Public and confidential.' 60 *Law Society's Gaz.* 261.
  Questions the need for secrecy in negotiations for reform of legal training.

Graveson, R. H. 'Legal education.' 234 *L.T.* 712.
  Report of an address by R. H. Graveson proposing the establishment of a new institution, a British Law School, by combining the College of Law and the Inns of Court School of Law.

Hughlin, L. 'Modernisation of the profession.' [Letter]. 60 *Law Society's Gaz.* 229.
  Giving details of the Association for the Modernisation of the Legal Profession, founded to improve relations between both sides of the profession.

1964.

House of Lords. Proceedings. 'Commonwealth law students—Training.' 114 *L.T.* 141.
  Report of statement by the Lord Chancellor that the Council of Legal Education was developing a post-final training course to prepare Commonwealth students for practice in a fused profession in their own countries.

Wickenden, C. D. 'Law reform: the solicitor's voice.' 61 *Law Society's Gaz.* 189.
  Recommends closer co-operation between the two branches.

1965.

Anon. 'Solicitors arise.' [Letter]. 115 *L.J.* 45.
  It is a pity that Eric Fletcher, appointed Minister without Portfolio to examine law reform, cannot be called Solicitor General because he is a solicitor.

Anon. 'Streamlining legal education.' 115 *L.J.* 457, 489.
  Editorial criticising lack of progress in setting up a common course of training for solicitors and barristers.

Anon. Current topics: 'Kind words at last.' 109 *Sol. Jo.* 182.
  Refers to article in *Sunday Express* by Colin Cross in favour of appointing solicitors to the bench.

Anon. Current topics: 'The leak.' 109 *Sol. Jo.* 421.
Refers to publication of memorandum of Council of the Law Society about restrictive practices of the bar.

Anon. 'The legal profession.' [Letter, signed: J.C.B.]. 109 *Sol. Jo.* 938.
As a continental lawyer practising as a solicitor in England, the writer points to the disadvantages of a divided legal profession if Britain joins the Common Market, particularly the problem of the right of audience for solicitors in the Community courts.

Gardiner, Lord. 'The Lord Chancellor talks to the editor.' 109 *Sol. Jo.* 139.
He is opposed to ultimate fusion of the two branches, and believes that the disadvantages of solicitors sitting on the county court bench would outweigh the advantages.

Geach, C. D. 'Worthy of his hire.' [Letter]. 109 *Sol. Jo.* 54.
Disagrees with statements (108 *Sol. Jo.* 1044) that the division of the profession into two branches is admirably designed to provide specialists in consultancy and advocacy, and that barristers are poorly paid. Considers that solicitor-advocates are superior to counsel.

Parker, A. 'The leak.' [Letter]. 109 *Sol. Jo.* 458.
Welcomes the Law Society's memorandum, adding that judges are chosen from among 2,000 barristers, although there are 20,000 solicitors equally well qualified.

Townshend-Roe, R. 'Frenzied solicitors?' [Letter]. 109 *Sol. Jo.* 218.
Commenting on a review of *The English Bar: a priesthood* which quotes the view that barristers are insulated from the heat and passion of the client, while solicitors are partisans. 'This hieratic view of counsel is nonsense.'

Travers, R. L. 'Worthy of his hire.' [Letter]. 109 *Sol. Jo.* 26.
Proposes that the section of the *Law List* devoted to counsel be arranged in classified order to make it easier for solicitors to find counsel with the right qualifications.

Yahuda, J., and others. [Letters]. 109 *Sol. Jo.* 328, 360, 397.
Yahuda (p. 328) and Wilkes (p. 397) argue in favour of solicitors' right of audience in the higher courts. H. J. Goldthorpe (p. 360) writes that solicitors do in fact have right of audience in the House of Lords, citing *Halsbury's Laws*, 3rd ed., Vol. 36, p. 45–49.

1966.

Anon. 'Legal learning: the case for research.' 116 *N.L.J.* 431.
Comments on the lack of research by the legal profession into its own affairs.

Anon. '1934 and all that.' 116 *N.L.J.* 518.
Quotes a question in the House of Commons whether any steps have been taken to implement the recommendations of the Legal Education Committee report (Cmd. 4663) of 1934.

Anon. 'Legal education: consumer research.' 116 *N.L.J.* 1069.
Comments on S.P.T.L. *Survey of legal education in the United Kingdom* which shows that the majority of solicitors and young barristers consider the present system of legal education inadequate.

Anon. 'Solicitors of the future: the cost of training.' 116 *N.L.J.* 1306.
Questions why solicitors have to bear the cost of training through the method of articled clerkship.

Anon. Current topics: 'Profession's reform.' 110 *Sol. Jo.* 138.
Quotes Harold Lever, speaking at the Oxford Union, criticising restrictive practices on both sides of the profession, and suggesting that the two branches be fused.

Anon. Current topics: 'Chance for comparison.' 110 *Sol. Jo.* 473.
Cites *Rondel* v. *Worsley* (*The Times*, June 14, 1966) in which the plaintiff appeared in person and submitted a brief prepared by his solicitor, M. Zander. 'Is this the first step towards fusion?' Zander replied (p. 523) that fusion was a red herring, the point being that the court accepted a written argument.

Cohn, E. J. 'Case for a divided legal profession.' *The Times*, April 19, 1966, p. 11.
Considers the divided profession in England to be more efficient than the unified profession in America, on the grounds that it provides the necessary specialisation.

Lund, Sir T. 'The future pattern of the profession.' 63 *Law Society's Gaz.* 127.
Questions the traditional separation between barristers and solicitors.

Napley, D. 'Mr. David Napley on persuasion.' 110 *Sol. Jo.* 802.
Summary of an address in which he questioned the view that the bar, as specialists, are better advocates and lawyers than solicitors, and suggested that counsel are needed only in cases where it is desired to obtain a second opinion, or where the points of law require prolonged research.

Reeves, P. 'Status of solicitors.' [Letter]. 110 *Sol. Jo.* 9.
With reference to the proposed County Court Divorce Bill, there is no logical reason to deny solicitors audience in the higher courts or to exclude many talented people from the judiciary.

Reeves, P. 'Extended right of audience.' [Letter]. 110 *Sol. Jo.* 389.
Argues for extending solicitors' rights of audience to meet the needs of the times.

Scott, J. R. 'Solicitors as judges?' [Letter]. 110 *Sol. Jo.* 315.
'Many solicitors have considerable experience of sitting on tribunals . . . and could fill many other appointments, including county court judgeships.'

Shawcross, Lord. 'Why the legal profession needs reform but not fusion.' *The Times*, June 21, 1966, p. 13.
Supports reform within the two branches, but opposes fusion.

1967.

Anon. 'Still overcrowded inns? What now?' 117 *N.L.J.* 640.
Refers to overcrowding in the Inner and Middle Temples, and urges provision of more accommodation for barristers and solicitors, but sees no solution in fusion.

Anon. 'Legal education: a fresh start?' 117 *N.L.J.* 1357.
Editorial comment on the appointment of the committee to advance legal education (the Ormrod Committee).

Anon. 'County courts: right of audience.' 111 *Sol. Jo.* 337.
The Attorney-General does not think it desirable to amend s. 89(c) of the County Courts Act, 1959.

Anon. 'American proposals for the English legal profession.' 111 *Sol. Jo.* 429.
Refers to *Lawyers and their work: an analysis of the legal profession in the United States and England*, by Q. Johnstone and D. Hopson, who are in favour of fusion.

Anon. 'Westminster and Whitehall.' 111 *Sol. Jo.* 854.
Quotes the Attorney-General who gave negative answers to appointment of solicitors to the bench, and to allowing solicitors to plead in the High Court (October 23, 1967).

Allen, D. C. 'Solicitors' right of audience.' [Letter]. 111 *Sol. Jo.* 377.
Demanding repeal of s. 89(c) of the County Courts Act, 1959.

Darby, T. E. 'Fusion.' [Letter]. 111 *Sol. Jo.* 720.
A solicitor writing in favour of fusion. If the bar and solicitors were united, the Law Officers would have more sympathy with the problems of the profession as a whole.

Dickinson, D. 'Fusion.' [Letter]. 111 *Sol. Jo.* 156.
Solicitor-advocates in county courts are at a disadvantage when opposed by a barrister, as their arguments carry less weight with judges. Legal aid certificates are often given for the purpose of taking counsel's opinion unnecessarily, and many solicitors are better qualified to give an authoritative opinion than some counsel.

Green, D. A. R. 'A case for fusion.' [Letter]. 64 *Law Society's Gaz.* 432.
Fusion at general practitioner level and separation of functions at specialist level would best serve the needs of the client.

Harris, D. 'Easier interchange.' [Letter]. 64 *Law Society's Gaz.* 559.
Proposes that solicitors and barristers should be able to sit exams of the other branch as external candidates.

Lipton, J. S. 'Suggested changes in American legal system.' [Letter]. 111 *Sol. Jo.* 639.
Quotes an article in *Playboy* by F. Lee Bailey in favour of splitting the American legal profession on the English model.

Martin, N. B. 'Solicitors' right of audience.' [Letter]. 111 *Sol. Jo.* 394.
Supports demand for repeal of s. 89(c) of the County Courts Act, 1959.

Reeves, P. 'Bar-imposed customs.' [Letter]. 111 *Sol. Jo.* 394.
Demands the abolition of archaic customs imposed by the division of the profession.

Wilson, J. F. 'Legal education. Reform of the structure of professional training.' 117 *N.L.J.* 1334, 1363.
Outlines a scheme for university-based legal education.

Zander, M. 'Legal education—priorities.' 117 *N.L.J.* 526.
Review of the inaugural lecture of Professor J. K. Grodecki who advocates a four-year LL.B. course as obligatory training for lawyers, as in continental countries, followed by a one-year course in practical skills at the professional school.

1968.

Anon. 'Solicitors as county court judges.' 118 *N.L.J.* 147.
Report of Lords debate on Administration of Justice Bill. Lord Goodman suggested that academic lawyers should be eligible for the High Court Bench, and solicitors be eligible for appointment as county court judges. The Lord Chancellor's reply was 'obscure and irrelevant. It consisted . . . of an attack on the notion of fusion'.

Anon. 'The profession to come.' 118 *N.L.J.* 457.
Editorial comment on the Law Society's special committee on 'The future of the profession' which proposes a common legal training for entrants to both branches.

Anon. 'Non-practising barristers.' 118 *N.L.J.* 743.
At the annual meeting of the Bar, it was argued that barristers in commerce or local government should not be subject to restraints imposed by the Bar Council.

Anon. 'Solicitors and the courts.' 118 *N.L.J.* 1129.
Review of British Legal Association's memorandum to the Royal Commission on Assizes and Quarter Sessions, that there is nothing so specialised about advocacy to entitle the Bar to resist the claim for solicitors' right of audience in these courts.

Anon. 'Social barrier removed.' 112 *Sol. Jo.* 161.
Approves the relaxation of certain rules governing conduct between barristers and solicitors.

Anon. Current topics: 'Out-dated custom.' 112 *Sol. Jo.* 405.
Refers to a case where the chairman of Leicestershire county quarter sessions rejected a solicitor's application for right of audience, relying on the 'ancient custom of this court'.

Anon. Current topics: 'Negligence after fusion.' 112 *Sol. Jo.* 510.
Cites the case *Miranda* v. *Khoo Yew Boon*, [1968] 1 MLJ 161, where it was held that a Malayan advocate, in a fused profession, could be sued for negligence because of contractual relationship with client. For English barristers this would be another argument against fusion.

Anon. Current topics: 'Hope for a joint legal education.' 112 *Sol. Jo.* 870.
Refers to memorandum submitted to the Ormrod Committee by the Senate of the Inns of Court, suggesting two stages of training, of which the first stage would be common to both branches.

Best, S. P. 'Legal education: five lost years.' 118 *N.L.J.* 760.
Proposes a system of common education, and redefines the division between solicitors who would deal with non-contentious work and advocates who would practise in the courts, including issuing proceedings and drafting pleadings.

Reeves, P., and others. 'Right of audience at Quarter Sessions.' [Letters]. 118 *N.L.J.* 819, 871.
Arguing that solicitors should have right of audience in Quarter Sessions. R. N. Hutchins (p. 871) mentions proposed amendment to the National Parks and Access to the Countryside Bill, 1949, which would have given solicitors right of audience in rights of way cases.

1969.

Anon. 'Instructions on undefended divorce petition.' 119 *N.L.J.* 794.

Criticises Bar Council for attempt to discourage solicitors from using their newly acquired right of audience in undefended divorce proceedings.

Anon. 'Functional demarcation and judicial office.' 119 *N.L.J.* 914.

Editorial supporting the division of the profession 'to the extent that it secures a proper distribution of functions between one branch and the other', but approves Beeching's recommendation that solicitors should not be excluded from judicial office in the lower tier of the proposed courts.

Anon. Current topics: 'Easier transfer to the Bar.' 113 *Sol. Jo.* 613.

Comments on new scheme to facilitate transfer of solicitors to the bar, which the Attorney-General hoped would end demarcation disputes about right of audience in quarter sessions.

Reeves, P. 'Right of audience before quarter sessions.' [Letter]. 113 *Sol. Jo.* 18.

Notes the British Legal Association's plan to put forward applications from solicitors for right of audience in all quarter sessions.

Reeves, P., and others. 'Demonstration at quarter sessions.' [Letter]. 119 *N.L.J.* 45.

Letter about the B.L.A.'s plan to secure right of audience for solicitors, and further correspondence from C. Lewis (p. 233), P. Reeves (p. 282), J. Fordham (p. 350), G. B. Bates (p. 397), J. Fordham (p. 447), G. B. Bates (p. 491) and P. Reeves (p. 772).

1970.

Anon. 'Judicial office—conditions of eligibility.' 120 *N.L.J.* 239.

Commenting on Lord Gardiner's lecture to the Bentham Club, '*Two lawyers or one?*', criticises him for ignoring the Beeching Commission's arguments in favour of appointing solicitors to the bench.

Anon. 'Post-Beeching bench—no solicitors.' 120 *N.L.J.* 1031.

Regrets that Beeching's proposal to make solicitors eligible for judicial office has not been included in the Courts Bill.

Anon. 'Solicitors as judges.' 120 *N.L.J.* 1077.

Further editorial comment.

Anon. 'Solicitors as circuit judges.' 120 *N.L.J.* 1096.

Statements from the Bar Council opposing, and from the Law Society supporting amendment of Courts Bill to make solicitors eligible for judicial appointment.

Anon. 'Right of audience—Quarter sessions.' 120 *N.L.J.* 1078.

The Law Society rejects fusion, but demands extended rights of audience for solicitors.

Anon. 'Playing extra time.' 120 *N.L.J.* 1125.

Commenting on Lord Tangley's amendment to the Courts Bill, which was withdrawn 'with misgivings', so that the Lord Chancellor might pursue the 'wise and statesmanlike approach' of discussing it with the Bar Council and the Law Society. 'Apart from the fact that the "natural timetable for discussions . . . between solicitors and barristers" was, in Lord Tangley's experience, of the order of sixteen years, the question of rights of audience was not one which "ought to be settled merely as a compromise between solicitors and barristers" when it was in fact a matter which involved the interests of the public.'

Anon. 'Solicitors as judges.' [Letter, signed: Avizandum]. 120 *N.L.J.* 1148.
Asking why the Scottish court system was omitted from the Beeching Commission's remit, and why no comparison was made with Scotland, 'where, for over a century, solicitors and advocates have enjoyed equally audience before and elevation to the bench of the sheriff court'.

Anon. ' "Chambers" in the county court.' [Signed: A.H.S.]. 114 *Sol. Jo.* 276.
RSC ord. 32 specifies that solicitors have right of audience before a High Court judge in chambers, but the County Court Rules are unclear.

Anon. Current topics: 'Solicitors for the bench.' 114 *Sol. Jo.* 873.
Commenting on amendments to the Courts Bill, that there is no justification for excluding solicitors from appointment to the new circuit bench. Supported in letters from D. C. Allen (p. 888) and 'A Village Hampden' (p. 902).

Anon. Current topics: 'Compromise fulfilled.' 114 *Sol. Jo.* 961.
Amendment to Courts Bill passed making solicitors and barristers of ten years' standing equally eligible for appointment as part-time recorders, and then after five years to the circuit bench.

Brown, D. 'Practice down under.' 114 *Sol. Jo.* 781.
Queensland and New South Wales have always had a divided legal profession, while South Australia, Tasmania and Western Australia are following the pattern of Victoria, where the profession is fused in law but divided in practice.

Courtauld, S. 'The law.' *The Times*, October 3, 1970, p. 21.
Defends the continued division of the profession against arguments for fusion.

Gardiner, Lord. 'Two lawyers or one?' 23 *Current Legal Problems 1970* 1.
Arguments for fusion rejected.

Goodman, Lord. 'Lord Goodman: reform of legal procedure.' 120 *N.L.J.* 905.
Report of address given at Law Society conference in which he argued that solicitors should be eligible for appointment as county court judges.

Goodman, Lord. 'Solicitors' spirit of indignation.' *The Times*, November 19, 1970, p. 10.
In support of appointing solicitors as judges.

Hailsham, Lord. 'Learning the law.' 120 *N.L.J.* 883.
Summary of lecture to the Society of Public Teachers of Law, in which he said, 'It was accepted that the legal profession had two branches . . . there was also a third—the jurists and teachers of law'.

Holland, J. A. 'Fusion.' [Letter]. 120 *N.L.J.* 282.
The Chairman of the Standing committee of young solicitors on fusion invites views from the profession.

1971.

Anon. 'Solicitor-judges—a Conservative view.' 121 *N.L.J.* 51.
Comments on the Society of Conservative Lawyers' interim report—'short, unoriginal and often superficially argued . . . regrettably selective in the authorities it cites'.

Anon. 'Solicitors and the Crown Court.' 121 *N.L.J.* 1111.
Of 100 new appointments to the post of recorder in the crown courts, only 13 were solicitors. The Lord Chancellor's direction under s. 12 of the Courts Act giving solicitors right of audience in the crown courts at Caernarvon, Barnstaple, Bodmin, Doncaster and Lincoln does not extend solicitors' rights, but merely continues the rights which they previously had in the quarter sessions in those towns.

Anon. Current topics: 'Judges on the box.' 115 *Sol. Jo.* 761.
Review of Thames Television's documentary 'The Judges'. 'We were glad to hear Mr. Kenneth Younger advocating the appointment of solicitors to the bench. No solicitor was interviewed . . . and the anonymous barrister with his American training . . . was a far from typical representative of the bar.'

Anon. 'Solicitor recorders.' 115 *Sol. Jo.* 769.
Out of 175 recorders appointed to the crown courts, 2 are solicitors.

Anon. 'Solicitor recorders.' 115 *Sol. Jo.* 934, 954.
Of another 100 recorders appointed to the crown courts, 13 are solicitors.

Anon. Notes and news: 'Solicitor recorders.' 115 *Sol. Jo.* 855.
The Lord Chancellor said that applicants from the solicitors' profession had been disappointingly few.

Arnold, J. 'Relations of bar with solicitors.' 121 *N.L.J.* 696.
Report of an address discussing issues of co-operation and fusion.

Blatch, C. 'The future of the profession.' 115 *Sol. Jo.* 71.
Proposes a scheme for fusion of the profession with common education and qualifications, and the option for lawyers to become general practitioners or specialists. Candidates for the bench should be picked at an earlier stage and given special training.

Reckitt, M. H. 'Solicitor-judges: the case for county court registrars.' 121 *N.L.J.* 231.
'It is at least arguable that the ultimate solution in the public interest is a fused profession.' The concession for solicitors to become circuit judges after five years as recorder is of no benefit to county court registrars who cannot be released from their other judicial functions to sit as recorders.

Reeves, P. 'Solicitors' right of audience.' 115 *Sol. Jo.* 80.
Comments that the provision in the Courts Bill empowering the Lord Chancellor to direct that solicitors might appear in crown courts is not sufficient.

1972.

Anon. 'Bench at the bar.' *The Economist*, May 20, 1972, 24, 27.
With reference to the Justice report on the judiciary, discusses barristers' and solicitors' rivalry over judicial appointments.

Anon. 'Tomorrow's lawyers.' 122 *N.L.J.* 365.
Review of Young Solicitors Group's report which, although not amounting to fusion in the sense which is usually understood, sets out a plan for a unified profession in which lawyers, after five years' general practice, could qualify to become counsel with exclusive rights of audience before the Privy Council and House of Lords, and the Court of Appeal.

Anon. Westminster & Whitehall: 'Legal profession: Organisation.' 116 *Sol. Jo.* 20.
The Attorney-General rejected the proposal that the two branches be fused in line with practice in E.E.C. countries, and denied that there would be any difficulties regarding audience before the European Court.

Anon. Current topics: 'Rights of audience.' 116 *Sol. Jo.* 129.
Commenting on the Lord Chancellor's Practice Direction extending solicitors' rights of audience to appeals from magistrates' courts in cases where they had appeared on client's behalf.

Anon. Current topics: 'Things legal to come?' 116 *Sol. Jo.* 301.
Reviewing the Young Solicitors Group's report *'Tomorrow's lawyers'* which merits serious attention.

Anon. 'Unification of French avocats and avoués.' 116 *Sol. Jo.* 329.
Profession of avoué is annulled, all former avocats and avoués will become members of the unified profession of avocat, and in future the avocat will be fully responsible for the preparation of cases and do all the work which was formerly the function of the avoué.

Anon. Current topics: 'Judiciary scrutinised.' 116 *Sol. Jo.* 381.
Commenting on the Justice report which recommends that priority be given to making solicitors eligible as circuit judges and academic lawyers as appellate judges.

Anon. 'Solicitor recorders.' 116 *Sol. Jo.* 924.
The Attorney-General answered that 23 solicitors had been appointed as recorders since the commencement of the Courts Act, 1971.

Anon. Current topics: 'Prosecuting solicitors.' 116 *Sol. Jo.* 573.
Urges extension of the system of salaried prosecuting solicitors attached to each police force.

Hailsham, Lord. 'Solicitors' rights of audience.' 69 *Law Society's Gaz.* 7, 1.
Statement by the Lord Chancellor in the House of Lords extending solicitors' rights of audience to appeals from magistrates' courts in cases where they had appeared for the defence, and refusing to make any further extensions of rights of audience in the Crown Court on a geographical basis. Followed by comment of Council of the Law Society.

Moiser, C. H. 'Prosecuting solicitors.' 116 *Sol. Jo.* 613.
Disagrees with the suggestion for a salaried prosecution service.

Olson, A. F. 'Prosecuting solicitors.' 116 *Sol. Jo.* 634.
Prosecuting solicitor for Durham Police writes in defence of full-time prosecutors. 32 out of 46 police authorities have prosecuting solicitors departments.

Reeves, P. 'Lawyers in Europe.' [Letter]. 116 *Sol. Jo.* 357.
Refers to the proposal, agreed by Bar Council and Law Society, to limit the rights of solicitors to make representations to the European Court.

1973.

Anon. Current topics: 'Judicial appointments for solicitors.' 117 *Sol. Jo.* 97.
Welcomes Lord Hailsham's proposal to allow the nomination of a solicitor as deputy circuit judge. Lord Gardiner complained of solicitors encroaching on the province of the bar while defending their own monopoly. 'An answer to Lord Gardiner is that there should be the widest choice of candidates available for appropriate judicial appointments.'

Anon. 'Living with barristers. Part I.' 70 *Law Society's Gaz.* 1836.
A solicitor's views on working with barristers.

Anon. 'Living with solicitors.' 70 *Law Society's Gaz.* 1705.
A barrister's views on working with solicitors.

Ashworth, W. 'Living with barristers. Part II. Working with barristers.' 70 *Law Society's Gaz.* 1989.
A solicitor's account of working with barristers.

Burger, W. E. 'The special skills of advocacy: are specialized training and certification of advocates essential to our system of justice?' 42 *Fordham Law Review* 227.
The United States Chief Justice praises the English system, and proposes special training and certification for lawyers who wish to become trial advocates, as a remedy for the low standards of advocacy in American courts.

Gordon, J. 'Solicitors' right of audience in the Crown Court.' [Letter]. 70 *Law Society's Gaz.* 1636.
A solicitor writes about the failure of counsel to appear in two Crown Court cases which he had prepared.

Hartley and Worstenholme. 'Solicitors' right of audience in the Crown Court.' [Letter]. 70 *Law Society's Gaz.* 1934.
Supporting full solicitors' rights of audience in Crown Court, because of shortage of barristers to cope with the volume of work.

Paice, R. D. 'Mixed partnerships.' 70 *Law Society's Gaz.* 1515.
Argues for allowing solicitors to form partnerships with allied professions, e.g. accountants and surveyors.

Zander, M. 'Clinical legal education.' 123 *N.L.J.* 181.
Describes schemes for law school students in U.S.A. to obtain practical experience by working in legal aid centres for the poor.

1974.

Anon. Current topics: 'Foreign solicitors.' 118 *Sol. Jo.* 505.
The Solicitors (Amendment) Act, 1974, removes the ban on aliens practising as solicitors, and the European Court in *Reyners* v.*The Belgian State* (*The Times*, July 1, 1974) rules that the Dutch plaintiff could not be refused admission to the Belgian bar.

Anon. Westminster & Whitehall: 'Legal profession: Scotland.' 118 *Sol. Jo*. 835.
The Lord Advocate declined to initiate steps to fuse the two branches in Scotland.

Burger, W. E. 'The special skills of advocacy.' 46 *N.Y. State B.J*. 89.
Argues in favour of introducing the English system in the U.S.A.

Cohen, H. 'The BLA 1964-74: some American comparisons and observations.' 118 *Sol. Jo*. 322.
'The English bar is a prime example of elitism. A young person can be admitted to the bar and still not be authorised to practise his profession because of the euphemistic "lack of space in chambers" '. Disagrees with Burger's praise of the English system (q.v.). 'There are barristers who are not good trial lawyers, yet there are solicitors who are fine advocates.'

1975.

Anon. 'Specialist cartels.' 125 *N.L.J*. 99.
Review of article by M. W. Mindes in *A.B.A. Journal* 'in which he expresses serious misgivings about the move to secure specialist accreditations in specific branches of legal practice in his own country'.

Anon. 'The week. No comment.' 125 *N.L.J*. 835.
In address at the Police College, Sir R. Mark made one criticism 'which seems entirely justified. In reference to research into the criminal process . . . at Birmingham University . . . he said that it was "sad indeed that of all those concerned with the administration of justice, the Bar alone has declined to take part".'

Mindes, M. W. 'Lawyer specialty certification: the Monopoly game.' 61 *A.B.A.J*. 42.
Examples from other professions indicate that specialists seek regulation through certification, and then debar uncertified persons from the specialised area.

Reeves, P. 'A fused profession?' [Letter]. 125 *N.L.J*. 731.
Announcing the intention to form a society to promote fusion.

Ross, S. D. 'The legal profession in Tasmania.' 5 *Univ. of Tasmania L.R*. 1.
As the state has only five Q.C.'s and three barristers, the legal profession in Tasmania is effectively composed of solicitors who have full rights of audience.

1976.

Anon. 'Divided we fall. . .' 126 *N.L.J*. 1054
Editorial dissenting from statement issued by leaders of the two branches of the profession in November 1975 'that the interests of the public are best served by a legal profession divided into two branches . . . of equal status but with different and complementary functions'. Supports the four prerequisites proposed by M. Zander at a meeting of the United Lawyers' Association.

Anon. 'Advertising.' 120 *Sol. Jo*. 529.
Comments on Monopolies Commission finding that the ban on advertising by solicitors is a restrictive practice and should be abolished.

Leggatt, A. 'Why fusion is a consummation not to be wished.' 73 *Law Society's Gaz.* 978.
   Response to Zander (q.v.) arguing that both branches have equality of status but different functions.

Rawlinson, Sir P. 'A Royal Commission to inquire into the legal profession.' 73 *Law Society's Gaz.* 341.
   Guidelines of evidence to be presented to the Royal Commission by the Bar include the principle of maintaining the Bar as a separate branch.

Reid, B. C. 'Fusion in the legal profession.' 73 *Law Society's Gaz.* 272.
   Result of partial survey of junior members of the bar about attitudes to fusion, and urging members of both branches to demand referendums to gauge opinion.

Webster, P. 'Lawyers social walfare law.' 73 *Law Society's Gaz.* 278.
   Memorandum for Bar Committee on Lawyers and Social Welfare Law, proposing that salaried barristers be employed in CABs and law centres, sponsored by chambers who would facilitate their return to practice. This amounts to 'fusion', but 'a need cannot be allowed to go unmet because of sectional interests involved in attempting to meet it'.

Zander, M. 'Why the Royal Commission is likely to recommend reform of the divided profession.' 73 *Law Society's Gaz.* 882.
   Argues against division because of overlapping functions, inefficiency and cost.

1977.

Anon. 'In my view . . .' [Signed: J.P.A.]. 74 *Law Society's Gaz.* 1114.
   Criticises the United Lawyers Association's arguments for fusion made on BBC2 Open Door programme, and supports proposals of the Young Solicitors' Group.

Anon. 'Memorandum of evidence presented by the Young Solicitors' Group of the Law Society to the Royal Commission on Legal Services.' 74 *Law Society's Gaz.* 767.
   Rejects fusion.

Anon. 'Fusion and the judges.' [Signed: Pendragon]. 74 *Law Society's Gaz.* 270.
   Commenting on the judges' evidence to the Benson Commission which, although predictably against fusion, should be given some weight. Because the characteristic of our trial system is wholly oral, judges need the assistance of experienced advocates to conduct cases expeditiously.

Anon. The Week: 'Solicitor-judges.' 127 *N.L.J.* 155.
   Notes the Lord Chancellor's apparent reluctance to appoint solicitors as Crown Court judges. Solicitors appointed as recorders under the Courts Act 1971 are now becoming eligible under the 5-year rule for elevation to the bench.

Anon. 'Fusion—judicially considered.' 127 *N.L.J.* 178.
   Comments on evidence of the judges' committee to the Benson Commission.

Burger, W. E. 'The special skills of advocacy.' 3 *J. Contemp. L.* 163. See also 1973, 1974.

Forbes, J. R. 'Division of the profession: ancient or scientific?' 74 *Law Society's Gaz.* 67.
Historical survey of division which is costly and inefficient.

Harvey, J. A. 'A conveyancing partner's views—II: the LAG.' 121 *Sol. Jo.* 539.
A vitriolic attack on Legal Action Group for giving evidence in support of fusion to the Royal Commission. Apparently a left-wing plot to undermine the legal system.

Lawton, J. S. 'Would fusion be a consummation?' 74 *Law Society's Gaz.* 50.
Dissents from Leggatt (1976, q.v.), and critical of inefficiency of barristers.

McNeil, D. 'The divided profession.' 74 *Law Society's Gaz.* 162.
Vice-Chairman of the Bar criticises articles on fusion by Forbes and Lawton.

Mann, F. A. 'Fusion of the legal professions?' 93 *L.Q.R.* 367.
Admitting that he was formerly in favour of fusion, he now believes that separation is an integral part of the legal system, and that comparison with other systems, e.g. U.S.A., Germany and France, is irrelevant.

Napley, Sir D. 'United Lawyers' Association.' 74 *Law Society's Gaz.* 550.
Report of address in which he argues the advantages and disadvantages of fusion without committing himself to either side, and urges that the public interest is paramount.

Nicholson, R. D. 'Inquiries into legal services in New South Wales and in the United Kingdom.' 51 *Austral. L.J.* 764.
Comparison of the terms of reference and aspects of the legal profession to be examined by the two commissions, discussing attitudes to fusion.

Stockler, W. T. 'Rechtsanwalt and fusion.' [Letter]. 121 *Sol. Jo.* 635.
Dissents from the conclusions of Williams' article on the West German system.

Williams, G. 'Rechtsanwalt: a fused profession.' 121 *Sol. Jo.* 553.
Description of the West German system, in which judges play a much more active role, and thus the legal profession is much larger than in England. The Rechtsanwalt acts as both legal adviser and advocate, and the only limit on his rights of audience is geographical. In criminal cases the defendant may be represented by a Rechtsanwalt from anywhere in the Federal Republic, or by a law professor or any other qualified lawyer. The English system in contrast is inefficient, costly and slow.

Williams, R. 'Fusion: an outsider's view.' 74 *Law Society's Gaz.* 278.
Canadian lawyer who has practised in England considers that fusion would not benefit solicitor or clients.

                                    1978.

Flynn, T. E. 'Fusion.' [Letter]. 128 *N.L.J.* 319.
Disadvantages in the present structure of the legal profession could be removed without recourse to fusion.

Anon. 'Rights of audience in the Crown Court.' 129 *N.L.J.* 206.
Editorial supporting the Senate's opposition to extending rights of audience. 'We would suggest that the Law Society has failed to make out a case.'

Anon. 'Expensive, remote, unlikely to inspire confidence.' 129 *N.L.J.* 330.
Editorial commenting on Lord Goodman's evidence to the Royal Commission in favour of fusion.

Anon. 'The bar on trial, edited by Robert Hazell.' [Book review]. 123 *Sol. Jo.* 63.
Includes a chapter on fusion.

Berlins, M. 'Rights of audience.' 129 *N.L.J.* 1116.
Criticises the Royal Commission for not recommending extension of solicitors' rights of audience.

Best, S. P. ' "The bar on trial".' 123 *Sol. Jo.* 94.
Commenting on the review of 'The bar on trial', points out that the authors have overlooked the fact that solicitors already have limited rights of audience.

Colvin, E. 'Division of legal labour.' 17 *Osgoode Hall L.J.* 595.
Not about the division of the legal profession, but a sociological study of the professionalisation of legal work. The profession is generally viewed as having failed to meet legal needs of all sections of society, and is unlikely to reform itself from within.

Disney, J. 'New areas and styles of practice.' 53 *Austral. L.J.* 348.
Discusses legal needs of society and how they should be met, in the light of N.S.W. Law Reform Commission's proposals. Refers to fusion.

Wilmarth, A. E. 'Lawyers and the practice of law in England: an American visitor's observations.' 13 *Internat. Lawyer* 719.
A description of the divided legal profession in England. Slightly critical, and does not accept the arguments in favour of division, but admires the system of practical training.

Zander, M. 'A Canadian preview of our Royal Commission report?' 129 *N.L.J.* 599.
Review of the Staff report of the Professional Organisations Committee which, *inter alia*, rejected the idea of a separate conveyancers' profession, and opposed specialty certification.

1980

Anon. 'Demarcation difficulties.' 130 *N.L.J.* 665.
Editorial commenting on the Royal Commission's recommendations about the rights of employed barristers.

Luckham, R. 'The Final Report of the Royal Commission on Legal Services: a sociologist's view.' 43 *M.L.R.* 543.
Criticises the Commission for being less concerned with economic and social effects than with protecting existing restrictive practices and professional autonomy.

Zander, M. 'Commission examines English legal profession.' 66 *A.B.A.J.* 568.
Summary of the Royal Commission's conclusions, including its decision against fusion, and the narrowly divided decision (8 to 7) against extending solicitors' rights of audience.

Zander, M. 'Scottish Royal Commission on Legal Services reports.' 66 *A.B.A.J.* 1092.
Summary of the Royal Commission's conclusions, and agreement with the English Royal Commission on fusion.

1981.

Anon. 'Drawing back the demarcation line.' 131 *N.L.J.* 250.
Editorial on the Law Society's memorandum on lack of provision in the Supreme Court Bill for appointing solicitor-circuit judges to the High Court bench, or to enable barristers to become eligible for position of Official Solicitor.

Anon. 'Solicitor-Puisne Judges.' 131 *N.L.J.* 273.
Editorial on Lord Mishcon's amendment to make service as a circuit judge an alternative qualification to ten years' standing as a barrister.

Anon. 'Fusion in New South Wales.' 131 *N.L.J.* 962.
Editorial commenting on discussion paper 'The structure of the profession' published by Law Reform Commission of N.S.W. Three of the four commissioners favour a more flexible structure, maintaining the existing two branches, but abolishing discrimination on rights of audience and other legal work, eligibility for appointment as judge, and other discriminatory practices.

Flood, J. 'Middlemen of the law: an ethnographic enquiry into the English legal profession.' 1981 *A.B.F. Research J.* 377.
Account of the difficulties experienced by the author in carrying out research for a thesis in sociolegal studies on the work of barristers' clerks.

1982
Anon. 'Solicitors as High Court Judges.' 132 *N.L.J.* 449.
Editorial commenting that the withdrawal of Lord Mishcon's amendment (q.v., 131 *N.L.J.* 273) has proved to be a mistake, making it easier for the Lord Chancellor to do nothing about extending the scope for recruitment to the High Court bench.

Best, S. 'A solicitor's reply to the bar.' 132 *N.L.J.* 803.
In reply to W. Goodhart's article (q.v.), refers to BLA's proposal of 'dual practice' to the Royal Commission.

Goodhart, W. 'Can the bar be saved?' 132 *N.L.J.* 717.
Fears that the best young legal minds are being attracted into the solicitors' profession. If solicitors can give expert legal advice, the bar will suffer.

Harrowes, D. 'Australia revisited.' 132 *N.L.J.* 738, 775.
Includes a description of the fused legal profession in Western Australia.

Samuels, A. 'Solicitor circuit judges as High Court judges.' 126 *Sol. Jo.* 843.
Reviews arguments against and for appointment of solicitor circuit judges to the High Court bench, concluding that the artificial division between county court and High Court cannot be justified in logic. All judges, whether barristers or solicitors, should be eligible for advancement according to aptitude, ability, knowledge and experience.

1983.
Anon. 'Fusion—is it the way forward?' 80 *Law Society's Gaz.* 2893.
Report of Law Society's annual conference debate on fusion.

Anon. 'Inquiry in Western Australia into future organization of the legal profession.' 57 *Austral. L.J.* 660.
Comment on report of the Committee of inquiry recommending the continuance of the existing fused profession in Western Australia.

Anon. 'Westminster and Whitehall. Questions: Solicitors and barristers.' 127 *Sol. Jo.* 734.

The Attorney-General replied 'No' to a question whether he would introduce measures to merge the two professions.

Garner, J. F. 'Judicial appointments for academic lawyers? [Letter]. 127 *Sol. Jo.* 33.

Commenting on A. Samuels's article (q.v., 126 *Sol. Jo.* 843). 'Why should not recruitment to the appellate courts (including the House of Lords) be thrown open to senior academic lawyers (barristers or solicitors) of proven ability?'

1984.

Anon. 'Bar still needed.' 128 *Sol. Jo.* 229.

Editorial dissenting from the Law Society's campaign for the removal of barristers' monopoly of rights of advocacy in the higher courts.

Anon. 'The preservation of an independent bar.' 58 *Austral. L.J.* 630.

Comment on a speech by M. McHugh, President of the Australian Bar Association, arguing that proposals for reform of the legal profession in New South Wales and Victoria are 'hostile to the continued independence of the bar and detrimental to the public interest'. Fusion would lead to the best advocates becoming 'in-house' trial lawyers working for big firms of solicitors.

Anon. 'Solicitors seek equal court rights with barristers.' 81 *Law Society's Gaz.* 858.

Statement of the Law Society's decision to press for the removal of the bar's monopoly of rights of advocacy in the higher courts.

Adams, P. 'The bar and the public interest.' 128 *Sol. Jo.* 296.

Commenting on the editorial 'Bar still needed', stresses that the proper test is the public interest, not the profession's interest.

Bennion, F. 'Appointing judges.' 134 *N.L.J.* 94.

On the career of Oliver Wendell Holmes as Harvard law professor and Supreme Court Justice.

Cullwick, S. 'The art of the advocate.' 81 *Law Society's Gaz.* 1414.

Solicitors exercising their right of audience in the Crown Court on appeal from the magistrates' court are liable to be treated with blatant antagonism and rudeness, and even prejudice, from the bench.

Hall, K. 'Solicitor-advocates.' [Letter]. 81 *Law Society's Gaz.* 3141.

Another solicitor relates his experience of discriminatory treatment by a Crown Court judge.

Law Society. 'Rights of audience in the new prosecution service.' 81 *Law society's Gaz.* 3004.

Paper presented by the Law Society arguing that in the interest of flexibility, cost and efficiency barristers employed by the service should be able to prosecute in the magistrates' courts, and both solicitors and barristers be available to appear in the Crown Court.

McFarlane, G. 'A fair deal for judges.' 128 *Sol. Jo.* 795.
A barrister expresses concern that poor remuneration of the criminal bar will not attract barristers of sufficient excellence to form the pool from which judges are chosen.

Mackenzie, J. 'Rights of audience—ill-judged.' [Letter]. 81 *Law Society's Gaz.* 2735.
A personal experience of blatant rudeness from a Crown Court judge to a solicitor making a bail application in chambers.

Martin, D. 'Equal rights.' [Letter]. 81 *Law Society's Gaz.1483.*
Considers the demand for equal rights in court to be 'childish, provocative and dangerous'.

Mason, A. F. 'The role of counsel and appellate advocacy.' 58 *Austral. L.J.* 537.
Believes that the proposal for common admission to the profession in New South Wales would not improve the professional competence of advocates, and quotes Burger's criticism of low standards of advocacy in American courts.

Merricks, W. 'Audience rights—the gloves come off.' 134 *N.L.J.* 302.
Commenting on the Law Society's statement of March 15 demanding extension of solicitors' rights of audience, particularly to criminal work in the Crown Court. Considers the case is not convincingly presented, and the statement is reticent about other restrictive practices which benefit solicitors.

Morton, J. 'Standards of advocacy.' 134 *N.L.J.* 210.
Criticism of poor advocacy by many solicitors in the magistrates' courts.

Pratt, J. 'An argument for fusion.' 81 *Law Society's Gaz.* 193.
Conference paper rejecting the Benson Commission's conclusion, and setting out the arguments for fusion.

Price, J. 'Rights of audience—fusion/confusion.' [Letter]. 81 *Law Society's Gaz.* 858.
Commenting on the Law Society's decision to press for rights of audience for solicitors, argues that the client should have an equal right to choose a barrister as his advocate without employing a solicitor.

Reeves, P. 'Solicitors' right of audience.' 81 *Law Society's Gaz.* 1507.
A history of the movement to extend solicitors' rights of audience and to end the barristers' monopoly of advocacy and preferment to the bench in the higher courts.

Roberts, D. 'Solicitor-advocates.' [Letter]. 81 *Law Society's Gaz.* 1723.
A solicitor who has experienced habitual courtesy and co-operation from bench, bar and court officials when appearing in the Crown Court.

Samuels, A. 'Appointing the judges.' 134 *N.L.J.* 85, 107.
Description of existing procedure, recommending a judicial commission to make appointments. Mentions prejudice against appointing academics, although 'In North America academics have proved to be outstandingly good judges', and that a large number of solicitors have been appointed recorders since 1972, some becoming circuit judges.

Simmons, M. 'Full ahead for fusion.' 81 *Law Society's Gaz.* 1836.

If a solicitor, since the Davy-Chiesman decision, is to be held liable for counsel's mistakes, as well as being responsible for collecting counsel's fees, why is it necessary to employ a barrister? Clients should be free to instruct a solicitor-advocate, or a barrister without a solicitor as intermediary.

Young Solicitors Group. 'Rights of audience—the Young Solicitors' view.' 81 *Law Society's Gaz.* 1779.

A cautious welcome for the decision to press for extended rights of audience, which will not inevitably pave the way to fusion, but which will end an outdated monopoly and benefit the client.

Index